G000055352

Blood, Sweat & Tears
of Joy

By Billy Ping

First Edition: March 2020
                   Printed by *20th Century Print*
Second Edition: December 2020

Copyright @ 2020 Bill Fearon.

Thank you to:

My wife Joni for her contributions on her Mum and Dad's lives, and their robust ancestors; her excellent spelling consultancy; energy-empowering, diet-friendly fruit cake, flapjacks and scones to name but a few; living with my writer's moods in addition to my other moods; and for a very great deal more.

Brother Tom for his contribution to the bit about him, his eye-witness accounts from the olden days, and the knowledge and wisdom that only a big brother can have.

Old family friend Bill for the information on his Indian family.

Old school buddy Marco for the information on his Italian family.

Lots of my cousins for their great memories of family stuff.

And mostly Mum for providing the inspiration, motivation and much of the source of the content in this little book.

A Dedication:

This book is dedicated to my cousin and friend *Tony Herbert* who was born four days before me in 1954. He was an exceptionally good and loving family man, and he was arranging for this little project to go to print when he died suddenly in January 2020. Rest peacefully Tony and may your good spirit live on always.

CONTENTS

King Edward VII spent much of his life waiting to be granted a Royal position and formal responsibilities by his Mother *Queen Victoria*. She became Britain's longest serving Monarch at the time.

The Prince of Wales said: "*I don't mind praying to the eternal Father, but I must be the only man in the country afflicted with an eternal Mother.*"

Edward and I had very different views about our Mothers. I will always love and admire my Mum and this quirky little book is written very much in that context.

~

PREFACE

Billy Ping is not the author's real name. It is a made-up writer's name rather like *JK Rowling's* pseudonym *Robert Galbraith* which she used when writing a series of excellent novels. JKR's reasons for doing so were different to mine, and while *Billy Ping* is not a pseudonym it is so much more. I am effectively 'deep under cover' while telling true-life stories of a unique generation of people who lived their young lives through the second World War.

Because the true author is a rather boring man, I refer to him as *'Lard'* which is a shortened version of *Dullard (*A synonym for a slow or stupid person. Other dictionary descriptions include idiot, fool, simpleton, ignoramus, oaf, dunce, dolt, moron, cretin and imbecile).*

Lard worked in the Public Sector for nearly 40 years, moving in his career from a young happy classroom schoolteacher to a Principal of a college of further education in a vocation that he loved. He was a very lucky man, however, a working lifetime in the education sector culminating in a decade of experience as the head of a successful college didn't prepare him for a sudden financial crisis following a merger which failed after two promising years, leaving him disenfranchised and his career at an end.

After a lifetime of working obsessively long hours he became one of those people who was required to 'spend more time with his family.' He blamed no-one for the college's financial problems, he was an experienced manager with a good track record who simply didn't have the capability to manage his final and biggest challenge.

To this day, *Lard* has no answers to some of the questions of the who, what, when, where and why of the calamity of the organisation he was head of. As the boss he had been happy to receive the plaudits on behalf of 'his' organisation, and it was his final and toughest duty to resign. Under other circumstances he would have wanted to remain on the Bridge and steer the sinking ship away from the ice-berg to the security of dry land for repair, re-fit and the commissioning of a new Captain, but at the time of the catastrophe, a health scare and Doctor's orders meant he had to pack his bag and go.

The outcome for *Lard* was a loss of self-confidence and self-respect in ways that he had never experienced before. He did spend more time with his family, initially in helping with the care and affairs of his own and his wife's elderly Mothers. He also realised that he now had an opportunity to commit to writing a book which would record some of the experiences in the extraordinary life of his Mum and her family, friends and people of her who hailed from the East End of London.

It's my view that the real-life author became aware and appreciative of people and life experiences in retirement that he made little or no time for in his career which began back in the 1970's. Once the author's initial research and writing got under way, I, *Billy Ping,* soon emerged as a character that allowed *Lard* to write in a more creative and light-hearted way than he could as himself. Through *Billy Ping, Lard* found he was able to express frivolous views, and it quickly became apparent to him that I was a form of '*alter ego*' that gave him freedom to write and care less about what the reader might think. And so, with the creation of *Billy, Lard* began to emerge from his depths.

~

You may justifiably consider that this book has been written by a 'barrow boy' from *Romford Market,* or a professional gentleman with a long career in Public service, as *Lard* was indeed both these characters. Sort of. He was never a proper barrow boy because he didn't work in the market so he can't lay claim to the title '*Barrow Boy,*' but he was a van driver's delivery boy and subsequently a driver for the family wholesale china and glass business during his school and college holidays. He pushed a barrow (Upright trolley) over the Roman cobbles in Romford marketplace carrying glassware and all manner of crockery* into a posh little shop in a market arcade (*Dishes, pots, plates, bowls, tea pots, cups and saucers etc*).

~

INTRODUCTION

This little book explores some of the multitude of things that can happen in any large family and it includes a glimpse of experiences of people from the *East End* in the Second World War at home in London and abroad in foreign lands. It is, however, mostly an account of 'love not war' and represents the typical family life experienced by a generation of people who were young in the long years of the War, and for those fortunate to survive, the many years after to the present day. Mum ('M') was just one little girl who grew successfully from childhood to young adulthood in the turmoil, anxiety, fear and fun of the time. Her time.

For the 15 years after Dad died, I would visit M on a Saturday morning and we would catch up with our news and the world at large. She would make me a fried breakfast, always delicious and cooked in less than 7 minutes while talking to me and clearing up the kitchen at the same time. On reflection, it was a 'happy hour' for both of us, we laughed a lot, often about silly, unimportant things and it was a battery re-charge for me at the start of a weekend. It's something I will always cherish.

Over a period of about ten years, when I got home after my Saturday visit, I would scribble down notes of some of the things we had talked about - mostly the funny/silly bits. After M passed away and I began to draft this little book I had a mountain of chaotic notes in all manner of notebooks and scraps of paper. I scribbled on paper napkins in cafes and pubs and if I had a sudden memory recall on a beach, up a hill/mountain or in the car, my wife Joni or I would write on whatever we could find (Excluding our ever-present dogs). As time passed, more of my notes were recorded in my phone but still in a chaotic, most unprofessional form for an aspiring writer.

When the time came to start drafting the book, I struggled to make sense of my jungle of notes and to drop them into a relevant pile of the many possible topics. The assimilation and writing process has taken six years to complete but it has proved to be a most enjoyable, therapeutic project, which helped lift me from the gloom of an unplanned end to my career and the loss of my dear old Mum in 2013.

This book is a veritable jumble of stuff and nonsense, with some serious and sombre accounts of a jam-packed life inspired by my Mum and Dad (M&D) and the people of their generation born in the 1920's and 30's. The book ebbs and flows in a carefully planned meander through M's life, and when it wanders into the woods it is simply reflecting her life's paths and experiences.

*Note: I make no apology for shortening 'Mum' to 'M', she had no connection whatsoever (As far as I am aware) to *James Bond* or the world of espionage, although she did have a bit if a crush on *Sean Connery* and she did a decent impersonation of his Scottish brogue. 'M' is quicker to write and read so saves time and helps the planet by saving on ink and paper.

Most Chapters have a chaotic '*Chats With M*' section which lurches from factually interesting and educational to sad and silly, sometimes in the space of one paragraph. Please forgive my ramblings about experiences and events in my life but they are stories that M was a part of or knew about for good or ill.

I have tried to provide a glimpse of a generation of ordinary people from the *East End* of London doing ordinary things and living lives that are truly quite extraordinary when you look back on them over their lifetimes.

~

"For Whom the Bell Tolled"
How does it feel to live in fear of losing a war and the consequences? Surely the stress and anxiety are much the same regardless of what the war is about, the kind of war it is, and where it is? World War II lasted 7 years from 1939-45, and people feared the worst for several years beforehand as the Nazis in Germany built a massive military force in order to create a new empire across the world.

I was going to place most of the War issues in a section towards the end of the book because I don't feel it sits comfortably with the light-hearted passages which describe the many random topics that M and I discussed over the years, however, the Chapter on '*The Second World War*' is a very significant part of the book as it gives a context and 'real' sense of what the people of M&D's generation experienced during what should have been some of the best years of their lives but which were lost to a long and brutal War. Consequently, the substantial war years Chapter features early on and provides a context for all that follows.

I write with great respect for the people of M's generation. If you can 'go with the flow' you may hopefully find something to tickle your fancy.

Good luck!

~

Notes For Folk From Overseas:
The *East End* of London has always been a multi-cultural area and when I first began to write this little book I felt the need to 'reach out' to folk from overseas who may have a connection or an interest in this most interesting dot on the map of the world. My aim has therefore been to create a book that can be read anywhere from a tree in the *Amazon Rain Forests*, a sandy hollow in the *Sahara*

Desert or a busy commuter train on a rainy day in *Beijing*. I do hope that this little book will attract interest and a wide range of noisy responses from around the world.

M's spoken English had its own words, expressions and phrases and some of the language that her generation used in their lives has been integral to the culture of the people from the *East End* of London over many generations. Consequently, it could be difficult for people, particularly from outside the UK to understand some of the language used, so in order to assist folk from overseas with an interest in England, London or the East End, I have included an explanatory guide within the text to help explain some of the spoken language of M's generation.

You will see '*Notes for Folk From Overseas*' *mostly* at the end of a Chapter, and explanations of specific words or phrases marked with an Asterix* (*A Greek word meaning a star*).

Good value for a little book I feel.

MUM & DAD

M&D were born in 1928 and 1922 respectively into working class families in the East End of London, which by today's material standards was very poor.

M&D's families were of varied, mostly working-class stock. You will see in what follows a very broad and varied ancestral family tree which supports the assertion that a good mixture of people from different gene pools and walks of life in a family dynasty can produce a bunch of top-class people.

Today, the divorce rate is around 1 in 3 marriages in London and the South East, higher than it was for M&D's generation. Their marriage inevitably faced challenges and stresses over nearly 50 years until Dad's death, but their bond was strong enough to endure them all. They had the potency of the *'Married for Life'* cocktail that is respect, friendship and love.

I had the awful task that many adult children have of emptying their parents' home after they have died. A note written in M's familiar hand fell from her address book which said: *"The way to make a happy life is to learn to live with disappointment."* Well, her generation had shedloads of disappointment and yet so many of them lived a very full and often happy life (I love sheds and currently enjoy two).

I will start to answer the question *'How did they do that'?* by firstly describing the circumstances in which they lived their young lives, and then will sketch a picture of the generation that has seen more change than any other in the history of mankind. This was a generation that from a very young age had to cope in the midst of great hardship including a world war that was eventually won against the odds, and who went on to find the energy and desire to work and play as hard as any generation before or since.

M&D were both raised as children and young adults in *Stepney* in East London. It is the only East London District to be entered in the *Domesday Book* and was once the capital of the East End. Stepney is now in the London Borough of *Tower Hamlets* which began as a Medieval village around *St Dunstan's* church and a 5th Century development of Mile End Road called *Stepney Green*.

In the 19th Century the area grew quickly to accommodate immigrant workers and poor Londoners requiring a home, and Stepney's reputation was one of poverty, violence and overcrowding. It was badly damaged in *the Blitz* during the second World War with over a third of all housing destroyed. In the 1960s, 'slum' clearance allowed the building of mostly residential tower blocks and new housing estates, today there is very little of the Georgian and Victorian architecture left but some terraced housing remains, and *Arbour Square* and the streets around *Matlock Street* are good examples.

In M&D's early years living in the East End by the docks, residents still lived to some extent like the Victorians ('*Dickensians*'), the toilet was out the back of the house, heat came from the gas oven and coal fires in fireplaces, and you went to the local baths (at *Poplar*) for a hot bath.

These experiences left their mark throughout M&D's lifetimes during which they were constantly introduced to potential new experiences, some of which they chose not to use. They included indoor flushing toilets; a household bath with hot running water; a personal shower (M always preferred a shower in a bath rather than a cubicle?); fitted carpets; central heating; television, initially in black and white, then in colour (Sadly not in time for the 1966 football *World Cup Final* when England triumphed); space travel for monkeys and men; self-propelled lawn mowers; micro-wave ovens; vacuum cleaners; electric blankets (Easy to burn yourself in bed if not careful), hair dryers, food mixers, washing machines, dishwashers, toothbrushes, tumble dryers, shavers and toasters; nylon clothes and bed linen (Yuk!); mobile phones; 'package' holidays abroad; double-glazing; the birth of the 'digital' world, the video cassette, CD, DVD and computers that were the size of large wardrobes that gobbled cardboard cards and spat out endless piles of paper a foot wide with holes down the side which together with other essential attachments filled large rooms; cars with 'suspension' and loads of knobs and gadgets; and the start of home-cooking exotic foreign meals (At home, ours was spaghetti bolognaise with a bottle of wine for the grown-ups - *Valpolicella* from the province of *Verona*). To name but a few.

They also witnessed the creation and dropping of the *Atom Bomb* and deployment of nuclear weapons under, on and above land and sea and in space.

~

Mum

A Sad Uplifting Day:

M's funeral is not a very cheerful subject for a mostly happy little book like this, but I came across the notes I made for the service which took place on a wintery February afternoon in 2015 at *Upminster Crematorium*. I intended to throw them away but then thought it would be appropriate to include some of my comments in a book that is inspired by her and her life.

The day M was cremated was chilly and overcast and around 80 people came to pay their respects to the old lady. We all went to the pub afterwards for a drink, some nibbles and a chat, just exactly as she would have wanted us to. I have never been strong and stoic at funerals, but this was an experience that really helped me to put things in perspective and to receive without embarrassment the genuine love and support of family and friends. There was a lot of laughter, and M's people who were present that day had clearly come to enjoy sharing their memories of her.

In the service, M's Grandchildren spoke about their Nan, some called her *Nanny Romf* and others *Nanny Peck* - she and Dad would sing to our kids the old song: "*I love you a bushel and a peck...*"

Here is the gist of what I said in the crowded gloomy Chapel that afternoon:

- A favourite Irish blessing of M's was: "*May you die in bed at 95, shot by a jealous spouse.*"
- M had a wonderful, long marriage to a man she loved.
- She had to begin her life again at 65 years of age when Dad died.
- She had a long and happy life in which friends were often her family and family were her friends.
- She was born in a tiny, terraced house in Stepney, East London and her older sister Jess was allowed to see the new baby upstairs in the bedroom when she was born. Jess took pride from the memory and shared it often through her life.
- M passed away in hospital with professional care and two generations of family around her bed.
- She was hard-wired to worry about her nearest and dearest and wasn't really happy if she had no-one to worry about.
- Her childhood and young adult years were very tough before, during and after a world war that echoed long after the seven years of conflict. After her experiences of those often bleak and frightening years she was forever appreciative of the smallest thing that was positive, pleasant or fun. She was always genuinely excited and grateful for the smallest things, like a phone call, a postcard, a home-made cake and a lunch in the pub.
- She felt very lucky to have been evacuated to a lovely family in *Reading* who treated her like a daughter, she loved them, never forgot them, and often spoke about them. She would travel back to Reading some weekends to sleep in peace away from the bombs of the German *Blitz*.
- She became a Granny at 48 years of age. She cherished all her naughty Grand/Great Grandchildren - 10 in total when she passed away (15 and growing now).
- She was a serious knitter, including crochet, and was famous for her colourful, stripy jumpers made from mountains of spare wool. She knitted for Romanian children, so she was unofficially an International Knitter for England.
- M was not always old. She lived a very active life and worked as a volunteer delivering 'meals on wheels,' and also in the local hospital Maternity unit arranging and delivering the flowers (Not the babies – but she would have done

if asked).

- She danced (Ballroom) with Dad on holiday and won first prize for England in Portugal. She was therefore also an unofficial International Dancer.
- She had a little electric organ at home, and we would sing along on the odd special occasion. She had a lovely singing voice and could play the organ but couldn't read music.
- Finally, while Mum was undergoing treatment for an ailing heart and cancer in the months before she passed away, she showed me a quote from Bob Monkhouse (Comedian and tv presenter) in one of her favourite women's magazines: "They say such lovely things about people at funerals, it's a shame I'm going to miss mine."

I couldn't find the courage to stand up and say a few words when Dad died in 1997 and my big brother Tom spoke from the heart and I felt very proud of him and Dad. Like many people, I was very relieved to speak at M's service without breaking down and she was right there with me. She came to the pub with all of us afterwards of course and is remembered every year on her Birthday by her family who raise a glass of Shiraz in her honour.

~

M was born in 1928 just two years after the Queen. Photos of them over the years (Never together) show a strong similarity in their smallish demeanour and the way they dressed. M was petite, but she made two XL size sons (One tall and slim the other becoming a little rotund but in a cuddly way). The Queen also clearly excelled in raising a bunch of healthy, boisterous children.

The Queen's wardrobe surpassed M's as you would expect a *Regent* to outshine a *subject,* but like the Queen, M was always nicely dressed when she left the house (She only ever had one house to live in at a time).

Their common denominator (*A feature shared by two or more people*) were the handbags they would carry on almost all public occasions. Special event hats, handbags and shoes were of broadly similar type, they were facially alike when young and as they got older their posture and occasional 'sombre' facial expression was a match.

The older the two of them grew the more alike they became to the extent that M could have been Her Majesty's stunt double, leaving from the front door to travel in the horse-drawn carriage or limousine while the Queen slipped out the back door to catch the latest *James Bond* film or whatever else floats her Majesty's cinematic boat? M mastered the Royal wave and would practice in her armchair when the major Royal occasions were on the telly (It never entered her mind that she could possibly become the Queen's stunt double, but if offered the job I'm sure she would have done it well and willingly without recompense, except perhaps for a signed photograph of Her Majesty).

M would have been uncomfortable to know that I had written about her in this way, she would have told me not to be ridiculous and that it was disrespectful to compare her with the Queen in such a way. Typical of her old neighbours from Stepney and the East End generally, she was always an ardent supporter of *Their Majesties the King and Queen.*

I had mixed feelings when we celebrated the Queen's 90th birthday in 2016 and felt a twinge of regret that M wasn't around to enjoy it. She would certainly have toasted *Her Majesty* and if leaving the house would have accessorised with a handbag, possibly some small earrings and green pastel overcoat but no hat. Her favourite pub for her last 20 years was *The Ship* in *Gidea Park, Romford* where never alone she would often enjoy a filet steak with all available trimmings and a glass or two of Shiraz, Merlot or "Cab Sav."

M was known as '*Little Green Nan'* by some of the friends of our kids on account of the green coat she wore over a number of years, seamlessly replacing the first one with an almost exact new replica without anyone noticing.

~

In 2014 when I told M that I would be writing a little book about her and her generation she wrote some notes for me. I asked her to focus on her early years, she had pleasant, tidy handwriting and wrote:

I think I was three when I started school and didn't like it at all, especially having to lay on a little bed for a sleep in the afternoon. I did like my teacher though as she was very pretty and played the piano which we had in our classroom.

I enjoyed the summer holidays when I was older when I lived in Stepney as I was allowed to go to Victoria Park (In Hackney) all day with a little "gang" and a bottle of water! On the way which seemed like miles we called in to the Bethnal Green Museum to stare at the "Mummies" in their coffins just to be very frightened.

Another treat was to trundle with a "gang" to Shadwell Park but were warned not to play in the sand pit, go down the stone steps that led straight into the river Thames, or go down to the Rotherhithe Tunnel. Of course, we did all three! We would walk through the tunnel to the South Bank.

I was eleven when the War started and spent 3 years with a lovely family in Reading. I was the only one to stick it out away from home for 3 years. My dad was in Reading for a while as he did war work for the American Army Air Corp laying tar runways for an Aerodrome. I remember him taking me home with him to Stepney a couple of times. We used to catch a Red double decker bus from Reading and would sit upstairs for the best view and he liked to smoke. I was in heaven being with my dad on a trip like that , but it was only for a couple of days. When we reached Hammersmith, I knew we had reached London.

Before I was an Evacuee and still lived in Stepney I went to the "penny pictures" once a week with my friend and her brother. On the way we passed a stall with apples for sale. My friend's brother whose name was Georgie used to pinch 3 apples for us to munch in the pictures. I later married his cousin so I guess we would have been in-laws but I believe he was killed in the war.

Another treat to the pictures was to meet my dad from work and go to 'The Troxy'*. It was a beautiful Cinema and the program consisted of two long films with a live variety show in between and an organ which came up out of the floor at the beginning. I was fascinated by the massive satin curtains that used to swish open before the show.

I wasn't quite 14 when I left school (still in Reading) as I had received a letter from my Mother to say I was to come home as my sister had got me a job in her office in London. My adopted Auntie who I loved was heart-broken and told me I didn't have to go and to stay with her as I was her little girl and she would always look after me.

Needless to say I had to go home as you did as you were told in those days! My Headmaster wasn't too pleased either as it wasn't the end of term, but I left and went back to London anyway. Buzz bombs and all.

*(Note: *The Troxy* was built in 1933 on the site of an old brewery, *The Commercial Brewery Company Ltd, Stepney,* at a cost of £250,000 (Over £16 million in today's money). Its interior was lavish with a capacity of 3,520, making it the largest cinema in England at the time. What a treat that must have been for little Mum!)

I soon had to grow up after leaving school with the help of my big sister Jess who changed my white socks and black lace up shoes for nylon stockings and court shoes with a little heel. She also showed me how to paint my nails and wear lipstick, which got me into trouble with my mother who was rather strict.

I soon settled into my work and loved it and always enjoyed going to work and going dancing at the Bow Palais on a Saturday night which cost about a shilling, I think. This was after my sister and I had cleaned the house then walked to the Public Baths as we didn't have one at home.

Sunday afternoon we used to go dancing at Covent Garden Opera house as they had changed it to a dance hall for the war. It was wonderful after working in the City of London with the Buzz bombs dropping all week. There was no alcohol sold at Covent Garden only tea and coffee or soft drinks which was just as well as there were forces from all over the world who came there.

We met some lovely young men but never knew if we would see them again as they were sent away to fight abroad. It was a long and horrible 6 and half years of war and you had to grow up quickly.

I don't know how our mother fed us, we were 7 in our family, one brother away and food was rationed. They tell us we were healthy on such a meagre diet, but I have my doubts.

Sometimes it was difficult to get to work through the bombing and the buses and trains were cut, and I remember one occasion when a lorry full of soldiers pulled up for me and my friend and yanked us up with them. "Great fun!"

When the war finished things settled down a bit and things got easier but not for a long time. I met my husband after the war at a church reunion we had both belonged to. He had been a Boy Scout and I was a Brownie, so we didn't know each other but he knew my sister. We soon put that right and were married within a couple of years.

~

We kept our spirits up during the war by singing a lot. We lived next door in Stepney to three old ladies. They all worked in a pickle factory and spent every evening in the pub around the corner having a drink!

The rocket bombs were dropping thick and fast at this time and our family had to sleep in a horrible air raid shelter built in the road. Our poor Mother had great difficulty getting Jessie (Sister) and myself out of bed to join everyone in the air raid shelter. We were so tired we just wanted to sleep in our own beds. I don't know how much safer we were in the air-raid shelter than our house. "None at all as far as I was concerned."

Later in the evenings the three "old ladies" slowly made their way home singing all the old songs and joining us in the dirty smelly air raid shelter reeking of pickles. We became very fond of them as they always cheered us up.

Sometimes on a Friday I would join my mum and dad in the pub around the corner. I didn't drink I was about 15 and had a lemonade, but I enjoyed being with them and we always had a good sing song.

One Friday my mother said she didn't want to go for some reason, but she didn't know why. Later-on that evening, we had a dreadful Air Raid and our little pub got a direct hit. Needless to say, a lot of people died in that pub that night. It was very close to where we lived, and all our windows were blown out and our dear dad was thrown right along our passage. It was a very near miss.
I soon had to grow up after leaving school.

~

A very dear nephew David, who lived in our house when I had left after the war looked after the last old lady for a long time till she died. He is still a lovely man. He was only a boy at the time but always had that very kind streak.
16

It sounds strange but the war seemed to bring the best out in people because we were all in it together.

End

On the 8th June 1946, *King George VI* sent a certificate with the *Royal Crest* on the front to all school children in Britain. M was 18 and working in London, so the certificate that she kept all her life must have been sent to young people who were at school or evacuated at some time between 1939 and 1946.

The King's message reads:

TODAY AS WE CELEBRATE VICTORY,
I send this personal message to you and all other boys and girls at school. For you have shared in the hardships and dangers of total war and you have shared no less in the triumph of the Allied Nations.

I know you will always feel proud to belong to a country which was capable of such supreme effort: proud, too, of parents and elder brothers and sisters who by their courage, endurance and enterprise brought victory. May these qualities be yours as you grow up and join in the common effort to establish among the nations of the world unity and peace.

~

On 19 December 1947, M received a written reference from her employer as she was leaving to be married to Dad and she never worked in paid full-time employment again. This was always a bone of contention as M wanted to go back to work after brother Tom and I were at school, but Dad wanted her to be a full-time mum and housewife. In those days, the Victorian ethic often prevailed and the opinion if not the legal ruling of the husband on his wife's vocation of 'housewife' usually carried most weight in M&D's community and circle of family and friends.

M's employer reference was from the *'Ministerie Van Verkeer'* (Netherland Ministry of Transport); *Bewindvoering Koopvaardijvloot-Groote Vaart* (Management Merchant Fleet-Deep Sea); *Crew Department.*

Her office was in *Moorgate*, London EC2 and she often spoke about the wonderful hardwood panelling throughout the building and how professional and polite the Dutch managers were. M's maiden name was *Smeeth* and the reference read:

To Whom It May Concern

Miss Jean Ivy Smeeth has been in our service from 27th July 1942 (*She was 14 years old when she started) till 31st December 1947 when she became redundant owing to the liquidation of our London office.

Miss Smeeth was originally employed as a junior clerk and subsequently promoted to position of Sundstrand accounting machine operator.

She has proved to be an efficient and conscientious worker, a good time-keeper and entirely trustworthy.

We have much pleasure in recommending Miss Smeeth for any responsible position for which she may make application.

Signed and stamped: *Netherlands Ministry of Shipping and Fisheries. Crew (Allotments Dept.)*

Well done my teenage Mum!

~

M was my 'Braveheart.' Braveheart is a successful film which is fictionally based on the 13th Century Scottish warrior William Wallace who led the Scots in the *First War of Scottish Independence* against *King Edward I* of England. In the film the Scottish warriors wore blue face paint, did not wear underpants, had hairy faces and chests etc, and shouted: "*Death to the Sassenachs*" (*A term used by Gaelic inhabitants of Britain to refer to the English*) and then they bashed people with mostly blunt instruments. M did once hit someone over the head with a packet of un-cooked spaghetti (Detailed information to follow), however, she was not Scottish and she did none of the things listed above.

M was a woman uniquely typical of her time and generation. Her ancestry is a rich mix of folk from different backgrounds but she never sought information on her family tree, however, when she was young, she was told at a fairground by a gypsy palm reader that she had been an Egyptian Princess in her previous life. M was comfortable with this. As a small boy I racked my brain to think of something she did that was obviously carried over from her life as an Egyptian or indeed any other sort of Princess and I was satisfied that I had found it when I saw her doing the '*hand- jive*'* at the *Collier Row British Legion* Christmas dance in 1961.

Note: The hand-jive which emerged in the 1940's Rhythm & Blues era can include thigh slapping, cross-wrist slapping, fist pumping, hand clapping and finger in the air/hitch-hike waving.

On reflection, I find the comparison a little stretched-to-fit, but it felt right in 1961. If the hand-jive sounds like fun to you dear reader, why not have a go! Practice privately and don't be constrained if you want to make up your own set of hand-jiving moves. Remove loose bracelets and bangles and other dangly bits from your wrists, or alternatively, wear eye goggles for protection.

M was very proud of her family, and would always say "my sister Jess/Ivy" and "my brother David/Fred." I used to think it was a bit odd to prefix their names with an explanation of who they were but I was missing the point, M was proud of her sisters and brothers and wanted people to know she had them, rather like wearing a badge of honour. My wife Joni is from the East End (Ilford) and she says the same thing when talking about her sister – a surviving East Enders custom maybe?

Unlike my Mother-in-law Jean, M would not have been comfortable with being described as the family *'Matriarchal figure' (*An older woman who is influential within a family or organization)* but she was much loved and respected by her family and loved receiving visits, letters, cards and phone calls from all of us. She would boast to anyone in ear shot about her latest holiday phone call from a grandson/daughter from a beach or mountain top in the UK or overseas. She particularly enjoyed being sung to by a crowd of rowdy young men who were fuelled by fresh air and cold drinks singing a communal chant to *'Nanny Romf' (*Romf* is of course short for *Romford*).

She grumbled about Dad not wanting her to go to work until the day she died but filled her time with voluntary work including as a *'Meals on Wheels'* driver for *Havering Social Services* where she would deliver a cooked lunch to elderly people in a little Council van. As a *'flower lady'* (*Think Audrey Hepburn in *'My Fair Lady'* but in *Harold Wood Hospital* in *Romford* and not *Covent Garden*) she would arrange the new mum's flowers in the maternity ward and would describe every baby she met as 'beautiful.'

In some of her middle years M was also a 'lady of leisure' who invariably attended an *Adult Education* class in the day or evening until she became too old to get herself there and back safely. Some of the classes she attended between 1956 and 1996 at various local schools and colleges included *Tailoring; Cookery; Physical Training* i.e. ladies bending and stretching and waving their arms and legs around in a small dusty hall; *'The History of Old Essex'* e.g. Henry XVIII hunting in Epping forest; Yoga; Dressmaking; Floral art; Crochet *(*Pronounced 'crowshay', not to be confused with 'crotchety');* Social Studies (I don't really know what this was about so please use your imagination?); *Embroidery; Basket work* i.e. make a basket to put things in when you take it home; *Decoupage* (*Making arty things with paper, scissors and glue)* - M was very good at this and made lots of 3D framed pictures of all manner of chocolate box scenes e.g. Dickensian-style characters, cute children and animals; and last but not least, *Disco Dancing,* while wearing an early form of Spandex-like leotard (Nice).

M was pretty smart, and I can't think of anything in her daily life that she was particularly bad at doing, she had a little touch of magic about her, and she could do several things quickly at once while also having a conversation. Her youngest sister Ivy called her *'Mrs Whip-it- quick',* for example, she could chat and make my breakfast in the blink of an eye when I called in on a Saturday morning - fried egg, tomato, baked beans, bacon or sausage, mug of tea and buttered toast - while clearing up the kitchen and making herself a single slice of toast with *Marmite* and a cup of tea which she said *"tastes better in a cup with a saucer."*

M made tea in a teapot if she had 'special guests,' not me, and wartime rationing of food made her squeeze every drop out of a tea-bag with a teaspoon into an old egg- cup that had no other purpose, and then pour the drips back into the cup. She fed the birds daily and would cut up food scraps and spills - their special treat was bacon rind. Nothing went off in the fridge as it was managed with military precision, portions were small, and the rubbish bag virtually empty every week.

When she opened her front door to me she would scan my face and summarise my state of health in a Nano second *(*One thousand-millionth of a second):* "Bill you look awful/tired/well etc."

M was instinctively a good mimic, mostly of the people in her life, she didn't do it to entertain but to illustrate the person she was talking about. Her voice and body language would change, I think without her necessarily being aware of it. Two of her best and most frequent characters were an elderly, nosey neighbour and a much loved, obstinate brother in-law. There are several good mimics in M's family and if I may say, I can still do a pretty good *Charlie Drake* singing *'My Boomerang Won't Come Back,'* 'Naughty' and 'Please Mr Custer.'

*Note: Charles Edward Springall (1925 - 2006) AKA Charlie Drake, was an English comedian, actor, writer and singer who was popular with children and was known for his catchphrase: "Hello, my darlins"!

Fortunately for me, M was someone who did 'suffer fools gladly' and she was always tolerant, except in extreme circumstances. She would be embarrassed when Dad, who occasionally could be less tolerant, confronted someone, like a political election candidate who knocked on our front door in the early 1970's to ask for support for his extreme right-wing political party. Dad spoke through his teeth which were firmly closed and said: "I am washing this doorstep with hot water and disinfectant in one minute, so you had better get off it and don't come back."

M didn't use a dish washer, computer or mobile phone and she became increasingly stubborn as she grew older about the 'modern' things she didn't want, but the television and radio were a central part of her life for pleasure and companionship.

Elderly M kept her false teeth in a plastic cup on the bathroom sink of whichever house she was sleeping in that night. She stayed with us quite often and I would move the cup on to the bath side to avoid an unwelcome toothy grin and she would always put them back on the sink. We never spoke of this differing viewpoint, we didn't need to, as we knew neither of us would give an inch (Tooth or nail), so discussion and negotiation was pointless.

She had an extended stay with us shortly before she died, and we were sparring partners across the full range of common issues like the heating (Up/down); choosing the programme on tv (Old films v live sport); swearing and being rude about people (That would be me); and the advantages and disadvantages of a glass of wine or two in the evening while taking 32 pills a day (M).

The sparring between us was the mild bickering of two people whose relationship was very close, and never involved a standing count or knock-out blow. In fact, I can only remember M hitting me once when I was about 11 cheeky years of age. I don't remember what I said but it was the wrong thing at the wrong time, and because M was holding a long packet of uncooked spaghetti in a blue grease-proof paper wrapper at that very moment, she hit me with it. She struck my shoulder and there was an explosion and scattering of bits of pasta, I laughed (The wrong thing to do at the wrong time) and she stomped off in frustration crunching through the pasta in the hallway causing me to laugh again. It was a good value strike because we laughed about it for ever more.

Even as an old lady in poor health, M had the energy and strength of will to (proverbially) box my ears. She had more than a fair share of medical troubles in her life and always tried to struggle on in her determined, dogged way. She didn't like to 'bother' her local doctors, claiming '*they are very busy.*' If she had an appointment at the doctors or hospital, which were frequent in the last few years of her life, she would constantly apologise to doctors and nurses alike for being a nuisance.

Weather permitting, she would go out to the shops every day, often tottering down to Romford town centre for exercise and some human interaction, with a shopping trolley on wheels that helped keep her upright. She suffered from *Angina* and would often need to sit on familiar front garden walls to catch her breath on her way there and back. She was a familiar figure in the neighbourhood and many people would regularly stop and chat while she sat on one of her rest-walls. She knew who the local people were, the names of their children and Grandchildren, dogs, cats and tortoises etc.

M retained the *East End* community spirit all her life and had no idea how well liked she was in her neighbourhood where chatting in the front garden or street became increasingly unusual in the 38 years she lived in her bungalow which was between *Romford Market Place* and *Raphael Park* where Dad's ashes were spread at the foot of his own dedicated cherry tree. M&D and I moved there in 1977 and she was the last of '*The Street of '77*' when she died in 2015.

A local homeless person kept his few possessions and many newspapers and magazines in a shopping trolley, he was a scruffy elderly man with hair befitting an eccentric *Doctor Who*, and he spoke only on rare occasions. M didn't like him being called 'a tramp' and told people that his name was Henry.

Note: Ref 'Henry.' I mentioned to M that her name for the homeless gentleman was indeed a King's name but also the description given to a floating poo (*A *'floater')* in the public swimming pools that I frequented as a child. The plaintive cry of: "*It's a Henry*"! would trigger the life-saving staff to blow a whistle and call everyone out of the water until it was captured in a net with a long pole. It usually signalled my early departure from the public baths as swimming no longer seemed so much fun after a Henry had been spotted.

Henry chose M's front wall as his main location on most days, she didn't like him sitting on her wall but wasn't intimidated by him and they would greet each other when they passed on the pavement and occasionally there would be a polite, brief conversation. M kept an eye on him, he declined hot or cold drinks and she was very worried, fearing the worst when he suddenly disappeared one day. Months later he reappeared looking "none the worse for wear" and normal service was resumed.

In 2015, M suffered a stroke while waiting for five hours in a hospital waiting room for a blood transfusion in preparation for forthcoming surgery. My brother Tom was with her and she was transferred to the intensive care ward at *Queen Elizabeth's Hospital* in *Romford* but died two days later on a cold, grey 1st of February Sunday with beloved family members with her.

M had been unwell for a number of years but remained very determinedly alive and independent, there were too many good things going on in her family life for her to want to die from poor health. On the Sunday that she passed away, she continued to battle on in hospital after the nurses removed her life support, and my wife Joni said to her 'it's ok to let go Mum.' She died soon after, at peace with a few of the very many people she had loved dearly in her long and eventful life.

Soon after she passed away, I listened to an '*Eastertide*' church service reading on the telly in which the speaker quoted *Adam L Gordon:*

"Life is mostly froth and bubbles, two things stand like stone, kindness in another's trouble; courage in your own."

Those words written by a stranger described my Mum very well.

~

M's Birthday Timeline:
February 21st is a big day in our family. M and Joni were both born, and Joni and I were married on this day. Other notable events on this significant date in the history of the world include the following:

1173 Pope Alexander III canonizes Thomas Becket, Archbishop of Canterbury.

1431 Joan of Arc's first day of interrogation during her trial for heresy.

1613 Michael Romanov, elected first *Russian Tsar* of the house of Romanov. *1746* British forces surrender Inverness Castle to Bonnie Prince Charlie and the Jacobite forces.

1804 The first steam locomotive runs for the first time, along the tramway of the *Penydarren Ironworks* in Merthyr Tydfil, Wales.

1848 Karl Marx and *Friedrich Engels* publish *"The Communist Manifesto"* in London.

1874 Benjamin Disraeli succeeds *William Gladstone* as British Prime Minister.

1910 Douglas R S Bader, British pilot WWII was born (We lived on the outskirts of *Hornchurch Airdrome* where he was based in the War).

1922 Britain declares Egypt a sovereign State.

1931 Alka Seltzer introduced (The original medication for a hang-over in our house).

1933 Nina Simone (Eunice Waymon), American singer was born (M liked her).

1937 Initial flight of the first 'flying car', *Waldo Waterman's Arrowbile.*(No further news was received after the flight?).

1946 Alan Rickman, English actor was born (*Robin Hood Prince of Thieves, Die Hard, Harry Potter*). He died too young.

1946 Tyne Daly, actress was born (*Cagney & Lacey* – a favourite show of Joni and I back in the day).

1955 Kelsey Grammer, American actor and Director was born (*'Cheers'* and *'Frasier'*) Another family favourite.

1964 UK flies 24,000 rolls of *Beatles* wallpaper to US; *1983 Donald Davis* runs 1 mile backwards in 6 minutes 7.1 seconds (No reason given?)

Dad

Dad was the third eldest of nine children from *Stepney* in the East End of London. He very much enjoyed and always remembered being a member of the *Cub and Boy Scout* movement, progressing to the 'rank' of *Ranger* (As did my big brother Tom). He often talked about his Scouting experiences and he loved travelling to different places for camps and other rumbustious outdoor activities. One trip in the 1930's was to a large wooden shed in the countryside where a bunch of Scouts slept in the garden of the bungalow of a senior Scouter in *Cranham* in rural Essex.

They practiced various activities such as *'Wood Craft', 'Backwoods Cooking'* (Cooking in the woods, not cooking backwards), *'Gardener Activity'* and *'Sportsmanship,'* and would then take the tests that gave Cubs and Scouts their traditional armful of cotton badges. One of Dad's favourite expressions which possibly came from his Scouting days emerged when someone dropped food on the floor and he would say: *"Pick it up and give it a wipe, there's nothing like a bit of good clean dirt."*

He ran a small business while soldiering in *North Africa* during the War where he would dry off the Army's used tea leaves in the sun and exchange them for all manner of produce from chocolate and footwear to alcohol and fruit with the local people and Allied troops.

In the 1980's when we were first married, Joni and I moved to *Cranham*, and while the senior Scouters bungalow was indeed still there, nothing much around it resembled the virgin countryside as Cranham sits at the very Eastern edge of the post-war *'Green Belt'* area which was intended to protect sub/urban development in the countryside.

Today, Cranham is home for the *London Underground* trains that run on the *District* line from *Upminster to Richmond* in the West of London. The full trip takes an estimated 88 minutes through 41 stations, and includes many iconic London locations including *Tower Bridge, The City of London ('The Square* Mile'), the River Thames Embankment, Westminster (Parliament and Big Ben), and the *West End* (The posh side of town).

~

Dad was a moderate *'socialist'* by nature who voted for the Labour or Liberal parties. I think that living in the East End with many neighbours and friends of different nationalities and religions, not least the Jewish families from Eastern Europe, developed in him a strong dislike of the extreme right-wing Fascists that grew in number and strength in his local neighbourhoods. The influence of the rise in the East End of *Oswald Mosely** was significant at the time as he was a black-shirted Fascist who looked to *Adolph Hitler* and the *Nazi* movement in Germany for his lead.

*Note: *Sir Oswald Mosley, 6th Baronet*, was an English politician who was the leader of the *British Union of Fascists* from 1932 to 1940. The Fascists would spread anti- Semitic propaganda and hold hostile demonstrations in the Jewish sections of East London wearing Nazi-style uniforms and insignia. A notorious clash took place in the *Battle of Cable Street* in the East End in October 1936 and Dad was involved (More details to follow).

~

The Chapter that follows is mostly about Dad's experiences during the long years of the Second World War, and within three years of coming home from the War, he set up a wholesale china and glass business called **Rontays Co Ltd**, with his best friend, fellow soldier and business partner, my Uncle Bill, who I was named after. They ran a small, successful business in *Chadwell Heath* between *Romford and Dagenham* for over 40 years, employing family members and others who mostly became lifelong friends of the family.

In the early days of the new business Bill and Dad took turns to drive together to the Potteries in *Stoke-on-Trent* and the very first load of china and glass headed for the warehouse in Chadwell Heath tipped over on a busy main road and had to be shovelled off the road with the help of the Police.

Rontays supplied many of the small shops that sold china and glass in the London and Essex areas including businesses such as *Fords* at Dagenham, pubs, hospitals, clubs, Universities and hotels. If you lived or worked in these areas at the time you may possibly recall the round dark brown glazed teapots called *'Rock'* teapots; *'Blue-Band'* cups, saucers and plates; pint and half pint beer glasses and D*imple* mugs; and dinner services like *'Poppy'* which was a

favourite pattern for many years. They held a small stock of *Wedgewood* china which was more securely stored than everything else in the warehouse and tended to finish up in Director's Board rooms.

Most of the stock came from the *Potteries* in *Stoke-on-Trent* and the most popular brands sold by *Rontays* included: *Alfred Meakins; Royal Dalton; Ellgrave; Alcock; Sadler; Wood; Bilton; WH Grindley; Percy James; Johnson Bros; Rathbone; Twyfords; Cartwright & Edwards; Tams; and Handcock.*

I remember the arrival of revolutionary glassware called *Pyrex*, and Dad drank his tea with a slice of lemon from a *Pyrex* beaker with a yellow plastic holder until the day he died. I also remember the arrival of a new source of cut glass from *Czechoslovakia which* was good quality and value and very popular.

Uncle Bill was renowned for his habit of buying large quantities of all sorts of china and glass memorabilia that was produced for every major Royal event such as the Queen's *Coronation in 1953*, weddings, and the *Queen Mother* and *Queen's* significant Birthdays. Much of it was cheap and there was always stock unsold after the event, to reduce the wastage, there was not a family member, friend, or customer who wasn't gifted 'something patriotic' from the leftovers.

The weekly Friday delivery from the *Potteries* came in a 10 ton lorry from *'Wass Transport'* in Stoke which squeezed up the alleyway off *Chadwell Heath High Street* opposite the *Coopers Arms* pub. Bricks would be placed under the wheels on one side to tip the lorry away from the shop window on the corner of the alleyway and on the other side to avoid a large rock which was firmly cemented in the driveway for no apparent good reason (Lorry drivers and customers were told it was a Milestone on the ancient original road confirming *'13 Miles To London'* (*Aldgate*)). Fortunately, the lorry was always well packed, the drivers very good and so the china and glass were rarely unloaded with breakages.

Much of the stock arrived in wooden tea-chests from Ceylon/Sri Lanka, lined with tin foil with a sprinkling of tealeaves in the bottom. They were packed and stacked up to four high and were returned to the *Potteries* on the delivery lorry when excess to requirements. Any breakages were put in tea-chests and used by local Scout groups and schools for their broken crockery stalls at summer fairs and fetes. Throwing wooden balls to smash china arranged on shelves was always a popular, therapeutic attraction.

The fresh fish shop two doors up (*Eric Russell's* I believe) was '*By Appointment*' to *Her Majesty the Queen* and the fishmonger was happy to tell customers that the *Duke of Edinburgh's* favourite fishy treat was a weekly delivery of jellied eels. Possible, but unlikely I suspect?

I worked part-time in the warehouse from when I could weald a broom until I was in my early 20's when I would drive a delivery van. My brother and some of our cousins also took a turn during school/college holidays to earn much needed pocket money.

Some of the footballers from *West Ham* and *Spurs* who lived in the area would visit the warehouse and secure a 'bargain.' Dad was a Spurs season ticket holder with his youngest brother Ron, and I suspect the *Rontays* staff had a good source for the purchase of match tickets?

The *Chadwell Heath* police station was just across the road from the warehouse and the Constabulary were always welcome at the warehouse, and the Firm's* bank manager seemed to enjoy popping in for the odd item or three (*Rontays was always referred to as 'The Firm' but it had no links with mobs or gangsters. Honest Officer!).

Dad and Uncle Bill closed their business in the early 1980's when they were in their 60's, at a time when supermarkets with big buying and selling power moved into china and glassware in earnest. In retirement, Dad stepped up his Magistrate Court, Youth Club and school Governor work (at *Campion School* in Hornchurch). Uncle Bill's 'retirement' is sketched out later in the book.

~

Dad played football for *Collier Row British Legion* for many years and when he couldn't get a game in the Second XI he started a third team consisting of mostly youngsters and played himself in goal. He also set up, played for and ran a cricket club under the name of the family business *Rontays Cricket Club*, which for a number of years in the 70's and 80's, occasionally had up to seven family members playing. Six of us were regulars for a few very enjoyable years. All boys, no girls sadly.

The cricket club outlived Dad and completed its final innings in 2010 after more than 50 years. It featured regularly in the sports pages of the *Romford Recorder* and built a reputation for good attacking cricket and even better après-cricket performances in the bars of cricket clubs throughout London and (mostly) the County of Essex.

When I played football for my school, *Romford Technical County High* (Red shirts with blue trim) Dad was one of the best attending parents on a Saturday morning. Until I grew up a bit, I would ask him not to come and watch because it was bad for my masculine reputation, but he came any way, usually in his sheepskin coat (Ref the famous football commentator *John Motson/Motty*), and would give me an honest appraisal after the game which was always helpful. On odd occasions, he would referee if a teacher wasn't available, and he was clearly good at it because he was pretty fit for a man of his age and there was never any controversy or complaints. Most importantly, my rugged aura remained intact.

One cold dank Saturday morning Dad refereed a school match and our goalie Steve, a friend to this day, had the task of collecting the ball back from the Cemetery behind his goal. He seemed to show off, diving head-first off the wall into the graveyard and we all laughed when his head reappeared impersonating a ghost. In fact, he had slipped off the wall and broken both his arms on a tombstone. Dad was first on the scene to help pull him back over the wall by his (Broken) arms. Oops! Fortunately, Steve went on to long successful careers as a chef and community policeman and he bears no grudge.

Dad would always chat on the touchline with the teachers and Headmaster *Mr Coomber*, a brusque Yorkshireman from *Leeds* who had paint speckles on his spectacles for two years when he arrived down south. I believe that Dad may have covered my (Bad behavioural) tracks on a few occasions but he never mentioned it so I can only surmise? When the Headmaster was reprimanding me he would say to me without fail: "*William! Your Father* (Pronounced "*Futher*") *wouldn't be proud of you, young man!*"

Dad played leisurely golf at *Romford Golf Club* and helped establish a group called '*The Scrubbers'* for those who would not be challenging the leaders in any form of competitive match. I believe it continues to this day.

Dad was a part-time Magistrate at the Romford Court for a number of years and because we lived only a stone's throw from the Police Station, they would knock on the door day and mostly night for a Magistrate's signature for an arrest and who knows what else? He used his network of contacts to support local Youth clubs in the area, helping to find funding and generally championing their cause.

Dad was of the generation of British men who wore a shirt, jacket and tie much of the time (But not on the beach). He was always smart within his generation's dress code 'genre' and if the occasion warranted, his favourite formal togs were an impressive yellow woollen Scottish waistcoat with a brown pinstripe and a pocket watch and chain. I realised some years ago that it was no coincidence that my choice of wristwatch, wallet and wedding ring was and remains very much in Dad's own taste. I think there must be a 'comfort' factor for me in those important everyday personal items. Thanks Dad.

M&D always enjoyed their holidays and while the UK was a favourite venue they were well travelled mostly in Europe, and Dad would seek out local bars and restaurants, often carrying his favoured 'Conversational Spanish, German, Italian or Greek Guide.' M was less keen to wander off the tourist pathways but it was Dad's instinctive desire to meet and chat with local people wherever they were. We had meals in the family homes of hotel waiters in Tunisia, Spain and Greece.

~

Dad's Timeline: Having listed some of the key events taking place on 21 February, M's Birthday, I should do likewise for Dad who was born on **July 17, 1921:**

1762 *Catherine II* becomes Tsarina of Russia following the murder of *Peter III* (An enduring *'Who Done It?'*); and *Napoleon* surrenders to the British at *Rochefort* (Well done the *Duke of Wellies* - this must surely be where the expression 'Give it some wellie!" comes from?).

1841 the satirical magazine "*Punch*" was first published.

1899 the American actor *James Cagney* was born, ref the film *Yankee Doodle Dandy*. One of Dad's favourite 'Yanks' along with *John Wayne*. Dad described all films of any type with guns and shooting including Sci-Fi movies as *'Cowboys and Indians.'*

1914 *New York Giants* baseball outfielder *Red Murray* is knocked unconscious by lightning after catching a flyball (*A ball that flies uncontrolled off the bat*), the *Giants* won 3-1 but I doubt *Red* knew or cared much about the result at the time.

1917 *King George V's* Royal Proclamation changes the name of the *Royal Family* from (German) *Saxe-Coburg-Gotha* to *Windsor (*Easier when filling out application forms and signing One's name). The first *World War began the following year.*

1918 The entire *Romanov Royal Family* were executed by a Bolshevik firing squad in a basement in Siberia.

1937 *Elmer Fudd*, *Warner Bros.* cartoon character made his bumbling debut in "*Egghead Rides Again*". His catchphrase was "*Shhh, be vewy quiet, I'm hunting wabbits."* His least favourite wabbit was *Bugs Bunny* They were a favourite pair in our house.

1947 *Camilla Parker Bowles* Duchess of Cornwall and wife of Prince Charles was born; 1952 American actor *David Hasselhoff, The Hoff*, was born (Ref *'Night Rider', and 'Baywatch')*.

1954 *Angela Merkel*, Chancellor of Germany, was born.1957 *The Cavern* club opened in Liverpool, and was soon to host a newly formed boy band called the Beatles. 1975 *Apollo 18* and *Soyuz 19* make the first US/USSR linkup in space. This relationship remains a work in progress.

~

Dad showed signs of dementia in his sixties and battled against *Alzheimer's* for the last 10 years of his life. He died suddenly of a heart attack in 1994 while sitting on a bench with Mum outside the *Dolphin Leisure Centre* on his way home from the Friday market in Romford.

~

The following Chapter on the Second *World War* gives glimpses of the brave, lucky young man and leader Dad was through the eight challenging years that he was a soldier (1939-46).

Dad is my hero. Lucky is a son who can say that.

THE SECOND WORLD WAR

I often wonder how a decade of worry and fear about World War II affected the health of those who experienced it? How did the stress of their generation compare with their own children's, who have experienced very different lives and lifestyles? We know that stress is a dangerous part of life even without the additional worry of a war in your own back yard with the prospect of an invasion by a mighty, conquering foe.

Right-wing extremists had bullied their way to political and economic power in the shambles that Germany found itself in at the end of the First World War and it had become a formidable enemy. Their well-publicised military might, aggressive doctrine, and ferocious Nazi rhetoric must have been a very threatening and frightening experience to all those that stood in their way.

The stories and information of the War in this Chapter are a mixture of factual accounts of people living through the War, official military records and journalism. There are a small range of facts about the action that my Dad survived over seven terrible years of warfare before he was demobbed in 1946. I list some staggeringly awful statistics of the War's dead and injured, and a small number of personal accounts of specific incidents and battles that Dad, best friend Bill, comrades and his brother Vic were in the thick of.

When a violent incident, fight, battle or war involves someone that you know, particularly family and friends, it becomes more real and sharpens your sense of awareness and some of my research for this book has been shocking and at times felt brutal. I knew a talented young family man who was killed in the 9/11 *Twin Towers* tragedy, and a young colleague whose husband was murdered in the London 7/7 bombings in 2005. Even from my very detached position these incidents remain a gut-wrenching memory and will stay with me and will always cast their shadow. How did Mum and Dad's generation endure the years of war, its build up and aftermath and then go on to lead 'normal' often seemingly care-free lives? I think it can only be described as a wonder of human and Mother nature.

In the early phase of the War in the summer of 1940, the British suffered a crushing defeat at *Dunkirk,* and the most likely outcome for much of the seven years of the War was defeat and ultimately invasion by a large, well organised and equipped unforgiving enemy. How do you cope with a threat like that, what did the people who lived during the war think about when they got out of bed in the morning or stopped during the day for a cup of tea? Did they think about the likely loss of life, their own and others, did they worry constantly about losing their homes, jobs, pets, pubs, cinema, favourite shoes, suit, photo albums, Grandad's watch, wedding ring, record collection and team photo signed by the entire West Ham United Football Club? (A local team).

It must have been very tough to cope in the circumstances in London and other major cities in the firing line in Britain during the War years, but the *Bulldog Spirit* of "*Keep Calm and Carry On*" was a very appropriate slogan for the time and circumstances. I hope I would have been able to 'carry on' like folk did during those years, but 'keeping calm' might have been easier said than done?

The War itself was very nearly lost several times before it finally ended in victory. M watched the *Battle of Britain* in the (often) blue sky above her between July and October 1940, and saw many airplanes and airmen blown apart in it or plummet from it. She was a sitting, standing or lying-down target throughout the German *'Blitz'* of London (*'Blitz' is from the word "Blitzkrieg" meaning "Lightning War" and it lasted from 1940-1941 during which German bombers dropped 18,000 tons of explosives on London*).

'*Shock and Awe*' is a military term that well describes the German bombing raids during World War 2, it was coined during the Iraq war in 2003 by the American General *Tommy Franks* who described USA tactics as: "*Rapid dominance over an adversary by the initial imposition of overwhelming force and firepower.*"

The threat of a bombing raid by aircraft or rocket never went away in M's London, which was the *East End* and *The City* (*Square Mile*). Today in 'peace time' Britain we have to deal with the problem of terrorism, a very real and worrying daily threat, but as yet we have not had to contend with the terror and horror of massive, continual bombing and all the physical and mental devastation that goes with it. The sound, sight and smell must surely stay with you forever?

This Chapter is not written as a war novel, screenplay, movie or tv adventure, there are no actors playing heroes or villains, background music, special effects, soft-lens photography or colour enhanced post-production. Only some of the true facts and a number of challenging, eye-witness anecdotes.

Newspaper Coverage of the War:
The British newspaper coverage throughout the War was day-to-day, blow-by-blow and when family members and friends were involved it must have made for nervous, compulsive reading as it was a critical source of detailed reporting often beyond the information provided by BBC radio and *Pathé News** at the Cinema. There has surely not been a period of such extended threat, fear and faith in the modern history of Britain as in the period 1939-45.
*Note: Pathé News produced newsreels and documentaries in the UK from 1910 until 1970 and its founder, Charles Pathé, was a pioneer of silent movies.

Here are a few examples of news headlines that were highly significant for my family and the world at large during the War:
July 7, 1940: *Nazi Field Marshall Hermann Goering* unleashed Germany's *Luftwaffe* bombers on cities in Britain. He said: "*This is the historic hour when our*

air force delivers its blows right into the enemy's heart."
My family were the enemy, and many lived and worked in central London at the heart of the Luftwaffe's targets. Around this time the existing peace treaty between Germany and Russia signed in 1939 began to look uncertain and the war against Germany would not have been won without the involvement of Russia, but nobody knew that in 1940.

September 27, 1940: Japan signed a ten-year economic and military alliance with Germany and Italy in Berlin forming the *Rome–Berlin–Tokyo 'Axis.'* This must have been a frightening alliance for the people of the Allied nations around the world.

November 14, 1940: The Luftwaffe used the *'Bombers Moon'* (**Strong light from a full moon*) and 449 bombers dropped 503 tons of bombs and 881 incendiaries (*A device designed to cause fire*) turning *Coventry* into an inferno, killing 554 people and seriously injuring 865. The ruins of the old Cathedral remain today in remembrance of those who died.

St Michael's Church was originally constructed between the late 14th and early 15th Century and was only one of a countless number of historic properties that were destroyed across the world throughout the War.

June 6, 1944: The *D-Day* Normandy landings by the Allies. "D" denotes the *day* of the invasion when 'the exact day when the attack has not yet been determined.' The need for secrecy was clearly essential.

September 11, 1944: The first Allied armed forces entered Germany. US troops under *General Bradley* progressed with *'Free French'* soldiers who had liberated Paris on August 25th. A week earlier British and US troops had freed *Brussels* and *Liege* in Belgium.

March 28, 1945: The last German *'V2 Rocket '* was dropped on Britain and it fell on the *East End* of London. Bomber pilots used the *River Thames* as a guide into *Docklands* and central London day and night. The German name for the rocket is *'Vergeltungswaffe 2'* translating to *'Retaliation Weapon'* referring to the very heavy Allied bombings on German cities where civilian casualties were extensive.

The V2 rocket was the first man-made object to travel into space on 20 June 1944, highlighting the advanced expertise of German scientists and engineers who successfully pioneered journey into space. The V2 rockets caused yet more fear and carnage, not least in London, and some of the same German engineers and scientists were instrumental in sending mankind to the Moon from the USA later in the 1960s.

~

Dad was Christened Thomas (No other name) and was effectively the archetypal *'British Tommy.'* He lied about his age and joined the *Territorial Army* in *Tower Hamlets* at the outbreak of the War. His Regiment was the *Rifle Brigade,* and he was in the *Signal Corps*. He was in service for the seven years of the War from 1939-45 and during 1946 for post-war duties. He fought with the 7th and 8th Armies in North Africa where he and his comrades were named the *'Desert Rats'* and following a hard-earned victory, embarked to Sicily moving on to fight in Italy.

Dad was a soldier from 18 to 25 years of age but never spoke about his combat experiences in any detail to me, M or anyone else as far as we knew. One story I do recall him talking about was an incident in Italy when he and his best friend Bill Taylor, who later became his brother in-law, found themselves accidently on the wrong side of the enemy lines while in a Bren-gun carrier (*Like a small open- top tank with a large machine gun - two sat in the front and about six could squeeze in the back with the gun*). They were chased by enemy soldiers but made their escape, a narrow one for the two friends and also ultimately for all of us who were in the families that the two lost soldiers created after the War.

~

Dad's Army Service Record:

Dad's *'Army Book 64. Soldier's Service and Pay Book'* is in his own handwriting and is so battered that it's not possible to read it all clearly, however, this is my best attempt:

May 1, 1939 - *Enlisted.* This was through *The Territorial Army* at *Bow* in Stepney. He was 17 years and 10 months old, so claimed he was 18 to satisfy the regulations. His *'Trade on enlistment'* was *Glass Beveller.*

September 1939 - *"Called to colours" by the Rifle Brigade, 2ⁿᵈ Tower Hamlets. 'Corps trade and grade': Driver Operator Class III.*

October 1939 - *Regimental Signal Instructors course in Clapham.*

May 1940 - *D&M* training course at Ford Factory Dagenham* (*Maybe 'Driving and Maintenance'?)

October 1940 - *PT* (Physical Training) *Instructors course at Hendon Police College.*

October 1940 - *"Classified Derv Opps"* (Maybe something to do with diesel engine vehicles?)

July 1941 - *Appointed Corporal with 10th Rifle Brigade.*

October 1941 - *W/T* (I don't know what this was?) *Instructors course at Bovington, Dorset.*
*(Note: Today, *'The Armour Centre'* in *Bovington* is the British Army's centre of excellence for training in the skills of armoured warfare. It trains soldiers in driving and maintaining armoured fighting vehicles (AFVs) and operating vehicle weapons' systems and communications equipment. There is also a tank museum at Bovington.)

November 26, 1942 - *Embarked to North Africa.* The Desert Rats were born.

July 31, 1943 - *Embarked to UK on Prisoner of War escort* (I believe this was following the death of his brother Vic from 'friendly fire' in November 1942).

September 1943 - *Returned to Regimental duty overseas* (North Africa).

September 28, 1943 - *Promoted to Lance Sergeant* (A Sergeant of the lowest rank, formerly a Corporal appointed to act as Sergeant without increase in pay - he's climbing the ladder).

March 12, 1944 - *Embarked to Italy* (See the notes below on the *Battle of Monte Cassino*).

May 1944 - *Appointed Signal Sergeant* (Temporary).

September 30, 1944 - *24 hours leave at the 8th Army Rest Camp in Naples.*

October 1944 - *Charged with 'contravention of censorship' regulations* (Re a letter home to his family. Dad's letters saved by his family are all positive and cheerful and give no information other than his own creature comforts and discomforts, like missing a home-made Sunday roast dinner.

December 17, 1944 - Promoted to Sergeant (Signalman).
In 1944, Dad's elder brother Arthur who was in the *Press Corps* on account of flat feet, had a number of celebrity acquaintances and he introduced Dad to *Laurence Olivier* on the set of the film '*Henry V*" while they were filming the *Battle of Agincourt*. Dad always enjoyed a good display of "swash and buckle" and said that Sir Larry was a 'very nice man who gave his time generously.'

March 1945 - Posted to 2nd Rifle Brigade.

June 21, 1945 - One week's leave in Venice. Including lunch in the Warrant Officers and Sergeants Club with grilled steak, mashed potatoes, French beans, fruit salad and cream, bread roll and tea - for 30 Lire. Dad kept the menu with lots of comments written on it from his buddies, only two of which make any sense: "It was smashing"; and "Good Luck Tommy boy, and BOH !!!" ('BOH'?) They were very grateful for this welcome break after the active service they had been through and I have a bunch of black and white photos of the band of brothers enjoying Venice - they were scrubbed clean in smart casual uniforms and very sun tanned.

August 1945 - Embarked to Egypt with 7th Rifle Brigade-Prisoner of War duties. This was the period of the War that Dad experienced some enjoyment and he talked about the good times they had including time spent talking with German prisoners of war who were glad their War was over. Dad was given responsibility for guarding a storage depot which he described as "a barn full of German liquor" and he had the enviable task of ensuring the contents were distributed to the British Army in order to raise morale.

April 13, 1946 - Embarked for final return to UK. How did the returning soldiers feel on this journey? What were their emotions when they saw Blighty for the first time for who knows how long? How did it feel to be back in civilisation on the journey to their homes?

~

Dad's official War records are sketchy from 1939-42 and I was told by the *War Office* that the official records may have been 'classified' (Top secret!) or they may have been destroyed in the London bombings. Dad was in North Africa from 1942 and the Special Air Service (SAS) began life in July 1941.

Lieutenant David Stirling, a *Commando* of the *Scots Guards* had the idea of 'forming small teams of parachute-trained soldiers who would operate behind enemy lines to destroy enemy aircraft, attack supply and reinforcement routes and gain intelligence.' There was already a *'deception unit'* in the Middle East area which wanted to form a *'phantom'* airborne brigade to threaten enemy plans. It was called *K Detachment Special Air Service Brigade* and Lieutenant Stirling's unit became *L Detachment Special Air Service Brigade*.

Their first mission in 1942 was an attack on *Bouerat*, a village in Western *Libiya* where they caused severe damage to the harbour, petrol tanks and storage facilities. They completed   many dangerous raids across North Africa and   in September were renamed *1st SAS Regiment* consisting of four British squadrons, one *Free French* and one *Greek Squadron* and the *Special Boat Section*.

Dad was in this area in 1942 and his Commanding Officer, *Anthony Pawson* (A *'Captain Marvel'* type character) mentions in his diary of the North Africa campaign, activities in *Bouarada* in neighbouring Tunisia at the time, so my fertile brain wonders if Dad had some training and/or involvement with the SAS in the period he was in North Africa? I'd like to think he was secretly a hero, but have no evidence of an SAS connection - he might just as easily have been co-opted by the *Catering Corps* to peel spuds?

Medals and Commendations:
Dad was authorised to wear the following medals by *Lieutenant-Colonel, Commanding 2nd Battalion, The Rifle Brigade:*
The 1939-45 Star for operational service, 3rd September 1939, and 2nd September 1945;
The Africa Star with Army Clasp (August 1944);
The Italy Star;
The 'France Germany' Star;
The Defence Medal; The Territorial Efficiency Medal;
The War Medal 1939-1945 (Which was awarded to all full-time service personnel).

The 'Star' medals were awarded for 'Gallantry,' and Dad was officially *'Mentioned in Despatches'* (MID) on 23 May 1946. It reads:
"War Office, May 1946. The KING has been graciously pleased to approve that the following be Mentioned in recognition of gallant and distinguished services in the Mediterranean Theatre."
Dad's name and rank (Sergeant) appears in a long list of military personnel from across the British Commonwealth. A MID is not an award of a medal but is a commendation of an act of gallantry or service. Dad's Superior Officers would have written a report for High Command which described his: *"Gallant or meritorious action in the face of the enemy."* All despatches were published in the London Gazette, a State newspaper which has existed since 1665.

In 1920, the *Army Order* authorised the issue of an *oak leaf* emblem decoration to be pinned or sewn diagonally on to the 'Victory' medal ribbon or the left breast of the formal dress uniform. Dad's *'King's Mention'* was for action in Italy, but I haven't been able to locate any details of what he did.

~

Brief History of *The Rifle Brigade*:
The British Military replaced the famous and historical *'Longbow'* (and arrows) with the *'Musket'* which developed into the *rifle*. Therefore, I consider my Dad who was an infantryman (The soldiers that did the fighting in the front line) to have been a latter-day *Longbowman* of which the *'Essex Longbowmen'* were feared by foreign enemies and admired by countless Queens and Kings. Furthermore, he was also a modern-day *'Musketeer'* as seen and glamorised in countless novels, tv series and movies. There was no glamour in the military training or action during
World War II:

The Regiment was formed in January 1800 as an *'Elite and experimental Corps of Riflemen.'* It drew recruits from a variety of British Regiments and initially they were armed with rifles which were more accurate with longer range than the musket but took longer to load. Not good when you have fired a shot and the enemy keep on coming.

The idea of individual soldiers hitting specific targets was largely unheard of in the 1800s with only the 'mass volley' being used. The Regiment was trained to use natural cover wearing green as camouflage instead of the traditional red, and riflemen worked in pairs and were encouraged to think for themselves in combat.

I have Dad's *Rifle Brigade* green beret stored in my bedroom wardrobe. When I was a kid, I wore it with a home-made uniform and a rifle that fired ping-pong balls. No-one was injured in my period of pretend soldiering. Not even next door's cat *Marjorie*.

The Regiment became an important element in most actions of the British Empire including *The American War of Independence 1775; The Battle of Waterloo 1815; The Crimean War 1854–1856; The Indian Mutiny 1857–1859; The American Civil War 1861–1865; Khartoum 1878–1898; and the Boer War in South Africa 1899-1902.* In 1861 on the death of its Colonel-in-Chief, *Prince Albert*, The Queen bestowed the title of '*The Prince Consort's Own Rifle Brigade'* on the Regiment.

In 1948 the Regiment was merged with The King's Royal Rifle Corps to form The Green Jackets Brigade, and in 1958 it amalgamated with The Oxfordshire and Buckinghamshire Light Infantry. In 1966 the three Regiments became the three Battalions of the Royal Green Jackets and in 2007 were merged with The Devonshire and Dorset Light Infantry, The Light Infantry and The Royal Gloucestershire, Berkshire and Wiltshire Light Infantry to become The Rifles.

~

The Main Campaigns That Dad Was Involved In:

North Africa:
History records battles in North Africa involving the Greeks, Romans, Arabs and Turks. Napoleon said that "Egypt is the most important country in the world." Suez is the land bridge connecting Africa with Asia and the Suez Canal, built in 1869, it was critically important in both World Wars.

For the Allies, the control of the Suez area and North African region was very challenging as France had collapsed and been occupied by Germany, and in June 1940 Italy entered the War on the side of the Germans. Consequently, a relatively small British force in the Middle East stood alone and had to beware in all directions, south to Italian East Africa, west to Italian Libya, and north-east towards Syria whose loyalties were not clear to the British. In addition, the British lines of communication through the Mediterranean were initially cut off. Apart from that everything was fine.

Tobruk:
Britain took control of *Tobruk* after routing the Italians in 1940 but the Germans reinforced the Italian troops with the *Afrika Korps* of *General Erwin Rommel,* the *Desert Fox,* who battled cleverly and continually with the British *Eighth Army* (*The Desert Rats* were considerably smaller than foxes*) around *Tobruk*, finally forcing them to retreat into Egypt. This left the Allied garrison at the port of *Tobruk* manned only by the *South African Division* which included the *Eleventh Indian Brigade.*

With artillery, dive-bombers and *Panzer* (Tank) forces, the Germans pushed past the Allies, and defeated South African *General Henrik Klopper* ordered the surrender on the morning of the 21st June 1942. Rommel took more than 33,000 prisoners one of whom was Dad's brother Vic, together with thousands of vehicles, fuel, and rations. *Rommel* was promoted by *Adolph Hitler* to *Field Marshall* and he turned his attention to *Suez*.

The *Siege of Tobruk* in Libya was one of the most significant battles in North Africa, the battle started on 11 April 1941 and lasted for 241 days. The Indian and South African Allies fought valiantly throughout.

Lieutenant Colonel R.H.W.S. Hastings 2nd Battalion Rifle Brigade, wrote an account of the battle:

The arrival in Africa of German armoured formations put a different complexion on the Western Desert problem. We looked forward to the coming offensive without undue apprehension. The advance on 18th November was unlike anything we had known before. In the usual clear desert sunlight the endless columns of tanks set out across a fresh stretch of featureless desert under the umbrella of aircraft such as we had not previously known, some of us were to remember that morning three years later when the convoys came out into the Channel beyond the Isle of White and saw across the sea to the west the line of ships leaving the shelter of Weymouth Bay (For the Normandy D-Day landings). The Germans duly attacked.

Their air force was active in dive-bombing and strafing. The squadron of 7th Hussars were set on fire one by one, all day the dust blew. For some, morale was lower than at any time before or since. Even in the black days after Dunkirk or the retreat to Alamein, where we were more nearly affected, things hardly seemed as bad as they did in that miserable dump. We had not eaten for two days or more

On 18th November we had thought ourselves wonderfully equipped with new tanks, and strong enough in armoured brigades and infantry divisions to march straight to Benghazi. Now the armour was shattered. It seemed that the Germans had defeated the best equipped army we had put in the field, and that we had no resources with which to hold even the frontier.

(*General Rommel* took 33,000 prisoners at Tobruk including 19,000 British troops including my uncle Vic).

Within six months the three (Officers from High Command) who had done so much to make any success possible were dead. All killed before any permanent settlement was achieved in the desert. We will remember those who had done so much with so little: of "Straffer," standing by his tank, his side hat worn straight on his head, like a Bishop's, making characteristic use of his unique humour; of "Jock," hoarse with energy expended, thrusting a huge hand into a vaster pocket, urging the columns to yet more offensive activities; and of Hugo, pictured curiously in a deckchair at Buq-Buq among the asphodel (*A Eurasian plant of the lily family*), reading a book with absorbing concentration, desperately longing to get to Cairo, knowing the endless troubles awaiting him when he got there.

El Alamein:

The *Battle of El Alamein* was the culmination of the North African campaign between British Empire forces and the German-Italian army. Having taken *Tobruk* in June 1942 *Rommel* advanced into Egypt but was defeated at *Alam Halfa* in September.

Rommel commanded 13 Divisions and 500 tanks with around 100,000 men. *'The Spartan General,' Lieutenant-General Bernard Law Montgomery, 'Monty' for short,* commanded approximately double the number of men and tanks with an army consisting of British, Australians, New Zealanders, Indians, and South Africans, French and Greek units. The Allies were also strong in the air.

In late August 1942 *Monty's* orders read: *"There will be no withdrawals-absolutely none-none whatsoever-none!"* On 30th August *Rommel* announced to his troops: *"We have the intention of completing the final annihilation of the Eighth Army."* Two of the greatest warrior-leaders of their time were ready to fight to the end. Had *Rommel* succeeded I would not be writing this little book and you would not be reading it.

The battle began on October 23 with an Allied bombardment of around 1,000 guns with air and armoured support. After ten days of ferocious fighting the Allies achieved a decisive victory. The German army avoided annihilation and withdrew. *El Alamein* was fought in the manner of a battle in the First World War using massed artillery with limited advances and the defeat of enemy counterattacks. The final battle of *El Alamein* was crucial, the *Panzer* divisions withdrew to Tunisia and within days Anglo-American forces landed in Morocco. By May 1943 the campaign was at an end and the Mediterranean dominated by the Allies.

Dad treasured a written account from The Rifle Brigade Chronicle 1946 entitled 'Some Men Have Nine Lives' by Major V.W.Street (By kind permission of W.Blackwoods Ltd) which typifies the activities and attitudes of the soldiers of all ranks in the Rifle Brigade.

In September 1942 a small group of volunteers were involved in 'under- cover' activities to disrupt operations behind enemy lines in the Suez area. They had been relatively successful, but numbers had dwindled to a handful of men who were attempting to get back to Brigade headquarters. Major Street reported:

An hour after daylight two Italian soldiers patrolling the seashore saw us and walked up to the spot where we were, their rifles slung on their backs and their hands in their pockets. They were as surprised to see us as we were to see them and appeared to think we were Germans. We encouraged them in their mistake, and they soon moved on, apparently quite unsuspecting. It was clear we could not remain in this vicinity (Shortly afterwards)......

Suddenly there was a burst of firing from behind and, on looking round, we saw three groups of men advancing towards us, gesticulating and shouting wildly in true Italian style , stopping now and again to take erratic pot shots at us with their rifles.

The four of us paused a minute. What could we do with our miserable pistols against 50 rifles? The open desert lay ahead of us and there seemed not the remotest chance of escape." We'll make a run for it" we said to each other, and took to our heels, two of us going left and two to the right. Any minute we shall be bowled over like a couple of shot rabbits, I thought as I panted along, but the shooting of those Italians was unbelievably inaccurate, and with lungs nearly bursting to our surprise we found two newly dug holes about three feet square and two feet deep. The Italians came within a few feet of us curled up in our holes. They were clearly quite unable to understand our apparent disappearance into thin air. Eventually they moved on and we were left undisturbed all that day. So, we smoked our pipes and played dominos until the sun set (I added the last sentence to enhance the archetypal 'Britishness' of the story).

~

In October 1940, American *Major Bonner Fellers* was assigned as military attaché to the U.S. Embassy in Egypt with responsibility for monitoring and reporting on British military operations in the Mediterranean and Middle East. Britain granted him access to their activities, plans and other key information. *Fellers* reported extensively to his superiors in the US including *President Roosevelt*, the Head of American Intelligence, and the *Joint Chiefs of Staff*.

Over a six-month period, his transmissions were intercepted by Axis agents and passed to Field Marshal Rommel giving 'The Desert Fox' invaluable secret information. This contributed hugely to catastrophic British and Allied defeats at *Gazala* and *Tobruk* . *Fellers* was known as a protégé of *General Douglas MacArthur*.

In his defence, *Fellers* had concerns about the security of the "*Black Code*" of the *U.S. State Department* and in February 1942, he reported: "*Believe that code compromised,*" but he was subsequently informed that it was secure and so he continued to send his reports by radio. In fact, unbeknown to the US, the details of the code were stolen from their Embassy in Italy by Italian spies during a night raid just prior to the US entering the war. Within eight hours the top-secret data on British troop positions, losses, equipment, reinforcements, strengths, supplies, field positions, transport, battle tactics and even morale were routinely in the hands of the German and Italian military.

Fellers' messages also alerted *Axis* to British convoy operations in the *Battle of the Mediterranean*. The Germans referred to *Fellers* as "*Die gute quelle*" ('*The good source*') and *Rommel* referred to him as "*the little fellow.*"

British Secret Service intercepts by its '*Ultra*' intelligence operation indicated the Germans were accessing critical information from a source in Egypt, and they considered *Fellers* as a possible source. On June 10, 1942, the British became convinced *Fellers'* reports were compromised because one intercept had criticised British tactics in comparison to US tactics. The British informed the Americans on June 12, and on June 14 the US confirmed that *Fellers'* reports were the source. He switched codes (15 days later) on June 29 and the leaks ceased.

Fellers was not blamed for the interception of his reports but he was transferred from Egypt on 7 July 1942. Upon returning to the US he was decorated with the *Distinguished Service Medal* (DSM) for his analysis and reporting of the North African theatre of war. He was also promoted to *Brigadier General* on December 4, 1942.

Fellers' reports were cited in his DSM as: "*Models of clarity and accuracy*" (I'm sure the Desert Fox agreed) and were very critical of British leadership, operations and weapons, for example: "*The Eighth Army has failed to maintain the morale of its troops; its tactical conceptions were always wrong; it neglected completely cooperation between the various arms; its reactions to the lightning changes in the battlefield were always slow.*"

Meanwhile, back on the battlefields of North Africa, the British Tommy's and their Allies continued to fight and die. These accounts of the North African campaign show the enormous influence of luck, good and bad, in a war.

A cemetery and memorial were constructed at *El Alamein* with generous support from Egypt. The *Alamein Memorial* commemorates soldiers and airmen of the British Commonwealth who died in Egypt and Libya together with the *Eighth Army* in Tunisia, Syria, Lebanon, Iraq and Persia.

11,945 people are remembered at the Memorial, and the casualties suffered show the true extent of a 'World War,' the essential commitment that Britain had from many true allies around the world, and the sacrifice they made for all of us through an extraordinary alliance of people from very different countries, cultures and religions:

Casualties	Land	Air Force
U.K	4,880	2,138
Australian	338	317
New Zealand	777	90
South African	795	460
Indian	1,788	-
Colonial and other	147	-
Canada	-	215

At the end of the El Alamein campaign Winston Churchill is quoted as saying: "Now this is not the end. It is not even the beginning of the end. But it is, perhaps, the end of the beginning." In retrospect, when you know the battles that followed in the War, you can better understand what he meant.

~

Dad sent the following *'Airgraph' (Letter)* home in April 1943, it was a month before the end of the North Africa campaign and it is striking to read his determination to send a happy, positive message home with the single purpose of easing his family's worries. Shortly after the letter was sent his Regiment moved on to Italy and the living hell of one of the worst extended battles of the entire war:

Airgraph: Sender: Corporal T Fearon, A C of 10th Brigade. R.B. B.N.A.F. (4.4.1943)
Dear Mum Dad and All,

My Sunday Bulletin. And thankful I am this time for the airgraph. Having written so much of late I could do little justice to a real letter. Again all is very well. Of course there was not the old Roast & Co. for dinner or apple pie but there's still no complaints having had a few days of rather dull weather. The old sun breaking through again to-day has been rather appreciated. Just by the way, in case at any time you think of me lying, knocked over by the heat, with someone waving a fan standing over me, I have learned from our own very good newspaper that in these particular parts the heat does not come up to the visualised tropical heat. You know! No frying eggs by the sun while listening to music hall. Last night Bill told me some more of those stories. Kitty – you'd be amazed. Good job there isn't room for me to pass them on. Space Fini & tea up. So Bye, Bye again loves, still smiling. Your Tommy xxxx Love to Fardy x

~

Fardy was Dad's Grandad who lived with the family.

*Note: The A*irgraph* was introduced in the WW2 to improve communication between Britain and the Middle East. It reduced letters on special forms on to microfilm and enlarged them at the destination point. *Kodak Ltd* managed the contract which allowed letters to be filmed in Cairo and enlarged in the UK.

~

The Death of a Brother:
Dad and his older brother Vic served in different Regiments at the same time in North Africa. Vic was killed in the War by what is insensitively described as 'friendly fire.' He was taken prisoner at the *Siege of Tobruk* in North Africa and while locked in the   hold of an Italian ship, *SS Scillin*, drowned when the ship was hit by a torpedo from a British submarine, *HMS Sahib*, ten miles north of *Cape Milazzo* in the *Tyrrhenian Sea* off the north-east corner of Sicily.

Immediately following the torpedo strike, *HMS Sahib* was fired on from a German escort ship and hit by depth charges from the Italian corvette *Gabbiano*, the *Sahib* was badly damaged and was later scuttled.

SS Scillin was a 1,591 Ton cargo steamship built in Scotland in 1903 which passed through a succession of owners of various nationalities. She was built as *H.M. Pellatt* but was subsequently named *Memling, Nicole Le Borgne, Giuliana Pagan* and *Scillin Secondo* before becoming *Scillin* in 1937.

Vic was only a year older than Dad and was the second oldest of seven brothers and two sisters. The two brothers were very close and the loss of Vic during the War was a crushing blow for the family. My Nan could never forgive the Germans or Italians for the War and the loss of her son, but in time Dad learned to take a different view.

The following are extracts from a report in the *London Evening Standard*:

A Stepney born survivor (**Sidney Adshead**) has given an account of the sinking of an Italian ship in which 800 British prisoners of war were being taken from North Africa to the Italian mainland in November 1942....it is almost certain that many of the 700 prisoners not accounted for referred to by Sir James Grigg, War Minister, in the House of Commons on February 1st (1943), were in the ship.
...the survivor was taken prisoner at Tobruk in June 1942, and his account was written for the benefit of the parents of his friend, Vic, who was a Lance Corporal in the *Royal Army Service Corps*. The War Office have now confirmed that Vic was on board the ship which was sunk and regret there can no longer be any

hope that he survived.

~

On the 7th February 1944, the following letter was sent to Dad by family friend *Edith Ramsey (MBE),* East End teacher and campaigner for the working class:

Dear Tom,

I had a long talk with Sidney Adshead this evening, and I have put down all the things he said in his own words about the last months he spent with Vic. I have typed it out and sent a copy to your mother. I was doubtful about doing this, for I know it will give her pain. And yet I hope it will comfort her too, for she would want to know everything she could about Vic. And as Adshead told it, it was not a depressing story – quite the reverse, for it gave one the inspiration that comes from a great achievement of the human spirit. In spite of everything being against them, those men could yet manage to make fun for themselves and for others. It is a lesson I shall not forget.

I feel very humble in face of such heroism and such sorrow. It is good that your mother has such strength and comfort in her other children.

God bless you Tom and keep you safe. Love to you from your friend, Tilly.

~

These lovely, inspiring words reflect very well the humility and quality of Tilly Ramsey. These are the notes she wrote:

An account of the period up to and during the loss of so many British prisoners of War:

TOLD BY SIDNEY ADSHEAD, A Survivor of The Italian Ship, SEILLON, which was torpedoed on 14 November 1942 when carrying English Prisoners from Tripoli to Italy (Sydney makes no reference to the fact that the attack was from an allied submarine).

Vic, Howard and I had always kept together in our unit and we were all taken prisoner on 20.6.42 at Tobruk, where we were kept for seven days. We spent another seven days at Derna, and went on to Benghazi, where we stayed for about three months, till on 17.10.42 we were taken to Tripoli.

The number of prisoners taken was between 25,000 and 30,000, and we had none of our equipment – only tropical shorts and boots – blankets and for two days no water. After that, we had tinned beans, sweets, jam and biscuits and 1 pint of water issued as rations every two days for the first week. At Derna we were packed tight – no room to lie down – and had daily rations of Italian bully beef and a packet of Italian biscuits. This continued as our rations except that for part of the time at Benghazi we could have cooked rice, tomato puree and cheese instead of bully. At Tripoli we were issued with three small Italian blankets each, and a dixey. At Benghazi once but only once we had a spoonful of coffee to share between two men. We had no shaving kit till we got to Benghazi, and no soap at any time. In spite of this we managed to keep clean by washing in water.

This sounds very grim but we had a lot of fun trying to make the best of it. Some men just let themselves go and were dirty and depressed but at least 90% of us kept ourselves clean and cheerful. Vic was always cheerful. He talked a lot about his mother and his home, and he had some photos which he used to look at. He was always a lively sort, leading in any sport to be had. We had to organise our own amusements. Four or five men had piano accordions, and concerts were held three times a week. Then we had auctions. Four of us – the fourth named Smith – used to share our rations. The meat had to be eaten as soon as it was taken out of the tin, for if it was left the flies got at it. But by sharing it with another man, we could have two meals a day. At Benghazi we were given five cigarettes every three days. Our ration should have been fifteen a week, but we had no contact with the Red Cross, and had neither parcels or letters.

We were classed 'in transit' all the time. Vic always led in the amusements we planned for ourselves. We had some good times in the desert, and it was just the same in the prison camp. Sometimes we would have an auction. One man who did not smoke would auction his cigarettes, and men would bid wallets, or any possessions they had for them. We arranged lectures too – on Horses, Poultry, Mechanics, or any subject on which we could find a speaker. Two or three times a week we had a religious service.

Then we got amusement out of making things with any material we could find. We would make an oven in the sand with a lump of tin, and cook pies to vary our rations. Men who were handy with a knife carved ash trays and once we held an 'Arts and Crafts Exhibition' and charged two cigarettes to go around and view all the skill of the craftsmen. It was a very good show.

We had to improvise all the time. Draft-boards and dart boards were made and competitions held. We got hold of some timber and made a board with rings and amused ourselves testing our aim by throwing little hoops onto these rings. Books were invaluable. We slept in little bivouacs about three feet high, and there were six men in each. Any book we could get was read from cover to cover by each of the men in a bivouac and then passed on to another. Except for the bivouacs there was no shade in the camp.

Six times during these months we were given P.c.s on which we could write our names and our home addresses and these ought to have got home. But one of mine arrived in England after I did, for a parcel of them was picked up after the English had got the country again.

At Benghazi we were taken out on fatigues and put to cleaning up barracks. We were glad to get out, but when we were asked to unload ammunition trains we refused, for we knew that was against international law. Some "South African Blacks" who were kept in separate camps were forced to do this, for they were told that unless they did they would have no food rations.

In the early days the men who had a little Egyptian money on them were able to obtain extra cigarettes, but the Italians charged abnormal prices for the cigarettes, and soon the money was spent.

At 3 p.m.. on the 13th November we set sail from Tripoli in an Italian ship, Scillin.

There were about 800 English prisoners on it. In charge were Italian guards. We were battened down in holds, and at 2.30pm on the 14th November, seven or eight shells hit the ship. I was standing by the stairs in the hold and ran up the stairs.

Stan, Howard and Vic were against the wall on the other side. At the top of the stairs, there was a rush of water. The ship seemed to split and I do not know whether I jumped into the water or fell. A torpedo had hit it. Half of the ship went down in forty or fifty seconds.

Twenty-six Englishmen and thirty-four Italians were picked up by the submarine and I was one of these survivors. Several of us had been wounded by shrapnel. We reached Malta on the 15th November. Officers came around and asked us forenames and numbers of any men we knew had been on the ship. We all gave from fifteen to twenty names. But all documents and records had gone down with the ship. Neither the Italians nor the English had any record of the men who were on it, and the War Office had no means of knowing. Nobody who knew Vic will ever forget what a splendid fellow he was, and he was happy all the time. He knew he had something worth fighting and dying for, and he was happy to be with his friends, cheering them on.

~

Here is the official record on Vic's Memorial held by the *Commonwealth War Graves Commission.*

Memorial: El Alamein War Cemetry:

234. Fearon Victor (23), Lance Corporal, SS Scillin, Royal Army Service Corps, 1 Support Group, 14/11/1942. Son of Arthur William and Catherine Fearon, of Romford, Essex.

~

That's all we have to officially mark Vic's sacrifice. It doesn't seem right that his military plaque sits in a far-off foreign field and his grave lies at the bottom of a distant ocean. The family are lucky to this day to have Tilly Ramsey's letter to Dad and the notes from Sid Adshead to stand as proud memories of Vic.

My cousin Cath, daughter of Kit, Dad's eldest sister, worked hard to have Vic's name added to the military War memorial in Romford near the Town Hall in the heart of Romford which honours local people who were killed in the two World Wars. It took until 1996 to persuade the 'authorities' to agree to the addition of one particular prisoner of war who was killed in 1942. Our Nan and the family were saddened and could not understand why Vic's name was omitted from the memorial until it was rededicated in 1996. It is possible that 'Governmental authorities' (Those well-known invisible people) decided it was not appropriate to recognise Vic's loss under the circumstances of his death.

~

What Really Happened?

While the ship was being loaded at the Spanish Quay in *Tripoli Harbour* the Captain protested about the excessive numbers being boarded. When 814 prisoners of war were aboard, the remaining 195 were sent along the Quay to board a later ship. It wasn't until the Commander of the British submarine *HMS Sahib* heard the survivors speaking that he realized that he had sunk a ship carrying British POWs. At a subsequent enquiry, the Commander was cleared of any wrongdoing as the *SS Scillin* with British prisoners aboard was unmarked and sailing at night without lights and the Commander believed that the ship was carrying Italian troops.

The Ministry of Defence kept the incident a secret for fifty-four years stating that those lost had died in Italian prisoner of war camps or were 'lost at sea.' Requests for information from the families of the prisoners killed were not met until 1996 when the truth was revealed. Hence, (Presumably) the agreement to add Vic's name to the memorial in Romford. Researchers claim that the circumstances of individual deaths have only been given to the most persistent families.

The account of the sinking and the casualty list were factually flawed and when the mistakes were pointed out the M.O.D. in 1996 they accepted the errors but to date no alterations have been made to the records and no official reason has ever been given for withholding the information? Records stated that 200 POWs were aboard the *Scillin* plus a Naval gun crew and 30 Italian guards. The true number was revealed by British intelligence (Known as *Ultra**) in a decrypted signal on 13 November 1942, the day the ship left *Tripoli.*

*Note: *Ultra* was the name adopted by British military intelligence in June 1941 for wartime intelligence that broke high-level encrypted radio and teleprinter communications from the enemy at the *Government Code and Cypher School* (GC&CS) at *Bletchley Park*. *Ultra* became the standard system for the Western Allies for all intelligence of this type. The name was agreed because the intelligence obtained was considered more important than that designated by the highest British security classification in use at the time, 'Most Secret,' and was defined as being 'Ultra' secret. I understand that all *Ultra* recommendations had to be personally seen and approved by the Prime Minister *Winston Churchill*. Ultra's existence was only publicly disclosed in the 1970s.

~

Ultra intelligence forecast the sailing of the *Scillin* and gave the course and timings in detail, amending the timings when the ship sailed three hours late. The reasons for the 'official' reticence to disclose the true facts for such a long period of time are not entirely clear to this day, but some (I know not who) have claimed that it was deemed necessary so as not to jeopardise the source of the intelligence that identified *SS Scillin* on that fateful night.

It has been suggested that it was considered essential to conceal the source of the *Ultra* intelligence service which had accurately reported the *Scillin's* position and schedule enabling *HMS Sahib* to intercept and sink her. It is claimed by researchers that the intelligence gathered included knowledge of the presence of prisoners of war on board.

The *Scillin* was the 6th ship in which POWs were lost over a 12month period with a total loss in excess of 2,000 prisoners. Researchers claim that *Ultra* intelligence had given advance information of the presence of the POWs movements in all cases.

Ultra was clearly 'top secret' and it was a priority of the Allies to prevent the enemy *Axis* countries from discovering that their signals were being read. Expert sources claim that if all of the ships that carried POWs had been protected from attack, it would have been obvious to the enemy that the Allies had prior knowledge of the cargo carried by *Axis* ships.

I find this set of circumstances worrying. If levels of intelligence continue to progress beyond *Ultra* to ever higher levels of secrecy, as surely they may have done since World War 2, at what point will matters of national security be determined by people (Or a person) outside the control of Government and the Crown? Perhaps *Big Brother* already exists, and we aren't aware of him/her. Why would we be?

That aside, it's surely not possible for people who have lost loved ones or indeed the public at large, to find peace with the loss of a life *"For King And Country?"* when the sacrifice is actually determined by an unknown intelligence service for a purpose unknown.

(***Source:** A significant amount of this information was researched from the BBC's service: *'WWII People's War. An archive of contributions written by the public.'*)

October 2014. Thank you *'Contributor ADM1991839.* I have a feeling that you have a close family connection with the sinking of *SS Scillin* in November 1942. I'm not sure if any of this information that I am divulging in this little book remains top secret, so if I mysteriously disappear overnight or am found in a ditch with an umbrella prick in my leg, you may wish to think the worse has happened to me.

~

In the same edition of *The Evening Standard* that reported the loss of the Italian ship SS Scillin, on the next page following the report of the sinking, the following article appeared:

Clark Gable in Car Crash Case:

Captain Clark Gable the film star (*Referred to as '*The King of Hollywood'* in his heyday in the 1930' and 40s) was involved in a £7,442 car crash case, reports Associated Press from Los Angeles.

A collision occurred last year when Gable stopped his car suddenly at a boulevard stop, and another car crashed into it. Two persons had concussion, a broken ankle, cuts and bruises.

~

When I read this, I thought it was typical of a 'big shot' film star and I felt a little resentful that it was virtually sitting alongside the tragic story of my Uncle Vic and his fellow soldiers. It seemed that the USA had contrived to make *Clark Gable* a Captain for no good reason. I looked up his War service record and saw that I was quite wrong.

The following account is based on information from '*Defence Media Network'*:
Gable volunteered for the *Army Air Forces*, went to the 13-week Officer Candidate School, and was trained as a photographer and aerial gunner. He was assigned to go to Britain to film '*Combat America*', a propaganda movie about air gunners.

A serving airman said "Gable was assigned to our squadron but not to a particular crew, and the group controlled his assignments. They wanted him to have an outer- wing aircraft with a clear view of the skies for his air-to-air photography. He stayed with us right up from 1942 to 1945 and I can tell you, they didn't put him on the milk runs. He took a lot of pictures of flak bursting beside his aircraft."

Gable and a cameramen and sound engineer followed the crew of a B-17, named "*Ain't It Gruesome,*" through 24 missions, including one where the aircraft was shot up by German Focke Wulf Fw 190 fighters and lost an engine, with the crew eventually bailing over a field in England when fog closed in.

Interviews with veterans debunk the myth that Gable wanted to die because of his grief over losing his wife Carole Lombard in an air crash, returning from a War Bonds tour during the War. They describe him as a sturdy man with unnaturally large hands who took his duties seriously, maintained a military posture, but was willing to party when appropriate.

~

The Battle of Monte Cassino:

Dad's war certainly didn't end with the victory in North Africa and soon with a heavy heart at the loss of his brother, he was embarking for Sicily and a deadly campaign in a barren, frozen, mountainous area in Italy.

In August 2012, *Dalya Alberge* wrote a summary in the *Independent* newspaper of the battle of *Monte Cassino* to highlight a new movie which was to be Directed by *John Irvin* (Ref. *'Tinker, Tailor, Soldier, Spy';* and *'The Dogs of War'*) to recognise the seventieth anniversary of the battle:

'Monte Cassino was one of the most bitter and bloody battles of the Second World War, causing tens of thousands of casualties over five months in 1943-44. Now, almost 70 years later, the bravery and sacrifice of soldiers who fought in it is to be told for the first time in an English film. It will be an overdue tribute to the "D-Day Dodgers" – so-called of the troops who during
the Italian campaign endured the worst close-quarter fighting since the First World War. They felt their extreme sacrifice was eclipsed by the D-Day landings at Normandy, about which many feature films have been made.
Irvin has long been fascinated by Monte Cassino and he told The Independent: "I think there is a sense of shame of the sheer cost and horror which was inflicted by questionable decisions leading to colossal casualties."
Monte Cassino was a mountain redoubt in the German defensive line, stretching across Italy and blocking the Allied advance to Rome. During the harshest Italian winter on record, and difficult terrain, the battle centred on the world-famous vast sixth-century abbey, an ideal defence for the Germans.
The Allied victory came at a high price. The Allies made repeated attacks on the abbey and some 200,000 soldiers on both sides – including British and Commonwealth - were killed or wounded. Many of those who survived were scarred mentally, like the comedian Spike Milligan.
The Germans, however, rescued the Abbey's treasures, and at first the Allies refrained from bombing the building, though they eventually were forced to destroy it. The redoubt was finally captured by Polish troops.
Dr Caddick-Adams told The Independent that the veterans of Monte Cassino are like the "forgotten army of Burma": "All the attention [of filmmakers] is on Normandy… Monte Cassino is perceived as a backwater in some ways. Had D-Day not been happening, this would have been the major Allied effort and therefore would have got its fair share of attention."
His book reflects the horrors of the battle. The troops lacked proper equipment to dig in in the mountainous terrain and the rocks shattered like glass when hit by any projectile, which "sent splinters of rock in all directions, and causing a horrifically high number of head, face and eye injuries". Men also died from heat and cold exposure.'

~

Basil Harvey wrote a book on the *Rifle Brigade* in a series entitled: *'Famous Regiments.'* He summarises the Italian Campaign as follows:

'The 10th Battalion went to Italy in March 1944, the 7th and 2nd following them in April to take their part in a new kind of warfare. Desperate battles were fought in great heat or intense cold, in mountains, river crossings on narrow rocky roads, with mud in winter and dust clouds in summer; it was different and much more uncomfortable than that fought in the desert.

The Germans in Italy could concentrate on defence, and it was only the constant pressure of the Fifth and Eighth Armies that prevented them from withdrawing significant numbers to reinforce other fronts. The new type of warfare demanded new formations, for motor battalions were unable to operate in their usual previous role with armour. They would now become normal infantry, the vehicles that carried the motor platoons being replaced by troop-carrying three ton lorries. Strong officer protests enabled extra vehicles along with a large number of wireless sets, which allowed the Battalions to continue to work efficiently with the armour and to exploit the Rifle Brigades' reputable qualities of quick thinking and urgent action. The 10th Battalion played its distinguished part in the great battle of Cassino and fought on through the Hitler line.'

Dad and Uncle Bill were in the thick of this campaign in the *Signal Corps*, with the main duty of supporting the infantry front lines with essential and effective communications.

~

Peter Caddick-Adams wrote *'Monte Cassino. Ten Armies in Hell.'* He writes:

'All had anticipated a land of sun, cherry blossom and grapes, but found something very different. If ever battle space was dominated by geology and combat directed by climate and terrain, then Monte Cassino provided an extreme example. Battle slid back to a medieval pace; hand-to-hand fighting was common; mules and horses were used in place of modern engines of war, as combatants on both sides found that the ground around Cassino was unforgiving. An ankle-twisting loose scree covered all gradients. The hard and brittle hills shattered like glass when hit by any projectile – shells, mortar rounds, hand grenades and bullets sent rock splinters in all directions causing a horrifically high number of head, face and eye injuries.

Troops found it impossible to dig foxholes and gun positions to protect themselves from enemy shelling or the elements. The infantry was issued with ridiculously small entrenching tools or picks, which made little impression on the rugged mountainsides. The only shelter to be found was in hillside natural caves or fissures. Burying the dead was all but impossible, the problem made worse in the summer months when the flies, rats and wild dogs provided a health threat of their own.

The terrain also magnified artillery fire acoustically, which was nerve-wracking in the extreme and left speech impossible. One German commander in the hills wrote that 'the demoralising effect of the intense bombardment was increased tenfold by the echoes in the valleys.' There was a terrible sense of feeling trapped when caught on a narrow mountain track by shellfire with nowhere to shelter. Much of the Italian landscape in the winter was shrouded in an eerie freezing fog, crippling the ability of all armies to fight, disorienting soldiers and playing on their fears.

No other campaign in Europe pulled in the same range of nationalities and cultures as that in Italy. The brutality of the fighting at times reached the worst extremes of the Russian Front, while the attrition rates often exceeded those of the Western Front. Failure to achieve a decisive result at Cassino in the first five months of 1944 condemned those in Italy to a further year of war. The casualties on both sides from September 1943 to May 1945 were excessive but balanced. The Allies suffered 312,000 killed, wounded and missing; the Germans lost 435,000, an average loss to both sides of 1,233 personnel every day, almost one for every minute of the 606 day long campaign. This attrition was most pronounced at Monte Cassino where 200,000 casualties were inflicted on Germans, Italians, French, Americans, British, Indians, New Zealanders, Poles, Canadians and South Africans during 129 days of hell.

The winter of 1943/44 was literally a killer, from October to December '43 very heavy rain fell in central Italy for fifty days turning all low ground into oceans of freezing mud swamping airfields and roads. On high ground rain turned to sleet and snow creating drifts up to 23 feet. Allied and Axis field hospitals were inundated with three times their capacity, from frostbite cases to combat casualties. Temperatures were so low that vehicle steering columns and engine components froze and fractured.

Conditions were merciless. Allied commanders found much to their surprise that the only reliable form of transport was horse or mule. Mules were generally stronger than horses, carrying 200lbs for up to 16 miles without rest. Generally, more patient when heavily laden than horses or donkeys, a mule's skin is harder and less sensitive than that of their parents and they also show a natural resistance to disease and insects; their hooves are smaller but harder than those of horses. They could wade through mud that would stop a jeep, were perfectly balanced to negotiate tiny, narrow winding trails that were everywhere on mountainsides and seemed to have the ability to just keep going at a steady pace, deaf to distractions.

They had the ability to haul everything from food, water, medicine, ammunition and weapons up – and the dead and wounded down – the phrase 'stubborn as a mule' acquired a new comforting meaning.'

Who would have thought that the heroes of *Monte Cassino* would include the common mule? There is no such thing as a dumb animal.

In December 1943, U.S. war reporter *Ernie Pyle* wrote of a mule train winding down from *Mount Sammucro* bearing Allied dead:

'I was at the foot of the mule train the night they brought the commander Captain Wasko's body down, soldiers made shadows in the moonlight as they walked. Dead men had been coming down all evening lashed to the backs of mules they came lying belly down across wooden pack saddles, their heads hanging down on the left side of the mule, their stiffened legs sticking out awkwardly from the other side bobbing as the mule walked. The Italian muleskinners were afraid to walk beside dead men, so Americans had to lead the mules down that night.

German artillery searched for likely locations for mule parks. The shelling killed and wounded many animals, whose distress played on the nerves of muleteers and soldiers alike. One American doctor described an attack when the entire mule train was destroyed. 'The Italian muleskinners are hysterical....... To treat them is impossible. None of them will hold still long enough to be bandaged. They scramble off the mountain leaving a trail of blood behind them'. The British soldier Victor Belves recalled the mule handlers looked after their animals ' in the same way we would look after our cat or dog' after a shell burst on the mountainside he recalled someone shouting and crying loudly I looked around and saw one of the mules with its intestines coming out desperately trying to get to its feet but losing the battle. I will never ever forget the mule-handler, calling out the mules' name as it got weaker, the poor soldier had both arms around the mules' neck and kept shouting its name as the tears rolled down his cheeks. After three minutes I heard a rifle shot, the poor mule had been put out of its misery.'

~

In addition to Italian combat units, by the time of the fourth and final Allied offensive of *Monte Cassino* in Spring 1944, half a million Italians also served formally and informally in uniform alongside the Allies performing essential tasks as mine clearers, drivers, and mule handlers, engineers, mechanics, labourers repairing roads, machinery and equipment, builders, cooks, hospital porters and working for the bureaucratic civil affairs of AMGOT (*Allied Military Government Of Occupied Territories*).

~

In December 1943 in the midst of the Allied slog, battling to take *Camino Hill* was Gunner *Spike Milligan* serving as a signaller, much as Dad did, and he described the build-up before the battle:

'A string of mules with Cypriot attendants pass slowly by...... ammunition is dumped by the guns, the pile of mustard coloured shells mounts up, mud is everywhere..... the fire plan takes over and we just sit and wait to be given targets from Operations. There are nearly one thousand guns savaging the night.'

~

Dad and Uncle Bill fought in this all-important campaign which extended from January 17th to May 18th 1944. Dad was promoted to Sergeant in May 1944, so while he was plain lucky to have survived, he also could not have performed too shabbily.

Monte Cassino is a rocky hill 130 kilometres southeast of Rome in the Latin Valley, west of the town of Cassino at an altitude of 520 metres. It was best known for its Abbey and was the first house of the Benedictine Order of Monks established around 529 AD.

The main Allied forces came from the U.S.A., Britain, New Zealand, India, France and Italy. The Allied casualties of 312,000 during the period of the four Cassino battles were followed in June 1944 with a further 105,000 casualties in the conclusion of the Anzio campaign which lead to the capture of Rome.

The following summary is another close-up witness perspective based on information from 'ThoughtCo.' and sourced from the BBC: 'Battle of Monte Cassino' and 'History: Battle of Monte Cassino':

"Landing in Italy in September 1943, Allied forces under General Sir Harold Alexander advanced on two fronts with the Lieutenant General Mark Clark's US Fifth Army on the east and Lieutenant General Sir Bernard Montgomery's British Eighth Army on the west of the Apennine Mountains (Dad and Bill were serving with the Eight Army).

Very poor weather, rough terrain, and a strong German defence slowed the Allies progress. The Germans retreated slowly in order to buy time to complete formation of their 'Winter Line' south of Rome. The British succeeded in penetrating the line and capturing Ortona in late December, but heavy snows prevented them from pushing west to reach Rome. At this time, Montgomery departed for Britain to aid in planning the invasion of Normandy and was replaced by Lieutenant General Oliver Leese.

The Rifle Brigade played a significant part in the second battle, specifically in the Liri Valley, Melfa Crossing and Monte Rotondo 'theatres of war.' ('Theatre' seems a strange use of what is usually such a pleasant leisure activity).

For the fourth decisive battle, Alexander ordered II Corps to push towards Rome, while the French attacked into the Aurunci Mountains on the west side of the Liri Valley. To the north, XIII Corps were to secure control of the Liri Valley. The Polish contingent circled behind Monte Cassino in order to isolate the Abbey ruins. Using a range of deceptive exercises, the Allies were able to ensure that the Germans were not aware of these troop movements.

The attack, named 'Operation Diadem,' began on all four fronts on May 11 with a bombardment of over 1,660 guns. II Corps met heavy resistance and made little headway, the French advanced quickly and penetrated the Aurunci Mountains before daylight. To the north, XIII Corps crossed the Rapido meeting a strong German defence, they pushed forward erecting bridges on the way. Significantly, this allowed the supporting armoured divisions to cross the water. In the mountains, Polish attacks were met with German counterattacks.

By late on May 12, XIII Corps' bridgeheads continued to grow despite determined counterattacks from the Germans. The next day, the Germans began to pull back to the *'Hitler Line'*, eight miles to the rear. On May 15, the British 78th Division passed through the bridgehead and began a turning movement to cut off the town from the Liri Valley. Two days later, the Poles renewed their efforts in the mountains, and they linked up with the 78th Division early on May 18. Later that morning, Polish forces cleared the Cassino Abbey ruins and hoisted the Polish flag.

Consequently, the British Eighth Army immediately tried to break through the *Hitler Line* but was pushed back. After reorganising, a major effort was made against the *Hitler Line* together with a breakout from the Anzio beachhead. Both efforts were successful, and the German Tenth Army was reeling and close to being completely surrounded. With VI Corps surging inland from Anzio, USA Lieutenant General Clark surprisingly ordered them to turn northwest for Rome rather than cut off and help the destruction of the remaining German troops. It is thought by some that Clark's action may have been the result of his concern that the British would enter the city of Rome first despite it being assigned in the battle plan to the Fifth Army? His troops occupied the City on June 4.

*Note: *The Hitler Line* was renamed on *Hitler's* insistence, *The Senger Line,* after *General von Senger und Etterlin* to minimise negative propaganda in the event the line was breached by the Allies. It was a second *Axis* line of defence behind the main *Gustav Line* about 80 km south of Rome reaching from Cassino to the West Italian coast. It formed the main barrier preventing the Allied *5th Army* linking up with the US *VI Corps* in the Anzio 'beach head.'

The Battle of Anzio took place from January to June 1944 ending with the capture of Rome. The operation was opposed by German forces in the areas of *Anzio* and Nettuno.

~

In the winter following *Monte Cassino* there was no cessation in the Italian campaign, and I found a single newspaper article which reported on the activities Dad's 6th Armoured Division in M&D's box full of mostly happy, family photos and memorabilia:

Newspaper Article (May 1943) (Thought to be from *The London Evening Standard*):

6th ARMOURED DIVISION: 3 MEMORABLE MONTHS

"The Sixth British Armoured Division, which played a major part in the initial breakthrough from Cassino and pursuit North into Tuscany has been fighting for three months as part of the Fifth Army in its bitter struggle through the central Apennines. The Infantry entered Benedetto taking the Germans by surprise, occupied the hills overlooking the road, and fought their way with carriers (Dad's vehicle) in daylight into the next village. Bitter weather and German demolition didn't hold up the advance. Sappers again played their part under shellfire and tanks of the Armoured Brigade charged along the Corniche Road to Bocconi, where they were met with bazooka fire from the houses. The Infantry occupied high ground relying entirely on jeeps and mules for their supply, the advance achieved 13,000 yards in a fortnight and the capture of Monte Cassino. Large numbers of Germans (approximately 50%) surrendered having been pinned down by heavy fire and surrounded on every side.

Measured in terms of difficulties of ground and enemy demolitions, mud and rain, cold and fatigue, the operations in the Gothic Line* have had no equal."

(*Note: The Gothic Line was a German defensive line of the Italian Campaign. It formed the last major line of defence along the summits of the northern part of the Apennine Mountains during the retreat of the German forces in Italy.)

"In February 1944 Harold Rupert Leofric George Alexander, Commander of the Allied Armies in Italy told his theatre of war Commander Jumbo Wilson, that he favoured the reintroduction of the death penalty for desertion. Across the British Army between October 1943 and September 1944, 16,892 soldiers deserted (six per thousand) which was similar to the experience of 1916/1918. The Eighth Army suffered the highest desertion rates, and the problem was a real concern because most deserters came from the infantry and though their numbers were small it represented a much larger percentage of the combat arm who were already in short supply. A total casualty rate (combat and sickness) for 1944 was 647 per 1,000 among British troops.

In May 1944 in the valley below the monastery at Monte Cassino in the Liri Valley the Allies had their main movement corridor stretching towards Rome. The ground was a maze of small hillocks, often surmounted by stone-built villages, confusing tracks, woodland and small rivers which ran across the valley as an obstruction. The US 36th Texans failed to cross the River Liri with almost 3,000 casualties and now the British 13th Corps were to try again with Major Russell's Eighth Indian Infantry Division on the left and the Fourth British Division on the right. At the moment of attack Royal Engineers were to erect 7 bridges along a ten mile stretch of the river.

The assault eventually succeeded in May 1944 with a link-up between the Casino and Anzio fronts 124 days after the first landing on 22nd January. US Commander Mark Clark was unable to resist a good photo opportunity and left immediately by jeep for Borgo Grappa and insisted the successful link-up be restaged for the camera this time with his own very personal appearance.

Captain Alan Whicker (Famous post-war TV broadcaster) of the British Army Film and Photographic Unit was on hand to record the moment. At the same time, the Canadians were battling their way across the Melfa River and a traffic jam of epic proportions was building in the Liri Valley (A veritable log jam)."

~

The *'D-Day'* Normandy landings took place two days after the completion of the successful occupation of Rome and consequently the Italian front was considered a *'Secondary theatre of the War.'* Controversially at the time, *Lady Nancy Astor** referred to the British servicemen serving in Italy in 1944 as: *"The D-Day Dodgers."* She was reportedly of the view that the forces fighting in Italy were having an easier time than those deployed to the Normandy campaign. To refute this, the so-called *"Dodgers"* created: *"The Ballad of the D-Day Dodgers"* which included some less than polite comments about the Lady Astor.

*Note: *Nancy Witcher Langhorne Astor, Viscountess Astor,* was an American citizen who came to England at age 26. She married *2nd Viscount Waldorf Astor,* and after he succeeded to the House of Lords, she entered politics in 1919 becoming the first woman to sit as a Member of Parliament (MP) in the *House of Commons.* She served as a Conservative Party MP for *Plymouth Sutton* until 1945, when she was persuaded to step down.

Winston Churchill is alleged to have made a number of comments about Her Ladyship including a response to her comment: "Winston, if I were your wife, I'd put poison in your coffee." Winston replied: "Nancy, if I were your husband, I'd drink it."

Here are some of the verses from 'The Ballad of the D-Day Dodgers,' sung to the tune of 'Lilli Marleen' (A German love song):

We are the D-Day Dodgers, out in Italy, Always on the vino, always on the spree,
Eighth Army skivers and their tanks, We go to war in ties like swanks,

For we're the D-Day Dodgers, in sunny Italy.
Dear Lady Astor, you think you know a lot, Standing on a platform and talking Tommy-rot,
Dear England's sweetheart and her pride,
We think your mouth is much too wide,

From the D-Day Dodgers, out in sunny Italy,

Look around the hillsides, through the mist and rain, See the scattered crosses, some that bear no name,

The heartbreak and toil and suffering gone,
The lads beneath, they slumber on,

They are the D-Day Dodgers, who'll stay in Italy.

~

Commanding Officer Henry, Anthony Pawson:
Dad spoke very respectfully about Tony Pawson, his senior officer for most of the years he spent in active service in the War. They played cricket together in the Army and after the War Dad played some representative games in the Army and Tony Pawson arranged a trial for him with Surrey County Cricket Club, whose home ground was the *Oval* in South London. Dad was offered an initial one-year contract but he reluctantly declined and many years later told his son Tom that a professional cricketer's salary was not generous at that time, saying: *"I'd had seven years off and I had to get a proper job."*

Kent County Cricket Club provided a heart-felt obituary of Tony when he died in October 2012 aged 91:
"He played for the County as an amateur from 1946 until 1953. He was also an outstanding amateur footballer, representing England in the immediate post-war period and as a member of the squad for the 1948 London Olympics. He became the World Fly-Fishing Champion and was made an OBE for his services to angling.
At Oxford University he won Blues for cricket and association football and captained the University cricket XI in 1948. His football career included two appearances for Charlton Athletic in the 1950s, playing on the right wing. In the first of those matches, against Tottenham Hotspur on Boxing Day (With Alf Ramsey, England's future World Cup-winning manager in the team) he scored two goals (He worked for Reed International Paper Group, but football wages were so low he wouldn't sign a contract). As a member of the Pegasus side, an amalgamation of Oxford and Cambridge players (Most of them, like him, war veterans) he won two FA amateur cup final medals.
He was an entertaining batsman, playing 43 matches for Kent, during which he scored two centuries. His best season was 1947 when he scored 437 runs at an average of 43.70. His running between the wickets, especially in partnership with Godfrey Evans (An England 'great' he was described by '*Wisden*' as *'arguably the best wicket-keeper the game has ever seen*,') was an entertainment in itself as was his fleet of foot fielding."

~

Tony's Obituary in *The Observer* was also wholehearted:
"Tony Pawson was a fluent, elegant sports-writer for the Observer. "Cricket, football and fishing were in my blood," he wrote in his autobiography, *Runs and Catches (1980)*.
Attending Winchester college led to Tony's opening the innings at Lord's for a public schools under-16 team against a CF Tufnell's XI. He was lucky twice not to be out in his first over, but went on to make 237, his best-ever score and a ground record for an under-18 batsman.

Following demobilisation at the end of the second World War, Pawson made his debut as a righthanded batsman for the Kent first team in summer 1946 and went to Christ Church College, Oxford, to study history. On his debut for the university cricket team in 1947 he made a century against Gloucestershire.

(In the 1952-53 season, Pegasus reached the FA Amateur Cup Final for the second time) Before the final at Wembley against Harwich and Parkeston, Pawson was taken ill. With a temperature of 102F, Pawson was advised not to play. Convinced that he would not be needed, he had eaten a heavy meal, but then found otherwise – and was plied at half time with brandy, whisky and champagne. Pegasus won 6-0.

Volunteering for the army at the outset of war, Pawson was involved in the North African campaign and the Battle of Monte Cassino, south-east of Rome. He finished as a Major with a mention in Dispatches, having played in the same army team as the great Tom Finney, one of the few English football stars not co-opted by domestically based physical training units.

His work for the Observer started in 1968, he was cricket correspondent for a decade, sometimes also reporting on football on the same day, and continued to contribute into the new Century, as well as writing a number of books on sport. In May 1984 he won the world individual fly-fishing championship, and after campaigning to improve access for disabled anglers was appointed OBE in 1988."

~

How impressive a man must Tony Pawson have been? Wow! He was surely a comic book and Disney hero rolled into one - choose your own characters - I choose *'Tough of the Track'* and *'Buzz Lightyear.'*

I came across some notes of a recorded discussion which Tony made in 2005, and while the following are only a rough set of shorthand notes of the interview it gives the best insight I have found into Dad's day to day, year to year experiences while in active service. Here is a selection of some of the information provided by Tony in the recording:

Ranks: Rifleman at the Rifle Brigade Depot in GB, 1940; officer cadet served with Officer Cadet Training Unit, Douglas in GB, 1940- 1942; officer served with 10th Rifle Brigade in GB, North Africa, Italy and Austria, 1942-1947.

Background in GB and Sudan, 1921-1940: Education including military training received while at *Winchester College*. Period as rifleman with Rifle Brigade Depot in GB, 1940, invasion scare on first night; details of Home Guard at *Horsted Down*; interview for officer training.

Aspects of period with Officer Cadet Training Unit, *Douglas, GB*, 1940-1942: problems with terrain; story of fishing with explosives. Aspects of period as officer with 10th Rifle Brigade in GB, 1942; story of exercise with carrier platoon; tactical training.

Aspects of voyage from GB to *Algeria*, November 1942: embarkation; Mother's war service and her hop-picking in Kent during war; malaria precautions; later problems with malaria before FA Amateur Cup Final; air raid during approach to Algiers.

Aspects of operations as officer with 10th Rifle Brigade in North Africa, 11/1942- 5/1943: march to tobacco warehouse; activities during wait for posting; nights on beach; posting to frontline; story of air raid against Royal Engineers; accommodation at Bouarada; patrols; details of situation at Two Tree Hill; description of activities of own section (Including Corporal Tommy Fearon); reflections on battle.

Accommodation and sleeping arrangements; story of German tank advance and action taken against them; mining of road; fire received from German tank; contact with French Foreign Legion troops; story of ambush against armoured car and motorbike while at Bouarada; withdrawal from ambush; story of night reconnaissance patrol at Bouarada and return to Allied positions through German lines; coping with situation and advice during Officer Cadet Training; return to Bouarada and reconnaissance patrols; support given to Americans in Kasserine Pass; story of firing on Valentine tank; withdrawal from position.

Approach of battle and reconnaissance undertaken; events during wait for expected German attack including near miss from shell; discovery of German withdrawal and reason for it; details of journey to coast and plan to cut-off Axis withdrawal at **El Alamein**; events during wait for attack; scenes of battle and German POWs; description of advance including crossing of wadi and attacks on tanks; patrols carried out by unit; attacks from Junkers Ju-87 Stukas; briefing for advance through minefield; description of advance into minefield gap including communications and dealing with wounded; activity of Welsh Guards.

Action of A Company and others beyond minefield; casualties; contact with American troops; re- organisation of unit; pass through minefield gap; description of anti- personnel mines and German position in minefield; forming-up of Allied forces; air activity; details of advance across plain including POWs taken; story of communications; journey to and night in cactus grove (Ouch!); destruction of knocked-out tanks; news from Colonel; Junkers Ju-87 Stuka attack on A Company; special order received from General Alexander, 21/4/1943; rest period; activity in hill position; shellfire received and treatment given to wounded; plans for attack on Tunis; wait for start of battle; description of a German defensive position.

Method of throwing grenades; advance during first day including capture of German troops; advance of tanks; infantry assistance given to tanks including story of attempt to communicate with a tank commander. Shelling of dressing station including treatment gained for knee; evacuation to Oran; casualties in absence and decision to avoid close friendships; account of the capture of Longstop; reason for change in Company Commander.

Plan for final attack; contact with Royal Engineers; air activity during advance; scenes of tank attack; Moorhead's account of meeting-up with 7th Armoured Division. Description of advance to Tunis; journey around Tunis including reception from civilians; night patrol in Tunis outskirts; situation in Hammam Lif; taking of Benzedrine; contact with civilians in Hammam Lif; description of tank attack on Hammam Lif including assistance given by infantry; return to trucks; story of Honey tank during journey to catch-up with main force; planning and description of attack on farm; opposition faced during advance toward Enfidaville; air activity; surrender of German forces.

Aspects of period as officer with 10th Rifle Brigade in North Africa, May 1943-March 1944: story of shooting rabid dog in POW Camp.

Aspects of operations as officer with 10th Rifle Brigade in Italy, March 1944-May 1945: arrival at Naples; stay in transit camp behind frontline at **Monte Cassino**; exercises; position taken near Monte Cassino; restrictions on movement during day; description of anti-personnel mines laid by Germans and Nebelwerfer fire; building and crossing of Bailey bridges on Rapido; use of artillery and smokescreen; advance beyond river; story of passing a German artillery position; reconnaissance work and position taken; details of German and Allied attacks; problems during journey to and wait at forming-up area; capture of Monte Cassino and German withdrawal.

Scenes during advance through battlefield; shelling from Germans; capture of bridge; fording of river and positions taken. Casualties from mines and mine clearance; period as Company Commander; discussion of contribution to D-Day; troops and equipment lost to Operations Overlord and Dragoon.

Successes and failures of 10th Rifle Brigade in Italy; description of battle near Perugia including casualties; writing to families of casualties; German counter-attack on D Company including problems with communication; casualties; reconnaissance and clearance of mines; reaction to award of mention in dispatches.

Advance beyond Rome; problems faced by Allied troops in Italy; reactions to D-Day dodgers remark; advance to Gothic Line; arrival and memories of General Temper; humour among troops including air activity; rations; story of pig caught for dinner; recovery of body from a river; capture of a German engineer; death and memories of John Bodley.

Reflections on outlook of officers including question of battle fatigue; home leave; capture of Argenta Gap (*The Battle of the Argenta Gap was part of the Allied Spring

1945 offensive during the Italian Campaign in the final stages of the War. It took place in northern Italy from 12–19 April 1945 between British V Corps and German Panzer Corps units).

Details of artillery barrage; description of advance beyond River Po; surrender of German forces and subsequent accidents; story of stopping an execution of a Cossack in Udine; scenes following end of war including story of German troops continuing to fight; journey to Austria. Aspects of period as officer with 10th Rifle Brigade in Austria and Italy, 1945-1947.

~

Finally, here are some extracts from Tony Pawson's recollections after the War had finished:

Work with Glasgow Herald; situation in Klagenfurt including story of armed SS troops; celebrations at end of war in Italy; story of Nikolai Tolstoy libel case; story of football match organised in Verona and subsequent trial; promotion to major; story of match in Padua with Tom Finney.

Scare of fight with Yugoslav partisans including problems with displaced persons in Austria; discussion of repatriation of Cossack troops and possible war with Yugoslav partisans; Nikolai Tolstoy's libel trial and later BBC programme made with Tolstoy; story of cricket trial; effect of army service on later sporting career; gaining entry and funding at Oxford University; story of appearance in 1944 film The Way Ahead; reflection on anger of troops over events at Anzio; father's service with Home Guard; opinion of basic training including boxing (Sergeants Tommy and Bill both boxed for the Army).

~

Dad's Release from the Army:

Letter of 15TH March 1946:

FROM THE OFFICER IN CHARGE - RIFLE BRIGADE

Military Conduct : Exemplary.

Testimonial:

Thomas has been in charge of Battalion Signals in a position of responsibility using intelligence and initiative. He has done this job very well. He is a good leader and will not lose his head in an emergency.

Thomas wishes to join the Police which is highly recommended. He is a good organiser.

~

It was short and concise as the senior officers had many letters to write. Well done young Dad, you were a credit to the Army and the folks back home.

~

Letter to The Soldiers of the 15th Army Group:

HEADQUARTERS 15 ARMY GROUP

From General Mark W Clark USA Commanding. May 1945

With a full and grateful heart, I hail and congratulate you in this hour of complete victory over the German enemy and join with you in thanks to

Almighty God.

Yours has been a long hard fight – the longest in this War of any Allied Troops fighting on the continent of Europe. You men of the Fifth and Eighth Armies have brought that fight to a successful conclusion by recent brilliant offensive operations which shattered the German forces opposing you.

You have demonstrated something new and remarkable in the annals of organised warfare: you have shown that the huge fighting force composed of units from many countries with diverse languages and customs, inspired, as you have always been, with a devotion to the cause of freedom, can become an effective and harmonious fighting team.

Our exultation in this moment is blended with sorrow as we pay tribute to the heroic allied soldiers who have fallen in battle in order that this victory might be achieved. The entire world will forever honour their memory.

(And now the bad news)

The War is not over.... There remains the all-important task of inflicting a similar complete defeat on our remaining enemy – Japan.

Men of the 15th Army Group I know you will face the task ahead with the same magnificent, generous and indomitable spirit you have shown in this long campaign. Forward, to final Victory. God Bless you all.

~

Letter from H R Alexander Field Marshall, Supreme Allied Commander:

ALLIED FORCE HEADQUARTERS 2ND May 1945
SPECIAL ORDER OF THE DAY

Soldiers, Sailors and Airman of the allied Forces in the Mediterranean Theatre, after nearly two years of hard and continuous fighting whi
ch started in Sicily in the summer of 1943, you stand to-day as the victors of the Italian Campaign.

You have won a victory which has ended in the complete and utter rout of the German armed forces in the Mediterranean. By clearing Italy of the last Nazi aggressor, you have liberated a country of over 40million people.

To-day the remnants of a once proud army have laid down their arms to you - close on a million men all their arms, equipment and impedimenta. You may well be proud of this great and victorious campaign which will long live in history as one of the greatest and most successful ever waged.

No praise is high enough for you sailors, soldiers, airmen and workers of the United Forces in Italy for your magnificent triumph.

My gratitude to you and my admiration is unbounded and only equalled by the pride which is mine is being your Commander in Chief.

~

Dad never spoke badly of the Germans or the Italians. In the 1960's he went to German conversation classes in the evening and took us on holiday to Germany where strangely we met and spent time with an ex *Luftwaffe* pilot and his family.

He was a bomber pilot in the Blitz on London and M was on the receiving end on the ground. I refer to the holiday later in the book but suffice to say that Dad always said he didn't feel animosity towards the people who were his previous enemy.

He never explained to me why someone such as he who had experienced the very worst of battle and death over a number of years could have such positive feelings towards the people who were the enemy. As I grew older, I began to recognise the strength he needed to be able to forgive (Not forget), look forward and move on after the War.

The War set the foundation of M&D's young lives and was an ever-decreasing backdrop against which the experiences of their lives played out in their little 'theatre of peace.'

~

My research for this little book was a big learning experience in many ways, and I feel I should add to my accounts of Dad's own war experiences with some information on Britain's Allies that is perhaps not generally well known or spoken of in the years since 1945. Dad lived and fought with a wide range of Britain's foreign Allies, and his respect for them was considerable.

The Allies of World War II were named the "*United Nations*" from the 1 January 1942, and the 'Big Four' Allies were the United States, Soviet Union, UK and China.
The following countries were occupied by *Axis* and had governments-in-exile:
France, Poland, Yugoslavia, Greece, Netherlands, Belgium, Norway, Czechoslovakia and Luxembourg. Other Allied 'combatant' states were India, Canada, Australia, New Zealand, South Africa, Nepal, Ethiopia, Brazil, Philippines, Mongolia, Mexico and Cuba.

Former *Axis* countries and '*co-belligerents*' were Italy (from 1943) and from 1944 Romania, Bulgaria and Finland.

All the Allied countries suffered significant numbers of killed and wounded, and without their total support the War would have been lost relatively quickly and on many other occasions as the war years rolled on. Some of the contributions of China and India are perhaps not generally well known because some of their actions and experiences were not officially recorded, reported in the media, written about in historical accounts or non-fiction books, or featured in tv and movie dramas and documentaries. Here is a little information on them.

India:

The main source of this information is *Yasmin Khan*, Associate Professor of History at the University of Oxford who wrote '*The Raj at War: A People's History of India's Second World War*'(Published by Random House).

During World War II India was controlled and occupied by the UK and provided American bases to support China, Southeast Asian and India-Burma theatres of war. Indians were often reported as fighting with distinction in Europe, North Africa, Italy, South Asia, Burma and in India against the Japanese.

During the War's most critical period, over 2.5 million Indian troops were fighting, and 17 Victoria Crosses were awarded. Forces included artillery, tank and airborne forces. By 1945 India provided the largest all-volunteer force ever with over 2.5 million recruits. Over 87,000 Indian soldiers, including those from Nepal, Pakistan and Bangladesh died. The British Commander-in-Chief of the Indian Army from 1942 stated that the British: "Couldn't have come through both wars if they hadn't had the Indian Army."

The Muslim League* also supported Britain and their Allies (*A political party established in the British Indian Empire during the early 20th century). Industrial, financial and military support from India was crucial in the defeat of Germany and Japan.

~

The 18th Brigade of the 8th Indian Division fought alongside the Desert Rats at El Alamein; Indian troops were known as Chindits and were central in crushing the Japanese invasion into South Asia, and consequently the British Army took back the occupied territories in spring 1945. India provided the 3rd largest Allied force in Italy and amongst them were the 43rd Gurkha Infantry Brigade who led several advances at the Battle of Monte Cassino and fought like tigers on the Gothic Line in 1944/45.

"Coolies" loaded cargo at ports and cleared land for aircraft runways; merchant seamen (Lascars) served in the Navy; in central India and Bihar, an East Indian State, thousands of women mined coal to support the war; and plantation labourers from southern India dug roads towards Burma and China in the mountains in the northeast. They dug with pickaxes and other very basic hand-held tools, and many thousands died of exhaustion and disease. Millions of South Asians toiled for the Allied war effort, but no records are available or were ever taken. More is the pity.

Industrial accidents were common like the massive explosion in 1944 in Bombay Harbour when a ship loaded with cotton and explosives caught fire and blew up warships leaving over 80,000 people without homes.

Yasmin Khan writes: "British officers wrote hundreds of accounts of their time in South Asia but there is not a single written memoir by an Indian rock-breaker, road builder or miner. The wartime history belongs to Nepal, Sri Lanka, Bangladesh and Pakistan as much as to India… Indian leaders, including Gandhi, Patel and Maulana Azad, denounced Nazism as well as British imperialism."

Yasmin also refers to a newspaper report which said: "*This was not the "forgotten army" but the "unknown army."*"

~

China:

China's resistance to Japan is one of the great untold stories of World War II. Although China was the first Allied power to fight the *Axis* it has received far less credit for its role in the *Pacific* than the US, Britain or even the Soviet Union which joined the war in Asia in August 1945. The Chinese contribution was overlooked soon after the conflict perhaps because it was an 'inconvenient' story in the acceptable narrative of the '*Cold War*'?

In the early 20th Century, China's desire for national sovereignty clashed with Japan's aim of increasing its territories in Asia. War broke out in July 1937 and during eight years of conflict the *Nationalist* forces of *Chiang Kai-shek* and to a lesser degree the Communists fighting with *Mao Zedong* proved to be fearsome resistance fighters.

Here are some shocking facts and figures on the contribution the Chinese made in the First World War and World War II:

Ref. the *South China Morning Post:* "In the First World War Chinese workers dug trenches. They repaired tanks in Normandy. They assembled shells for artillery. They transported munitions in Dannes. They unloaded supplies and war material in the port of Dunkirk. *Basra*, in Southern Iraq, contains the graves of hundreds of Chinese workers who died carrying water for British troops in battles with the *Ottoman Empire.*"

Around 140,000 Chinese people worked for American, British and French troops in France and about half a million provided manual labour on the Eastern front for *Tsarist Russia* before the Empire fell in the 1917 *Communist Revolution.*

Once in France the Chinese worked in ports, mines, farms and munitions factories, they repaired roads, transported supplies and dug trenches near the front lines, many were killed. About 3,000 Chinese workers died in France on their way to the Western front in Northern France and while returning to China between 1916 and 1920, and approximately 30,000 Chinese died on the Russian front.

The estimated recruitment figures of Chinese workers in the First War are:

USA (Via France) - 11,500; France - 37,000; Britain - 94,500; Russia - 200-500,000 (*Source: Christian Koller, Immigrants and Minorities Vol.26*).

According to Chinese Government statistics the total number of military and non-military casualties was circa 35 million, with 20 million dead and 15 million wounded. In addition, the War led to in excess of 90 million refugees. The Japanese Army '*Three Alls*' policy in China ("*Burn all, loot all, kill all*") killed more than 2 million Chinese civilians.

China played a significant part in World War II despite being much poorer and militarily weaker than the USA and the British Empire. Around 40,000 Chinese soldiers fought in *Burma* with American and British troops in 1944 to secure the *Stilwell Road* linking *Lashio* to *Assam* in India. Fighting within China itself forced Japan to commit around 800,000 soldiers.

There were many atrocities rendered on the Chines people including the *Rape of Nanking* in 1937 and less well recorded massacres including the sacking of *Xuzhou* in 1938; the 1939 'carpet bombing' of *Chongqing* which killed more than 4,000 people in two days of air raids; and the '*Three Alls*' campaign in 1941 destroyed Communist regions in the north. The Nationalists did most of the fighting against Japan when compared to the Communists.

During both World Wars hundreds of thousands of Chinese seamen and workers were recruited and many were killed and injured on British ships. Chinese seamen received less pay and fewer rights than their British counterparts. Chinese seamen in London launched a campaign and following a strike in 1942 they secured a wartime *'Danger bonus'* equal to that granted to British seamen. Hoorah!

After World War II, faced with the break-up of the *British Empire* the British Government and shipping companies colluded to forcibly repatriate thousands of Chinese seamen. Most Chinese seamen were employed by the *Anglo-Saxon Petroleum Co Ltd* and the *Blue Funnel Line*. In 1946, to legally enable the expatriation of their Chinese seaman, the two Companies forced Chinese workers to move from the UK back to Asian-based ports within the influence of the *British Empire* which were mainly *Hong Kong, Shanghai and Singapore*.

If seaman refused to be repatriated, they were issued with deportation orders by the Police and the Courts. Once repatriated in Asia most of the Chinese crews were fired. Many of the seamen who were based in Britain left behind wives and mixed-race children who they never saw again. Over 50 years later in 2006 a memorial plaque was erected on *Liverpool's Pier Head* in remembrance of the Chinese seamen. This is not a proud episode in British history.

~

MUM & DAD's FAMILY AFTER THE WAR

My apologies for a rather sombre Chapter on the vagaries and misery of war. I will hopefully raise the reader's spirits a little in some of what lies ahead in the oft jolly meander of this little book with an account of members of M&D's family who appeared after the war.

Joni (My Wife and best grown-up):

Joni (Pronounced 'Jonnie' or you're in trouble with her Mum) is the love of my life and will remain so through death (fingers crossed?) She is a few years younger than me and M described her as 'the daughter I never had.' Joni was a clear favourite whenever there was the slightest difference of opinion between wife and husband. She went to school at three years of age and was an exceptionally good reader through her school days. The same standards weren't quite so lofty when it came to doing her 'sums.'

Her favourite teacher ever was *Mrs Maile* in Primary school, who helped create Joni's lifelong interest in history. Mrs Maile would make models from 'wattle and daub' (* *A building material used for making walls in which a lattice of wooden strips, 'wattle' is 'daubed' with a sticky substance usually made of a combination of wet soil, clay, sand, animal dung or straw).* Wattle and daub were used for over 6,000 years. Mrs Maile's most memorable creation was a *'Dark Age'** village with *Roundhouses,* fireplaces for cooking, weaving frames and ducks on a pond etc.

Note: The 'Dark Age' is a historical period in Western Europe in the 'Middle Ages' that recognises a demographic, cultural and economic deterioration following the decline of the Roman Empire. A later Dark Age began in English football in 1996 after Germany defeated England in a penalty shoot-out at Wembley Stadium in the European semi-finals.

When aged four, Joni's Dad John was concerned that she had been unusually quiet for a few days and asked her if there was anything worrying her. She said she was upset that a schoolteacher had told her that she was a "*Blasphemer.*" John asked her what she thought 'blasphemy' meant and she said: "Shitty knickers." John consequently suffered sore ribs caused by excessive laughing.

Joni passed her *'11Plus'* exam and went to a Convent school in Ilford. The experience of being taught by strict Nuns did not lead to a life of religion, reverence, gravitas or consistently good behaviour. This partly explains the behavioural traits of our three children - information to follow later. Our little family unit had a mother and eldest daughter like *Beryl the Peril* (In the comic *The Topper);* a kid daughter like *Minnie the Minx* (In *The Beano* - *real name Hermione Makepeace);* and a son like *Dennis The Menace* (Also of *The Beano*) with his trusty dog *Gnasher* who was our little mixed-breed (*Mutt*) called *Kipper.* It was never dull at home.

I was very surprised when Joni seemed to show a glimmer of interest in me when we were first introduced by mutual friends in 1979 at *The Unicorn* pub in *Gidea Park, Romford*. And while our relationship has changed a great deal due to life's experiences and the ageing process, not a day passes without me being eternally grateful for my good fortune.

Joni has outstanding levels of concentration, when she is focusing on something the world passes her by, so if she is e.g. reading, cooking or driving, it becomes her single focal point and her expectation is that everyone else will be alert to her thought processes. It is advisable to get out of the way as she moves around the kitchen while cooking, although strangely she is happy for any number of dogs to lie on the kitchen floor while she works and steps over them backwards with alacrity, whereas if I'm in the way I need to beware.

An early sign of her concentration conviction was while I was up a step ladder painting the ceiling with a brush in one hand and a pot of paint in the other. She approached with a large, hot mug of tea and shoved it under my nose. I confirmed that my only option was for her to unzip my trousers and hang it on my willy, at which point she came into my world and recognised my difficulty. My zip remained closed.

Joni is a very good and committed cook/baker who enjoys feeding her family so they can face the challenges of life. She instinctively feels the need to feed those she loves any time any place, and her concentration level equips her well to avoid distraction such as a World-ending Apocalypse, while making a roast dinner with apple pie and custard for her family.

Joni feels the need to move the furniture around in the house regularly, she does it when I'm not around and manages to do so because she is exceptionally strong, probably due to her family's war-faring gene pool and the swimming she has done throughout her life. She was the *Essex County 200 metre Backstroke Champion* in 1998 in the 38-42 years age group, but she had no idea until three months later when she was given a Certificate by her club coach at *Romford Town Swimming Club*.

Her furniture removal genes allow large, heavy items to be moved by her alone in *Iron Woman* mode. We have always had dogs in our family and they and Joni consider the house to be a large kennel (But no dogs are allowed upstairs!). Consequently, the only personal item of furniture that is mine alone is a comfy armchair which moves around the living room like a wooden horse on a Carousel (When I'm not on it). I can leave my comfy chair with the best view of the tv and return later to a view of the compost heap in the back garden.

Our kids have always referred to our house as "Mum's house," and now in their 30's, they still go to '*Mum's house*' for lunch/dinner, for a bath/shower or to stay over. I've always had a seat in the living room and a toothbrush in the bathroom, but I often need to inform people that I live there as well.

~

Brother Tom:

There could be no better big brother, and while we have much in common, we are also quite different in many ways. We both enjoy watching a variety of sports as the ability to participate has been stifled as the years have rolled by and while I have always enjoyed exercise and keeping moderately fit for my age Tom will tell you: *"If I feel the need for exercise I lie down until the feeling has passed,"* and if you ask him in a pub if he would like another drink he will answer: *"Have I got a hole in my arse"?*

He enjoys beer (Preferably ale) and with age and experience he has tempered the temptation to drink to excess and now only serves penance on a Sunday when he exists in a silent bubble on the settee with newspapers and rehydrating drinks. If he feels the necessity, he will walk off a hangover by moving from the bed or settee to the dining table.

I asked Tom for some early life memories for this little book. Here they are:

'I was born in 1950, the milkman had a horse and cart, we had coal fires and the coal was delivered in sacks and tipped into a coal shed by a man black from head to toe in coal dust.

Of the huge amount of change since then perhaps the one that stands out is the freedom children had to be outdoors. Mum took me to school on my first day and after that I walked about ¾ of a mile on my own. These days if I collect a Grandchild from school they aren't allowed to leave unless accompanied.

I have fond memories as a kid living in *Elm Park, Hornchurch,* of hours and hours playing outside, we would go to a nearby derelict farm (A large housing estate since the 60's), the park, or just roam the streets (I remember being told to knock on front doors and run away when I was 4 years old – the big kids called it '*Knock down Ginger*').

Fast forward a few years and I was in the *Boy Scouts*, one Easter about ten of us went to *Snowdonia* for the weekend. The van we were in broke down in Wales and so we were split into pairs and told to hitch-hike home. We made it to *Piccadilly Circus* by about midnight where we were approached by two Canadian men claiming to be 'adventurers' sympathetic to boy Scouts. They offered to take us back to their place for the night, public transport had finished for the day and my Scout mate Graham thought this was a good idea. I did not.

There was a policeman nearby and I went to speak to him and point out our two Canadian friends but they had scarpered. We were taken to *West End Police Station* in *Saville Row* and the desk *Sergeant* looked up and said, *"You won't get no bob-a-jobs ere"!* I phoned Dad who drove from home (15 miles) and took us home.'

~

Tom was an excellent Scout becoming a *'Rover,'* and he went to the *12th World Jamboree* at *Farragut State Park* in the *Rocky Mountains, Idaho.* 12,011 Scouts attended from 105 countries and VIP visitors included the *World Chief Scout, Olave Baden-Powell,* actor *James Stewart* and *Vice President* of the *USA, Hubert H. Humphrey* among whose famous quotes is: *"Never answer a question from a farmer"*?

Tom continues:

'Another fast forward and I'm in the pub (**Late '60's**) and beer was two 'bob' (***Shillings/10 new pence**) a pint, that's ten pints for £1. Sometimes these days when I pay £5 for a pint I tell the bar person I would have got 50 pints for that in the old   days and they look at me like I'm daft.

I was on holiday on the *Isle of White* in 1970 and we saw that there was a music festival with *Bob Dylan* headlining, so we turned up and got tickets at the gate for 'sod all' (***Very little cost**). We could turn up at the 'Upper Cut' in Forest Gate on $aturday night, pay on the door and see, for example, Jimi Hendrix or Stevie Wonder.

These days, things are very different, but they are just as good or better. Happy days'!

~

Tom enjoys music and he mentions the *Upper Cut* in Forest Gate, East London, but he also frequented a bunch of clubs in East London including *The Ilford Palais* (6 old pennies for a pint of cloudy *Scrumpy* cider in the little pub opposite); *The Lotus Rooms*; *Oscars* where he saw *Tina Turner, David Essex* and *Cream* (Eric Clapton, Ginger Baker and Jack Bruce); and various soul singers and groups at *The Room At The Top, Ilford* where *Gladys Knight, The Four Tops* and *The Temptations* strutted their stuff back in the day.

Tom also met Dave and some of his *'Dave Clark Five'* on a holiday in 1969 and they invited him and his friend, also a Dave, to join them on their extended holiday in Morocco but sadly work beckoned back home.

Tom worked hard in a long career as a Solicitor and was respected as a reliable, thorough lawyer who got the job done. It wasn't his biggest case, but he did assist in the transfer of a professional footballer, *Ricky Heppolette,* who was born in *Bhusawal,* India and was quite possibly the only Asian player in the Football

League at the time. Tom said that Ricky was a nice fella and he ensured the legalities were completed for a transfer from *Leyton Orient* to *Chesterfield* in 1976. The contract signing was conducted in the usual way in the 1970's in a petrol station service area on a main road between London and Chesterfield, probably with a cup of tea and maybe egg on toast or a burger? I don't think it's done like that any more?

Tom was a good hockey goalkeeper and played for *Ilford* and *Westcliffe* in Southend-on-Sea. In his playing days, hockey goalkeepers wore kit like a *Samurai* warrior with pads from thigh to feet, a leather thong on the head and motorbike gauntlets/gloves. His talent emerged on wet days when the mud was thick and he could slide feet-first into anyone he could see through his visor (He wore specs or contact lenses so his vision was not always 20/20). Opponents, team- mates, spectators and the referee were all fair game when Tom executed one of his mud slides. It was a horrible and wonderous sight and he would disentangle himself and emerge from the mud pile-up and quietly trudge back to his beloved goal line to wait for the next opportunity to launch himself on the unsuspecting.

~

Mum's Grandchildren:

M had seven Grandchildren and three Great Grandchildren when she died. She missed her fourth Great Grandson by nine days. He's a cuddly one and the two of them would have been good mates.

When they were younger, I often found myself denying that my three children Dave, Noo and Small were mine, this was on account of their bad behaviour. M would recount stories of their antics to her friends and family who almost certainly heard them more than once. Here are a few of her favourite memories with a little background for context:

Dave is my son and his sisters' older brother. People called Dave don't usually have a nick name as they rightly carry their name as a badge of honour. Our Dave was named after two Dave's in the family, they could not be called *Mr.Perfect* and *Mr.Goody-two-shoes* but both were/are jolly good fellas.

Dave was large, bright and robust from a very young age. His first profound words were: *"Daddy I'm ignoring a worm"* - an older boy had shown him how to dig up worms and put them in his toy tip-up truck but Dave was observed by his Mum chewing one and it was my duty to tell him off and ensure he understood that he should not collect and chew earth worms

At two years old he generally greeted the people he passed in the street and for a short while called all Asian people "Doctor" (Our doctor was an Asian woman); he escaped out the front door in his baby-walker machine lifting it up and carrying it over the threshold; and at 3 years climbed silently out the back window of the car almost on to the roof while we were stationery at traffic lights on a very busy main road - thanks go to the inventor of the car horn.

Dave has always been injury prone and if there was an NHS season ticket for Accident & Emergency hospitals, we would have bought one annually. Our local Doctor was popular and friendly, however, I am sure I was the only patient on her books that she greeted with a deep groan when I walked into her office. I believe the reason was that she held me responsible for my son's many scrapes, gashes, scratches, rashes, bruises, sprains and broken bones etc.

At 5 months old we would hang Dave from a door frame to bounce up and down in a harness and he would bounce to open the cupboard door under the stairs and swing in like *Tarzan* in the jungle with different sound effects. Eventually the door frame came away from the wall. Dave enjoyed that.

Dave was raised alongside a pet dog and when he could first walk/toddle he would squat like a dog to have a pee or a poo. This was ok unless he had no nappy on which was the case outside a crowded beach bar on holiday in Spain. Fortunately, his effort resembled chocolate *Maltesers* and I was able to pick them up and bury them in the sand with an air of 'he's dropped his *Maltesers* again.'

The day Dad was cremated Dave and I arrived home just in time for the departure of the funeral cars as Dave had been punched on the nose at school, requiring a trip to A&E. Dave apologised constantly for having blood stained clothes at his Grandad's funeral (It was mostly on his white shirt) but seemed to enjoy the event, riding in the front hearse with Grandad and then eating a mountain of cocktail sausages, chicken drum sticks, assorted sandwiches and a comprehensive selection of cakes. His Grandad would have expected nothing less.

Dave has been present on four occasions to-date when someone has passed away in close proximity, the closest being 3 inches away nose-to-nose either side of a tennis court fence. By contrast, it's not uncommon for a bird to land on Dave while he is outdoors - I witnessed a Robin on his shoulder while he was mowing the lawn in our back garden. Dave appears to offer no threat to man or beast despite his 6'5" and size 13.5 feet.

Most Dave's are generally good blokes (*Fellas/geezers*) and travel constantly up and down a '*Dave Spectrum*' from '*Hopelessly Lazy* to '*Outstandingly selfless,*' but Shakespeare could not have been referring to Daves when he said: '*Love them all but trust a few.*'

Beware '*Wantaway*' Daves who call themselves '*David*' because they secretly wish they were called George, Edward or some other more pretentious name. Beware these shallow *'Don't-Wannabe Daves'* as they have a tendency to self-aggrandizement (*A desire to enhance their reputation beyond what is justified by the facts)

~

Our Middle Child ('Noo'):

Unlike her big brother who at his birth, mostly on account of his large head, was stuck at the point of exit for 36 hours, his sister Noo burst forth into the world like a torpedo from a submarine surprising nurses and her mother alike. My cricket skills helped me catch her before she hit the floor in the Maternity ward. Her lungs worked well from minute one; she sucked her first *McDonald's* burger (Cheese no gherkin) at three months; and skipped crawling and walking and went straight to running, making loud thumping sounds upstairs like a charging Rhino.

Noo is the 'problem middle child' and she excels in this role to this day. M loved all children of the world and had no family favourites, but she was always quick to support Noo regardless of her frequent challenging behaviour. M loved and laughed at her first ever granddaughter's dress sense which has always leaned towards the avant-garde (*Favouring new and experimental ideas and methods). She was a very mature 18month-old and she liked to wear a tea-cosy on her head and her red wellington boots on the wrong feet.

One-day when she was very small, we realised that she behaved in the form of a combination of unsavoury characters from *Eastenders* on the tv. This enduring *soap* has much to answer for as Dave insisted on spinning round to the theme tune and one evening while giddy, fell on the brick mantelpiece and split his head which again required hospital stitching at the local A&E.

The day that Noo decided she would use a potty for the first time was a Christmas Day, she missed and found the carpet and the wall in the same movement and at the same moment Auntie Dot (At her 87th Christmas dinner), resplendent in a pink paper hat, choked on her roast turkey which had been carefully diced to avoid her choking, had to be given the 'Heimlich Manoeuvre'* to remove the blockage (*Stand behind the victim, link your hands between their tummy button and the bottom of their chest with your lower hand clenched in a fist and give up to five abdominal thrusts).

As soon as Noo could use a small pair of scissors at about 16 months old she cut her own hair, applied her mum's face make-up and chose her clothes from things she found in the house. Consequently, thereafter I possessed mostly odd socks and my (Clean) underpants would intermittently disappear and reappear until she moved out in her twenties. I have no idea what she did with them? Do other children covet their father's underpants?

In adulthood Noo very much enjoys the benefit of two fine loving sons and the eldest from seven years of age has helped her to tell her left from her right and to assist her in reading maps e.g. when driving to her mum's house. Noo's map-reading genes are from her Nanny Jean (Joni's Mum) who has no sense of direction and must always turn a map in the direction she is travelling to have any chance of guessing wrongly where she is and where to go.

Like her mum and little sister, Noo has always enjoyed playing netball, and one of M's favourite enduring boasts was when her granddaughter was invited to an England under 19's training camp. During a Saturday morning visit I heard M relay the proud news to her neighbour over the fence, her sister Jess on the phone and the window cleaner when he knocked for his money.

~

Our Kid ('Small'):

Small is a combination of mostly angel with a smidgeon of devil. She is a lovely young person but has a mischievous streak which is inherited from her Mother's 'Black Douglas' ancestral line (See more details in 'Mother In-Law' below). This fact combines with a childhood spent in the company of black Labradors and terrier breed dogs, which showed itself in her early speech which was mostly snuffling, panting and occasionally growling.

She spoke her first proper words when knocked over in the supermarket by a careless trolley-pusher. She struggled up in a long winter coat, scarf, gloves and woolly hat and shouted at the careless pusher: "Dick Head!"

The first time Small dressed herself to go to Infants school, Joni received a phone call to say that she was acting strangely and wouldn't stand up to get off the story mat. It transpired she had inadvertently stepped into an upside-down jumper (Crop-top) thinking it was her knickers, so she was travelling 'Al Fresco' when she left the house.

While propped in front of the tv when she was one year old, Small pointed at the screen and declared: "Gan-Gan Gorbachov!" She had studied this elderly man and decided that he was someone's Grandad. He had two Granddaughters at the time, Ksenia and Anastasia who are of similar age to Small. How did she know?

What an interesting man Mikhail Gorbachev is, he said: "Imagine a country that flies into space, launches Sputniks, creates such a defence system and it can't resolve the problem of women's pantyhose."

He also said: "If people don't like Marxism, they should blame the British Museum." I don't really know what he means but tend to agree with him.

*Note: Mikhail Sergeyevich Gorbachev, born 1931 in Stavropol Kray in the North

Caucasus region of Southern Russia, he was the *General Secretary of the Communist Party of the Soviet Union (CPSU)* from 1985 to 1991 and *President of the Soviet Union* in 1990–91. He was awarded the *Nobel Prize for Peace* in 1990 as his policies of *Glasnost* ("Openness") and *Perestroika* ("Restructuring") contributed significantly to the end of the *Cold War*.

~

Uncle Bill:

I am proud to have been named after my uncle Bill, he was born in Stepney in 1921 and remained true to his Cockney roots throughout his life. He had three sisters and his Mum died before he was a teenager, his Dad was a merchant seaman whose second wife had four stepchildren. Bill took on a fatherly role from a very young age.

His stepbrother George spoke with heartfelt sincerity at Bill's funeral in 2002 and said: "With our Father away at sea much of the time, it fell to Bill and sister Alice to bear many of the daily chores. Bill did his jobs without complaining such as the weekly trip with the pram to pick up six pennyworth of coke (Coal), raking out the fireplace every day, and his least favourite job was cleaning out the daily family porridge pot!

Bill helped me with my homework, introduced me to cricket and took me to the *Oval* to watch England in a Test Match, to the *Royal Albert Hall* to watch world Championship boxing, and to *The Valley* and made me into a lifelong *Charlton Athletic* supporter."

Bill was blessed with enormous energy and he went to work at 13 years of age in *Millers*, a hardware store, and took up boxing. He was paid to box for a few years under the name '*Nipper Taylor*' and he was 18 when the War broke out. Dad met Bill at school, and they joined the *Tower Hamlets Rifle Brigade* and fought together in North Africa and Italy. Bill was also '*Mentioned in Despatches.*' Heroes both!

They were both demobbed in 1946 and went together to a '*Welcome Home*' dance at a local church in Stepney where they met two sisters, Jess and Jean and in 1948 the four of them shared a double Wedding at the church on the hill in *Chigwell*. In the year they were married, Bill and Dad took a big risk and started the family wholesale china and glass business, '*Rontays*' (From their combined surnames).

Bill and Jess had three children and lived happily in *Elm Park* in *Hornchurch* for 17 years from 1952. Many of my happiest childhood memories are of times with my cousins from Elm Park, Melvyn (6 years older than me and looking like Elvis when he was a teenager), Susan (The sensible one) and Gary the baby.

Bill was a Life Member of the *London Ex-Boxers Association* and together with an ex-Champion boxer, *Terry Downes*, organised many charitable events through the *Lords Taverners* and the *Variety Club* to fund *Sunshine Coaches* for disadvantaged youngsters. Bill also organised a trip for 100 ex boxers to New York, the wives and girlfriends (*WAGS*) were on the trip and it was a great success raising substantial funds.

After the War, Bill and Dad played football for *Collier Row British Legion* and Bill continued to manage the team which later became *Ashrow FC* for many years. I made my debut in 'grown-ups' football playing in my uncle Bill's *Ashrow* second team. I scored very few goals in my football 'career' (I was an instinctively clumsy defender) but I scored my best-ever goal in that very debut game. We played in thick mud at *Stubbers Outdoor Pursuits Centre* in *North Ockendon* and I dribbled like the great *Jimmy Greaves* (Spurs and England) around seven defenders (It may have been three?) and smashed the ball into the roof of the net (It may have bobbled over the goal line?) and while I was completing this wonderful piece of skill my Uncle Bill was standing on the side-line giving a loud commentary on my progress to goal scoring glory.

I'm comfortable boasting about this sporting success because even the referee congratulated me on my goal that day which never happened again in any game I ever played. Quite the contrary, most games of football that I subsequently played involved me being spoken to in a mostly negative way by a referee. As *Forest Gump* might have said: *"Clumsy is as clumsy does."*

Bill and Jess worked with their sons Melvyn and Gary in a chain of three family hardware shops in *Dagenham* and *Collier Row* between 1973 and 2001. Thousands of local people will have shopped for their household bits and bobs at *Taylors Hardware* stores.

Bill and Jess had been married for 54 years when Bill died, and they enjoyed ten Grandchildren in what is now a veritable family *Dynasty*. Like many other veterans of war, Bill and Dad managed somehow to put the horrors of war behind them and went on to live full lives. Tom and Bill knew they were very lucky to have survived to build loving families and they drew essential comfort from each other's friendship after the War. They sat, stood, ran, crawled, climbed, laughed and cried side by side in the War and sat, stood, laboured, laughed, argued and moaned side by side in their business. They didn't talk to their families about their experiences in the War, and I have no idea if they ever spoke to each other about their experiences.

It's nice to think that the day I was born in 1954 marked the birth of Tommy and Billy Mark 2.

~

The In-laws:

My in-laws Jean and John are of the same generation as Mum and Dad. A strong memory of my mother and father in-law is back in the 1980's when Joni and I decided to get married. There was no special romantic moment with me down on one knee, I had previously enquired if she would like to become 'engaged' to be married and she said: *"I can't be doing with waiting around, let's get on with it and get married or just not bother."* I like to think of myself as the romantic partner in our marriage.

Soon after my non-proposal, which was accepted, we went to Joni's house after an evening out so that I could formally ask John's permission to marry his daughter. If he had said no, we would have done it anyway. When we entered the living room at around midnight, John was sitting on the sofa with his legs over Jean's shoulders while she sat on the floor cutting his toenails. It was only a mildly shocking scene as I knew them reasonably well by then, so I took the plunge and asked for John's blessing to marry his daughter. He was happy to do so and the four of us shared a bottle of warm *Cava* (Fizzy white wine from Spain) - John preferred it to *Champagne* (And it was a lot cheaper).

Joni and I are currently approaching 40 years of much happiness in our marriage, surely proving that a good, strong marriage doesn't need a romantic proposal and expensive, chilled celebratory wine. It probably doesn't need freshly cut toenails scattered on the living room floor either.

~

Mother In-Law:

Joni's mum Jean's maiden name is *Douglas* (Scottish Warrior Clan) and the information that follows in the Chapter on '*Ancestery*' will help explain some of the unusual things you will learn about her in this Chapter. Jean had fiery ginger hair and a temperament to match and now in her 90's, her hair is grey and she has mellowed a little due to the vagaries of old age but still has her moments which can terrify innocent by-standers/sitters. A characteristic outburst was in a quiet country pub a few years ago, when she grew tired of waiting over nine minutes for her dinner and hailed the waitress with a loud cry of: *"Oi ! Where's my dinner !?"* This was swiftly followed with the confirmation that: *"I don't like mashed potatoes!"* Puzzling for all those within earshot?

Apart from mashed potatoes she claims never to have liked little boys, this is despite quite clearly loving her Grandson, three Great Grandsons and any number of other little boys who she has encountered. M was wrong-footed when she first heard this claim by Jean and was never really able to fathom it. She said: *"Jean has some strange opinions, but she has a kind heart."*

Jean's father was born in 1869 and was 60 when she was born. It's interesting to reflect that Jean's Father was a child when the daily newspapers reported 'Custer's Last Stand at Little Big Horn.' When she was a young child the family left Manor Park in East London and went to live in Herne Bay, Kent, for the benefit of her Father's health. She attended the Ursuline Convent in Westgate where the Nuns were very strict. We have learned from our own kids' experiences the impact that one teacher in a school can have on a child in both a positive and negative way.

Jean's family returned to Clavering Road in Manor Park before the War but when she was 8 years old her Father hanged himself in the cellar of the family home. He had a rare disease, a thickening of the skull which caused immense pain. He left a note which said that he didn't want to be a worry or a nuisance to his family and he couldn't cope any longer with the pain. The family kept the suicide a secret because it was considered a crime in those days. Jean recalls the family had very little money to live on after the bread winner had gone and her Mother would take her daughters over Wanstead Park to look for loose change on the ground, including in the bushes? The mind boggles.

After her Father's death Jean's Mother became very devout and preoccupied with the Church and consequently Jean says she became "A little wild." She was a very small child but grew rapidly from the age of 12 (Reason not known?). She stopped growing at 5ft 9" and can project an aura reflective of her fearsome Scottish warrior ancestry, the 'Black' Douglas clan, but Jean can also be very self-deprecating and describes her youthful self as: "Skinny, ginger, with buck teeth, big green eyes, shockingly short-sighted with unflattering glasses, very clumsy and ugly."

During the War when all the local children were evacuated, Jean was equipped with her label, gas mask and cardboard attaché case and was ready to go but her mother decided she "Had best stay home with me," so Jean and her older sister Marie were never evacuated.

The family had an army anti-aircraft gun station at the bottom of their garden on common land which was also a 'holding camp' for soldiers before they were shipped overseas. Jean was ten when war broke out and she and her sister would dress up in old clothes and climb onto the scullery* roof (*A small kitchen or room at the back of a house used for washing dishes and other dirty household chores) to sing and dance for the soldiers. It sounds like fun for all, but Jean's adult voice is like an off-key Marlene Dietrich (With her head in a bucket). Maybe the troops used the experience as a form of torture endurance training?

During the bombing of London, landmines fell in Jean's road and most houses had their windows blown out and some were destroyed. Jean often stayed at a wealthy school friend's large house whose Father was "Something big in the City." The two girls slept in a bedroom in the cellar and they would read 'The
80

Girl's Crystal' magazines and copy the heroines which meant going out at night in the bombing 'Blackout' looking for spies:

"We would creep about in houses that had been bombed out, eat fruit and vegetables in abandoned greenhouses, and watch searchlights trying to highlight the bombers, the flashing torrents of 'flak' from the anti-aircraft guns and sporadic RAF fighters, all this noisily in the air over our heads day and night."

Jean was coming home from school on the bus when a *Doodlebug** fell on *Wanstead Flats*, a 'common' area of land where troops mustered and trained for battle. The driver stopped the bus and he and the conductor escorted their passengers onto the Flats beneath the barbed wire to take cover, and Jean recalls watching a City Gent calmly unpicking lace from a woman companion's hat that was caught in the barbed wire, and was impressed by how unfazed the pair of them were and said it was 'a typical example of the British stiff upper lip.'

(*Note: The Doodlebug or 'buzz bomb' was the V-1 flying bomb ('V' for vengeance) an early cruise missile, and the only jet powered aircraft at the time.)

Both Jean's elder brothers worked in the *Post Office* and they were co-opted into the *Signal Corps* and served in North Africa, both surviving. My Dad and Jean's younger brother Ron were both with the 8th Army in North Africa and I remember a conversation in the late 1980's between the two old soldiers at a family party. Ron was a personal aid to some of the senior officers including Field Marshall Montgomery (Monty) and Dad was an enlisted infantry soldier with absolutely no close contact with the 'Top Brass.'

The conversation didn't seem to exhibit much soldierly camaraderie and the exchange was relatively brief. I asked Dad what they discussed and he said: '*Ron was talking about the places he'd been and the battles he'd fought in North Africa but we had very different jobs in the Army, Ron was generally stationed miles behind the line of fire at HQ and I was usually in the middle of it.*' Clearly, memories remained vivid and feelings strong more than 40 years after the end of the War.

In 1942 when Jean was 13 she worked for the *National Bank of India* (NBI) and recounts: *"When there was an air raid our manager used to walk up and down the office whilst we were under the desks with a metal waste paper bin on his head yelling encouragement to us and death threats to the Germans."*

After the War Jean decided that she 'wanted to meet a man,' she had a friend Jean with ginger hair, bespectacled with buck teeth who was 4'11" tall and called 'Lofty': *"We were identical twins with a 10" difference in height and we were not a pretty sight at dances."* In 1950 during a *"Ladies Excuse Me"* at *Stratford Palais* Jean met the man she would live with happily-ever-after. She had taken her glasses off to appear more attractive while carrying the burden of extreme short-sightedness (A good word for '*Scrabble*' enthusiasts). She inadvertently tapped the wrong gentleman on the shoulder and so got to dance by accident with John her husband-to-be (Fate or fatal depending on your viewpoint).

John had travelled directly to the dance by motorbike from *Aberdeen* where he was stationed with the Navy and was with his older brother Steve who was officially classified as a '*lady's man*.' John had no such classification he was a diver who spent a lot of time in a diving suit and apparatus including the top-heavy brass helmet and lead boots. His eight-hour, bum-bruising motorbike ride from *Aberdeen* had turned his face purple which complemented his *Tintin** blond hair and large pointed scarlet ears. Consequently, Jean didn't want to dance with him but had little choice, and they continued to dance and romance until his death in 2010.

*Note: *'The Adventures of Tintin' was written by Belgian cartoonist Hergé, real name Georges Remi, and was one of the most popular European comics of the 20th Century.*

Jean and M were of the same generation and both lived on the East side of Central London for most of their lives. They were similar in many ways but also different in just as many. Jean was more forthright, particularly when she didn't like something or someone, for example, in her happy admission of her dislike of music and mash potatoes (Taken separately or together). M was milder in her views and would signal a lack of agreement or interest in a conversation by saying "*That's nice Dear*," which meant 'let's talk about something else.'

~

Father In-Law:

Mine was **John Breeze**. The Breeze surname is historically *Old Norse* for *Bear (*To be avoided when it is in possession of a sore head).* A once famous ancestor was *Louis Breeze, Master Botanist (MB),* John's Great, Great, Great Uncle, and a portrait photo of him is the spitting image of the present-day celebrity and Master Baker *Paul Hollywood.* Queen Victoria was reputedly amongst Louis Breeze's clientele and there is some interesting and unusual information to be found on him in the following Chapter on '*Ancestors.*'

John was born in 1929 in *Stratford,* East London, the second of four boys who were as close in age as the Bible infers is acceptable. Their mum *Gertie* was a District Nurse and Dad *Victor* was a Chemist. His parents described John as very light-hearted, tall, fair, naughty and un-manageable, hence, he was sent to live with an uncle in *East Ham* at 8 years of age because his parents couldn't cope with him at home. A month before his 10th birthday England were at war with Germany, his Father joined up leaving his three brothers in Gertie's care. John remained with his Uncle *Harrald* (Dutch spelling) and during the War years he re-joined his brothers and was evacuated to various places in the East and

South-West of England. The reason the four brothers were frequently moved around was not on account of their good behaviour.

The Breeze boys were billeted at *Harold Bass's* farm near *Canewdon* in Essex (Famous for witchcraft) where John confirmed: *"We faced regular punch-ups with the locals on the way to and from school."* John claimed the brothers weren't intimidated by their foe except when *Moggie Pugh, a* very large local girl joined in. He also reported that *"During our stay in Canewdon we secured our teacher's arrest for signalling to German planes."* The teacher was quickly released without charge.

The brothers would poach with local tinkers, and while racing on his grocery boy's delivery bike John was catapulted through the front of a car windscreen (It was a screen in two sections that lifted up) exiting through the side passenger window with only minor cuts and bruises. This incident was the final straw for the Parish Council and the evacuees were sent back to London. They were reassigned, the oldest and the youngest together in *Reading* and the other two brothers sent to *Helston* in Cornwall where they went to school, had part-time jobs and generally had a much happier time.

John was called back from *Helston* and thought he was going back to *Water Lane School*, Stratford because he had passed his *11+* test some years earlier and had enjoyed his time there. He sang in the choir and played cricket, losing his four top front teeth, struck while fielding by a ball from a game on the next pitch. He also recalled tying a girl called Barbara to a small tree in the woodland by the school playground by her plaits,* and leaving her there when the air-raid siren sounded. She survived and married his brother Peter, and so became John's Sister in Law.

Peter died in the 1960's and Barbara later married his youngest brother Andrew. I would like to report that John and Barbara grew up and developed a great friendship in adulthood, but they didn't. Toleration was the best they could muster.
*Note: Plaits are a length of hair that is divided into three parts which are crossed over each other in a pattern.

John arrived back from *Helston* and was met at *Paddington Station* by his Uncle Harrald, who told him that he wouldn't be going back to school because his parents had signed papers for him to join the *Royal Navy* at the *Chatham Dockyard* in Kent as a 'Boy Seaman.' He was aged thirteen and his childhood was over.

Uncle Harrald told John that life in the Navy would make or break him. John described a little of his experiences: *"Boy seamen didn't wear shoes on training ships or at sea, in winter the soles of our feet froze to the decks and quaysides, we had no privileges, were at the mercy of all manner of 'challenging' people and we were expected to work hard on our studies."*

John made the best of his situation, learned to play trumpet in the band and became a bugler (*Don't confuse with 'burglar') and a *'Button-boy'* standing at the top of the Mast during sequenced rope climbing and seamanship displays. He was also a Gun Carrier and a *Ship's Marksman* and although not old enough to play an active part in World War II saw service in the *Mediterranean* and *Palestine*. If his rotten parents were not proud of their son, I certainly am.

John served 12 years sailing around the world and became a Navy deep sea diver when he was eighteen. This was a highly dangerous profession which involved defusing mines and frequently bringing to the surface the dead from World War II. He was blown up on one occasion by a hand grenade in an ammunition dump overseas. It left him with spaghetti-like veins on his legs and he grew 2" in height following the traction received in hospital. Shrapnel emerged from his body for many years afterwards.

As a *Duty Boat Officer* in *Malta* he had to politely tell the *Duke of Edinburgh* that he wasn't allowed to smoke on board. John encountered the *Duke* on a number of occasions while they were both serving in the Royal Navy and was very complimentary about *His Majesty* as a sailor and a man. Such a commendation from John was rare and the Duke impressed with his *"Approachability and good sense of humour."*

In the course of his duties in various ports around the Mediterranean which included ferrying VIP's to and from their boats, he made acquaintances among the rich and famous including *Humphrey Bogarde* and *Erroll Flynn,* he also met *Princess Margaret* and was struck by *Princess Elizabeth* who he said was *"Really lovely, with a great sense of humour."* Compliments from John were mostly saved for Royalty.

As a diver he assisted with the camera work on the film '*Morning Departure*' (Released as '*Operation Disaster*' in the USA), a 1950 British naval drama about life aboard a sunken submarine starring *John Mills, Richard Attenborough, Victor Madden, Kenneth More* and *Michael Caine* as a 'teaboy' *('Uncredited')* in probably his first film. John always claimed his leg and flipper can be seen in an underwater shot and was very proud of it. I have reviewed the black and white film in question and could only identify a fleeting glimpse of a small part of a solitary flipper. Nonetheless, it's one more movie appearance than I can claim, although I was clearly seen for three seconds in a tv episode of '*Crackerjack*' in 1965 while on a school trip.

John was also a Navy diver/camera operator for the undersea wildlife conservationists *Hans* and *Lotte Hass* who hosted two British television series, '*Diving to Adventure*' and '*The Undersea World of Adventure.*'

Lotte and Hans pioneered the concept of the underwater documentary series.

Hans was an Austrian biologist and an early champion of the environment, he helped develop the *Aqualung* and popularised coral reefs, Sharks and Sting Rays on the tv. John also met *Jacques Cousteau* whose tv fame followed Hans and Lotte.

John and Jean were married in 1954 (The year that *Lard* was born) but she wouldn't allow him to sign a lucrative contract extension as a diver because of the very high accident and death risks and the impact it had on the divers' life expectancy. Consequently, he trained to be a Distiller with *Tanqueray Gordon* until his retirement, he became one of only seven people in the world who had the famous *Gordon's Gin* recipe.

He travelled the world for his work for most of his married life and I have a theory that his absence made the marriage grow fonder. He was often in Spain at *'Domecq,'* the sherry and wine producer in *Requena,* a Municipality in the Province of *Valencia.* In the UK *Domecq* is probably best known for its sherry but it acquired its first winery in 1730. How much would a bottle of that cost today?

Palacio Domecq is a highly impressive example of 18th century *Baroque* architecture in *Jerez,* home of the Domecq family since 1885 whose winemaking reputation remains one of the finest in Spain. The origins of the family date back to 1385 in southern France in the region of *Bearn.* In 1666, *Juan de Domecq* received a pair of white gloves and a sword as a token of appreciation for his help to the Crown from *Louis XIV,* the *Sun King,* and the symbols remain in the family crest which are in the Coat of Arms on the Palace's main façade.

The head of the family from 1917 to 2005 was *Don Álvaro Domecq y Díez* who distinguished himself as a fighter pilot in the Spanish Civil War on the Nationalist's side and re-introduced bullfighting on horseback to Spain. The Don invited John to *Palacio Domecq* for a convivial business dinner from time to time and during his first visit when his spoken Spanish was in its infancy, while at the dining table he tried out a Spanish phrase and asked the great man if he could please tell him where the toilet was. This caused much mirth amongst the Spaniards and the Don explained to John that he had just asked the way to "the shit house."

Jamaica was also a regular destination for maintenance and repair of the gin stills and the local workers said John looked like *Michael Caine,* so much so that he appeared in a West Indies *Gordons' Gin* advertising campaign in newspapers, magazines and posters in the 1970's in a *Michael Caine* look-alike pose. 'Not a lot of people know that' (See John's 'Michael Caine' photograph in the attached gallery).

John was both a popular and occasionally un-popular man depending on your point of view, he had a dry, cheeky sense of humour but first and foremost, despite a very tough childhood that often left him fending for himself, he was a good, loving family man. John and Jean had a holiday home on the *Costa Blanca* in Spain from 1984 and spent much of his 25 years in retirement on the Mediterranean coast which he loved.

John had researched the Spanish location well over the years and the hot weather helped his arthritis pain, they enjoyed a busy social life with ex-pat friends from all over Europe, but mainly Germany, doing all the obvious things we Brits do in Spain. He smoked all his life from a very young age often pretending to the family that he didn't and died of lung cancer at the age of 80.

~

Moi:

Last and least is me. The name Billy is obviously from 'William' which is a fine, historic name often used by Royalty, for example, in 1174 *King William The Lion of Scotland* (Known by the nickname* *Garbh/The Rough*) led the charge into battle outside *Alnwick Castle, Northumberland.* In typical 'William' style he roared: "*Now we shall see which of us are good Knights!*" Then someone knocked him off his horse and he was captured.

There's nothing much else to say as I am an alter ego and the real me, *Lard*, is very dull by nature. So I will simply confirm some of the things that happened in 1954, the year he was born:
-The **BBC** broadcast its **first television news bulletin**.
-The U.S. Supreme Court banned **segregation in Public Schools** (They took their time).
-**Roger Bannister** became the first person to break the four minute mile at *Iffley Road, Oxford.*
-The first **atomic power station** opened in *Obninsk*, near Moscow.
-RCA manufactured the **first colour TV** set (12½" screen).
-The U.S. launched the world's first **Nuclear-Powered submarine**.
-Bill Haley and the Comets recorded "**Rock Around Clock.**"
-**Angela Merkel** (German Chancellor) was born.
-**Chris Evert** (US tennis champion) is five days younger than Lard, they are fellow *Sagittarians* and haven't met, but he believes they share the view that "*The star sign stuff is a lot of tosh.*"
-The **pocket-sized transistor radio** was invented by *Texas Instruments.*

What strikes me about *Lard's* year of birth is the gloomy influence of the *Cold War* and the frightening increase in nuclear activity in the USA and Russia. Thank goodness for Bill Hayley! Interestingly, *Chubby Checker's* 1960 single '*The Twist*' must have had an influence on him at 6 years of age as he remains a very enthusiastic closet 'twister', although he admits some of his more impressive moves and shapes have had to be scaled down with the onset of older age.

~

Note For Folk From Overseas:

Definition of a 'nickname': It's common to give your family and friends '*nicknames*' e.g. my daughters are '*Noo'* and *'Small.'* It is an informal name for someone usually based on their real name e.g. Mrs.Smith/*Smithy* or Thomas/*Tommo*. Your nickname can also be based on your prominent 'personality trait,' character or characteristic e.g. *Grumpy, Smelly* and *Jar Head.*

The *Middle English* word *eke*, meaning 'also' or 'in addition' was joined with *'name'* to form *ekename* which means "also-name" in the late *Middle Ages*. E*kename* became *nickname* because *Nick* became a more familiar alternative to the word's original spelling. Simple.

~

ANCESTORS

Mum's Ancestors:

The Norman conquest in 1066 saw the widespread introduction of surnames in Britain but M's maiden name was *Smeeth* which allegedly originates from an *Anglo Saxon* 7th Century village in Kent and means: *"dweller on smooth land."* Today, *Smeeth* remains a rural village and Parish east of *Ashford* in Kent. M's Dad was Fred (Frederick Horace) and he lived all his life in or near East London, mostly in *Stepney,* he was much loved by his five children, not least his second youngest, Jean (Mum).

Grandad Fred was born in 1892 and died in 1953 and he married Ada, my Nan in 1920 at *St Thomas'* Church in *Stepney*. Fred was a builder's labourer who worked in and around the *Docklands* area of East London and served in the *Royal Artillery* in the First World War. He was in the *Royal Field Artillery 17th Divisional Ammunition Column* (London DAC).

During the World War I the *Royal Regiment of Artillery* were made up of three elements of which Grandad's unit was the largest arm and was responsible for the medium calibre guns and *howitzers* which operated close to the front line. The guns were horse-drawn and while Fred was enlisted as a 'Gunner,' he only spoke of the time he spent working with the horses which he loved.

Fred's *17th Divisional Artillery Column* embarked to France and undertook trench familiarisation training in southern *Ypres* before taking over the front line. In Spring 1916 they moved south to *The Somme* where their action included *The Battle of Albert* followed by *The Battle of Delville Wood* (15 July- 3 September 1916) which was a series of engagements between the German and British, South African and Indian Allies.

Delville Wood (Bois d'Elville) was a thick tangle of trees with dense hazel thickets and grassy ridges to the east of *Longueval*. As part of a major offensive on 14 July known as *The Battle of Bazentin Ridge* (14-17 July) *General Douglas Haig, Commander of the British Expeditionary Force* (A highly controversial figure) ordered the capture of the German position, the attack was successful but at considerable cost to life.

Fighting in and around the wood continued for 7 weeks until finally the *1st South African Infantry Brigade* captured *Delville Wood.* Throughout July and August both sides struggled for control of the wood and village, but wet weather reduced visibility and made the movement of troops and supplies very difficult. Ammunition shortages and high casualties reduced both sides to sporadic attacks including hand-to-hand fighting in what became a battlefield swamp of mud.

To this day *Delville Wood* is well preserved with the remains of trenches, a museum and a National Memorial to the *South African Brigade.*

In 1917 Fred's *17th Division* moved to *Arras* to fight in *The Battles of the Scarpe* and the capture of *Roeux.* In late summer they moved to *Flanders* and fought in the first and second *Battles of Passchendaele.* In 1918 they fought in ten further battles and were close to *Maubeuge* at the very moment *'The Armistice'* was signed on the *"Eleventh hour of the eleventh day of the eleventh month"* of 1918. The Division was quickly withdrawn to the west of *Le Cateau* which was very fortunate because the US Intelligence service reported that shelling from both sides continued for the rest of *Armistice Day* only ending at nightfall by which time many more casualties were suffered.

The *Armistice* expired after a period of 36 days and had to be extended several times. The formal peace agreement was finally reached when *The Treaty of Versailles* was signed in 1919.

At some stage in the *Western Front* campaign, Fred was gassed in the trenches as it penetrated the gaiters on his legs, an injury that caused him pain for the rest of his life. M recalled when she was a child that he asked his children not to bring pear drop sweets home as the smell reminded him of the gas in the trenches.

Working class *Private Fred Smeeth* served with the *Royal Field Artillery* in some of the most horrendous battles in one of the worst War's in history. He was injured, survived and went back to his home in *Stepney* in East London and worked hard in and around the docks to make a good and contented life with his wife and five children. Thank you always Grandad Fred.

~

Grandad Fred's Dad was *Philip Richard Smeeth*, baptised in *Aldgate* East London and he lived from 1865 to 1937. Philip is recorded in Fred's marriage record as a *'Wharf Hand'* meaning he was a London docker. His wife was *Hannah Scott**, born in *Mile End* in 1865, she died in 1906, early by today's life expectancy. Hannah's Dad was a *'Cooper'* (*A maker or repairer of barrels and casks*) and member of *'The Worshipful Company of Coopers,** one of the *Livery* companies in the City of London.

Like their son Fred, my Great Grandparents (I'm certain they were great) were also married in *St. Thomas'* Church in *Stepney* in December 1887. My Great, Great, Grandad was *Frederick John Smeeth* who lived from 1838 to 1890. There are lots of Freds in my ancestral chain and I continue the tradition by virtue of my middle name.

*Note: *Scott* is a surname first attributed to *Uchtredus Filius Scoti* who is mentioned in the *Charter* which recorded the foundation of *Holyrood Abbey* and *Selkirk* in 1120, and was also a name amongst the *Clans* who settled in *Peebleshire* in the 10th Century. Scoti (*Scott*) is an ethnic or geographical name signifying a native from Scotland or a person who spoke *Gaelic*. It was originally a generic name given by the *Romans* to *Gaelic* raiders from *Ireland*).

*Note: Re '*The Worshipful Company of Coopers,*' the original site of a school established by the *Coopers' Company* in 1552 is still traceable in *School House Lane* in *Stepney*. After various developments and amalgamations, the school moved from its location in *Bow Road* in the *Borough of Tower Hamlets* to *Upminster* in Essex. *Tower Hamlets* covers much of the traditional East End and was formed in 1965 from the merger of the former Metropolitan Boroughs of *Stepney, Poplar and Bethnal Green.*

The school moved (Sedately) from East London between 1971 and 1973 and became *The Coopers' Company & Coburn School* and today is a most excellent school at which two of my children attended (One mostly well behaved and one not so). My slightly older cousin Cath Peck was a Deputy Head teacher at the school, she was much admired and respected (A school 'legend'), serving from the early days in Upminster until her retirement. Any and all grammatical inaccuracies will undoubtedly be corrected by Mrs Peck when she reads this little book.

The school has many well-known ex pupils including the actors *Jack Warner* (Re tv's *Dixon Of Dock Green*) and *Bernard Bresslaw* of '*Carry On…*' movie fame. Two current celebrities were in my daughter *Small's* year, *Rochelle Humes*, broadcaster and singer in the pop group *The Saturdays*, and *Rylan Clark-Neal*, broadcaster and occasional singer who had a slightly different name and persona when a schoolboy. *Small* enjoyed *Rylan's* company possibly a little more than my legendry cousin the Deputy Head teacher?

~

M's Mum's maiden name was Aida Eliza *Clifford* and her Father's name was *Augustus Thomas* Clifford. Aida spoke in hushed terms of her family's 'bastard' descendance from *King George*, she didn't specify which *King George,* but it could only 'conceivably' have been the 4th (IV). Nan was born in 1895 and so this could possibly have made him my Nan's secret Great Grandad. I am quite happy to believe that I am descended from a bastard child of George IV or most any other Royal, but my limited research skills are not good enough to claim this with certainty. If I had evidence of the true facts, I might be disappointed at my findings, so I am happy to live in the possibility that a tiny proportion of me is a right Royal

Bastard.

For the purposes of this little book I am allowing the hushed family rumour to pass me by on its way up (Or down) the 'family tree' hopefully growing stronger and more mythical, eventually being made into a Block Buster movie. Perhaps *George Clooney* could play the part of me (However, I feel he may be insufficiently ruggedly handsome), I am willing to play a minor, non-speaking role in the movie as I have successfully played *King Herod* (A baddy) and *Sir Gavin Greensleeves** in school plays (*A goodly Knight in shining Papier-mâché armour with white tights). Indeed, I was also primed and rehearsed to play *Joseph* in Primary school but fell ill with *Tonsillitis* and my costume, made by M from old curtains with a tea towel headdress was given to another boy called Lesley who wasn't even as tall as me!

Ada's Mum *Emily* was born in *Walthamstow* in 1856 and her Dad, *Augustus* in *Stepney* in 1853. Augustus and his family lived in *Mile End* and *Stepney* where he was a 'Dock Labourer.' There was a famous *Admiral Sir Augustus William James Clifford, 1st Baronet* (1788- 1877) who was a *British Royal Navy Officer, Court Official,* and '*Usher of the Black Rod'* in the *Houses of Parliament at Westminster. Sir Augustus* is a slightly more plausible family connection than *King George,* but he would have had to be a frisky 65year-old to have fathered Ada's Dad Augustus.

What follows is a veritable feast of ancestral stuff which if you should find a little turgid, I recommend you download the theme tune to *'Bonanza'* the tv cowboy series from 1959-1973, and then you are sure to gallop through at a pace.

It wasn't until I studied my family tree for this little book that I realised why American families frequently pass the same names on down the male line, for example, *'Elmer Armstrong Custer-Capone the 4th.* The reason is that they are following the long-established British Aristocratic* tradition (**Aristocratic** unofficially means *'Posh').*

~

Sir Augustus W J Clifford was born in France in 1788, the illegitimate son of *Baron William (Billy) Cavendish, 5th Duke of Devonshire* (1748–1811) who was born 206 years and 2 days before me - we never met. Augustus' Mother was *Lady Elizabeth Foster* (1759–1824) and soon after his birth she brought him to England to be wet-nursed by *Louisa Augusta Marshall,* wife of the *Rev John Marshall.* Augustus was educated at *Harrow* School (Posh).

In 1813 he married *Lady Elizabeth Frances Townshend* (1789-1862) and each of their three sons, *Captain William, Robert* and *Charles* succeeded their Father as the second, third and fourth Baronets respectively.

Sir Augustus JW joined the Navy as a *Midshipman* in 1800 and was made Captain in 1812 (A good year for a musical *Overture).* He became a *Rear-Admiral* in 1848 retiring in 1866. From 1818 he was a *Member of Parliament* in Ireland for *Bandon* (Cork) *and Dungarvan* (Waterford) and was Knighted in 1830 and created a Baronet in 1838 (Didn't he do well!)

'*A Naval Biographical Dictionary*' records one of Sir Augustus' naval escapades:

"On the evening of 4 July 1811, he voluntarily, and in a most handsome manner, being at the time in company with the 36-gun frigate Unite' , led into the anchorage, between Civita Vecchia and the mouth of the Tiber, and there, having anchored under the fire of a battery of four 9 and 6 pounders, which was quickly silenced, headed the boats of the two ships, and, without the slightest loss, brought out three merchant vessels, although exposed to a smart fire of musketry from their crews, and from a party of soldiers drawn up on a height above."

He was clearly an adventurous man with plenty of '*swash and buckle*' (*Swashbuckling - to engage in daring adventures with bravado, typified by the use of a sword, acrobatics and chivalric ideals)*. The archetypal Swashbuckling character was created in the movies and made famous by the likes of *Errol Flynn* (1909-1959) and more recently, *Johnny Depp* as *Captain Jack Sparrow* in '*Pirates of The Caribbean*' (2003).

Sir Augustus JW was a Patron of the arts with a unique collection of paintings, sculpture, etchings, engravings and '*bijouterie*'* (*A collection of trinkets and jewellery* - in the East End this is called '*bric-a-brac*' and both my Nans, Ada and Catherine would have called the entire collection "*Dusterlabras*").

Sir Augustus Clifford's Father, *William Cavendish*, was a British nobleman, aristocrat, and politician. He was the eldest son of *William Cavendish, 4th Duke of Devonshire* and his Mother was *Lady Charlotte Boyle, Baroness Clifford. The Duke* was *Lord High Treasurer of Ireland* and *Governor of Cork* and *Lord Lieutenant of Derbyshire*. He certainly kept himself busy.

The 4th Duke of Devonshire was a '*Whig*'* Statesman and was briefly made the *Prime Minister, he* was the first son of *William Cavendish, 3rd Duke of Devonshire* and was a supporter of *Sir Robert Walpole* (The first British *Prime Minister* in 1721).

*Note: The *Whigs* were a political party who between the 1680s and 1850s competed for power with the *Tories*. The *Whigs* preferred a political '*Constitution*' where the *legislature* has the main control over power rather than the *Monarchy*. The *Whigs* were enemies of the *Stuart Kings* in the Revolution in 1688 and took full control of the Government in 1715 and remained in power until *King George III* allowed the Tories to return in the 1760s.

So, M's possible grandiose ancestors were on the left (Labour) side of politics. Power to the people!

William Cavendish, 1st Duke of Devonshire (1640-1707) was an English soldier and another *Whig* politician, and he inherited his Father's peerage as *Earl of Devonshire*. He was part of the "*Immortal Seven*" who invited *William III, Prince of Orange* to depose *James II* of England as monarch during the '*Glorious Revolution*' and was rewarded with the title of *Duke* in 1694. Religion was clearly a major factor in *Billy Cavendish's* life.

The *1st Earl William* (1552-1626) a fine name for an Earl I think, was the first to put his foot on the 'titled' *Cavendish* ladder and of course he was a Nobleman, politician, and Courtier* (*Someone who hangs around the King or Queen*). The Earl was *Knighted* at Whitehall in 1609 and was considered to be an early celebrity and 'leader of Court society' and he was an 'intimate' friend of the impecunious* (*Having little or no money*) *King James I* from whom he purchased his Knighthood. I can picture *Earl Billy* in a Swashbuckling movie or Broadway musical but I'm not sure that he would be the good guy?

The *1st Earl* was the son of *Sir William Cavendish* MP (1505-1557) who was, you guessed it, a politician, Knight (No Papier-mâché) and Courtier who became one of *Thomas Cromwell's* "*Visitors Of The Monasteries*" (Not to be confused with the '*Spanish Inquisition*') in the period when Catholic monasteries, priories and convents were disbanded in England, Wales and Ireland in order to make *Henry VIII* '*Supreme Head of the Church in England*' in 1534. In 1552, with his wife *Bess of Hardwick*, *Sir Billy* began the construction of *Chatsworth House*.

So, the *Cavendish* Dynasty who fathered *Sir Augustus William Clifford* were a pretty powerful, influential bunch and I can occasionally see some of the *swash and buckle* in myself, for example, when hacking and plundering while removing a large bush or tangle of weeds from the garden or when I played football in my youth causing referees to constantly blow their whistle as my arms, head, elbows and legs thrashed about uncontrollably. I think I was probably more buckle than swash?

By way of contrast to the *Cavendish* line of M's mildly alleged ancestral tree, I would like to return briefly to the family dynasty that is '*Clifford*' to share some of the historical achievements of the namesakes* (*A person that has the same name as another*) of my Nan *Ada Eliza Clifford*. If you are wondering why I'm doing this I refer you to popular tv programmes like '*Who Do You Think You Are?*' that follow the ancestral roots of well-known celebrities and say to you dear reader 'if it's good enough for them it's good enough for me!' (If you find it dull, maybe listen to the *Bonanza* theme tune one more time?)

Historical Cliffords:

There are lots of influential members of the *Clifford Dynasty* with lots of *Ladies* and *Sirs* from the *1st Baron de Clifford* in 1274 to the present day with *Miles Edward*

Southwell Russell, 28th Baron de Clifford, who at the time of writing has not yet made his claim to appear on the *Peerage Roll.*

These well-endowed Ladies & Gentleman of grandeur must have had enormous patience through the generations when signing their name for a parcel delivery at the front door, regardless of whether they used a feather quill or fingernail on a screen.

The ancient Norman family which later took the name *de Clifford* arrived in England during the Norman Conquest of 1066 and became feudal *Barons of Clifford,* first settling at *Clifford Castle in Herefordshire.*

Robert de Clifford, 3rd Baron de Clifford, also *3rd Lord of Skipton* (1305-1344) was the Member of Parliament for *Skipton* and his title was restored to him in 1327 after being forfeited by his elder brother *Roger de Clifford, 2nd Baron de Clifford* who was hanged for treason (Oops!).

In 1391, T*homas de Clifford, 6th Baron de Clifford and 6th Lord of Skipton* was in the *Baltic* and was involved in a brawl (He clearly liked a god tear-up) with *Sir William Douglas,* (Bastard) son of the *Earl of Douglas.* Douglas was killed and Tom, full of remorse, set off on a Pilgrimage to *Jerusalem* and died in 1391 on an unknown Mediterranean island. This is significant as we will discover later when reviewing my Mother in-law's *'Douglas'* family tree.

The tv actor *Danny Dyer* (Ref *'Eastenders')* was born in *Custom House* just down the road from *Stepney* and he has a most impressive family ancestry stretching back to *King Edward III* (1312-1377). Danny is proper proud of his ancestors, not least the castles they owned, however, my little M's alleged links through her own Mother's maiden name, *Clifford,* is right up there in the same league with its historical ancestry of Diamond Geezers and a proper bunch of castles. Just four branches down Danny Dyer's family tree from *Edward III* is *John Clifford* (1389-1422), *7th Baron de Clifford, 7th Lord of Skipton, Appleby Castle, Brougham Castle and Skipton Castle* (An impressive pile of Manors) who was unfortunately killed at the *Siege of Meaux, Seine-et-Marne,* France.

John married *Elizabeth Percy,* the daughter of *Sir Henry Hotspur,* referred to as *Harry Hotspur,* the famous Knight in shining armour who sported an infamous pair of ferocious spurs and who of course gave his name to a very good football team in North London who to this very day sing *"Come Along You Spurs!"* in remembrance of *Sir Henry.* One current *Spurs* favourite and highest scoring players is a Harry, *Harry Kane,* Captain of England and a true *Lion Heart.*

The next notch down on Danny's family tree from *Lord John Clifford* was *Mary Clifford* who married *Sir Philip Wentworth* (1424-1464) who was the Great Grandfather of *Jane Seymour,* third wife of *King Henry VIII.* Phil was beheaded at *Middleham* in Yorkshire ("I say *'Oops upside your head'* again"!) which happened frequently in those days (Although you could only be beheaded once of course).

The *Cliffords* depart Danny Dyer's tree at this point. Hopefully they were able to use a ladder and not a snake.

John Clifford, 9th Baron Clifford, 9th Lord of Skipton (1435-1461) was a strong Lancastrian leader during the *Wars of the Roses*. Indeed, the *Clifford* family was one of the most prominent 15th Century families in northern English history. Johnny was orphaned at 20 years of age when his Father was 'put to the sword' by partisans of the House of York at the very first battle of the Wars of the Roses, the Battle of St Albans (1455).

As a friend and ally of the son of the *Earl of Northumberland*, Johnny took part in a feud against the *Neville* family (Who have always been available for a good punch-up), the *Percy family's* main rivals in Yorkshire who were closely allied with the *Duke of York*. This included a series of armed raids, assaults and skirmishes and notably an ambush on one of the younger *Neville's'* Wedding Reception in 1453 (One of the earliest and most disgraceful recorded 'Wedding crashing' incidents). These attacks were made in a period of so-called 'Truce' and were adjudged to be 'un-gentlemanly conduct.' The *Neville* family have continued to prosper and can be seen actively involved today in top level sports like football and netball. Tracey Neville is a particularly fine coach.

Henry Clifford, 1st Earl of Cumberland (1493-1542) was *seated* (Presumably with a cushion) at *Skipton Castle* and was a close friend of *King Henry VIII*. He spent time at the King's Court and was Knighted at Henry's Coronation in 1509. He was appointed *Sheriff of Yorkshire* in 1522 and became *Sheriff of Westmorland*. We had *Sheriffs* and *Deputies* in England long before they were introduced in the *Wild West* of the USA.

The *Clifford* family has been described as: "*One of the greatest 15th Century families never to receive an Earldom.*" Worse things happen at sea I say.

Finally, I turn to one of the most colourful *Clifford's* of his time, *Sir George Clifford, 3rd Earl of Cumberland, 13th Baron de Clifford, 13th Lord of Skipton* (1558-1605), who was an English Peer in the *House of Lords*, a Naval *Commander*, and *Courtier of Queen Elizabeth I*. In 1577, Georgie married *Lady Margaret Russell*. He was known at Court for his jousting and impressive armour, he became *Queen Elizabeth's Champion and she* made him a *Knight of the Garter* and he sat as a Peer in the trial of *Mary Queen of Scots* (An unenviable task).

He rather suddenly and unusually switched to sailing as a career and was renowned for his battles against the Spanish fleet, particularly in the Caribbean. He set up an expedition with *Sir Walter Raleigh** which led to the capture of the very wealthy ship, the '*Carrack Madre de Deus.*'

(*Raleigh was a 'Landed Gentleman,' writer, poet, soldier, politician, courtier, spy and explorer. Amongst other things he is known for introducing tobacco in England and was one of the most notable celebrities of the Elizabethan era.)

Sir George owned a 38-gun ship, The Scourge of Malice, and his buccaneering* earned him great wealth but he lost so much at his jousting and horse racing hobbies that he had no option but to sell his inherited lands. (*Buccaneering- a pirate, ruthless speculator or adventurer)

Georgie also participated in the formation of the highly influential and powerful East India Company and his tournament armour is considered the finest surviving garniture* of the Tudor period. It was made at the Greenwich Armoury established by King Henry VIII and can be seen at the Metropolitan Museum of Art in New York. It was designed to show the Earl's support for Queen Elizabeth I and is emblazoned with the Tudor Rose (*Garniture is decoration, trim or embellishment).

There is a strong resonance of Georgie in the character 'Blackadder' portrayed by the actor Rowan Atkinson in the Elizabethan period of the popular tv series Blackadder.

Sadly, Sir George neglected his estates in the North of England and on his death left a long running succession dispute between his heirs. George's two sons, Robert and Francis had both died young and his daughter became his sole heiress. Lady Anne Clifford eventually became Countess Dowager of Dorset, Pembroke and Montgomery, 14th Baroness de Clifford, she was also High Sheriff of Westmorland from 1653 to 1676. She married twice, firstly in 1609 to Richard Sackville, 3rd Earl of Dorset and they had five children, three sons who all died young and two daughters and co-heiresses. The eldest was Lady Margaret Sackville wife of John Tufton, 2nd Earl of Thanet with whom she had eleven children, consequently the title Baron de Clifford passed to the Tufton family.

Lady Anne retained boundless energy and in 1630 married Philip Herbert, 4th Earl of Pembroke and 1st Earl of Montgomery. She was a strong, hands-on landlady who, a little like our own Royal Family today, rotated her home across her properties/castles, usually living in each for up to a year.

Lady Anne died aged 86 at Brougham Castle in the room in which her Father had been born and her Mother had died. What a magnificent woman!

My family retain a close connection to her husband's family as my Dad's sister June married Tony Herbert and they begat my cousins Karen and her older brother Tony, to whom this book is dedicated.

So, after Lady Anne passed away, the Clifford line then progressed with Nicholas Tufton, 3rd Earl of Thanet, 15th Baron de Clifford, who claimed the Baronial title in 1678. The lineage then passed through five generations of Tuftons and on to

Edward Southwell, 20th Baron de Clifford in 1776 and remained in the *Southwell* family up to 1832, then on to *Sophia Coussmaker, 22nd Baroness de Clifford* in 1874, and subsequently to the *Southwell Russell* Baronial Dynasty up to the present day.

There you have it, an intriguing family tree steeped in history, much of it involving battles, wars and all manner of anger and aggression. My Nan Ada was a woman of substance not to be taken lightly, with a great respect for people of good breeding. Hence, her tendency to whisper when mention was made of her (alleged) bastard family history.

I am filled with admiration for how much people in 'the olden days' crammed into their relatively short lives. None of them had a truly healthy diet, gym workout or the type of leisure time and medical services we enjoy these days and yet many had the energy and motivation to squeeze the maximum from their lives, often effectively dying of old age in their 30's and 40's.

~

Dad's Ancestors:

Dad's Father was *Arthur William Fearon*, called 'Pop' by his family, he was born in Ben Johnson Road, *Stepney* in February 1892 and died in *Romford* in 1963. Pop's Dad was John, 1867-1942, married to *Sarah Anne Gore*, 1856-1896. Sarah's Dad was a cigar maker and John's Dad was *John Lawrence,* a fishmonger born in 1836 whose Mum, *Mary Ann* was a laundress.

Pop married my Nan *Catherine Grey* (1900-1990) in *Mile End*, East London in 1917. Nan was born in *Whitechapel* and living in *Stepney* at the time. As a child she lived in *Blackwall Buildings* in *Thomas Street*. Nan's Dad was *Thomas Grey*, born in *Bethnal Green* in 1873 and he died in 1957 in *Romford* aged 85. At the time of his marriage he was a 'mustard manufacturer' and later became a 'paper presser.' Thomas's Dad, *William*, was a Blacksmith, in the longstanding family tradition.

My Nan's Mum was *Catherine Doyle*, born in *Shoreditch* in 1874 and she was a 'Chocolate Moulder' (Tough job but someone has to do it). Catherine Doyle's Mum was *Judith Nolan* and her Dad was *John Doyle* a labourer who moved his family to London's East End from Ireland.

Nan's parents were married in 1894 and the *1911 Census* records the family living in *Charles Street, Stepney.* Her Dad, Thomas (*Fardy*), lived with Nan and Grandad and their children after his wife Catherine died and he was known as '*Fardy*' because one of his Grandchildren found it an easier name to say than 'Grandfather.' He was much loved.

Dad's close family were three generations who lived and worked in and around

Stepney. They were good, honest working-class folk who for a substantial number of years toiled loyally in the Reign of *Queen Victoria.*

The First World War:

Grandad (Pop) fought in the First World War and served in the *Cavalry* with the *19th Royal Hussars.* A *'Hussar'* is a soldier in a light cavalry regiment which originally had adopted a dress uniform modelled on the *Hungarian Hussars* with characteristic tight *Dolman* jacket - lots of gold braid (Think Turkish cassock jacket or 1980's pop group *'Adam And the Ants')* with a loose-hanging *Pelisse** over-jacket (**A short fur trimmed jacket worn hanging over the left shoulder to look 'debonair' and prevent sword cuts*). The jacket was 'accessorised' by a *Busby** hat.

(**'Busby'* is the English name for the Hungarian Prémes Csákó or Kucsma. In its original Hungarian form the busby was a cylindrical fur cap with a bag of coloured cloth hanging from the top with the end of the bag attached to the right shoulder to cushion sabre cuts.) If I had been a *Hussar,* I think I would have reinforced the cloth bag with more than cloth to be sure of keeping my shoulder and arm attached.

The *19th Royal Hussars (Queen Alexandra's Own)* was a Cavalry regiment of the British Army created in 1858, at the outbreak of the First World War the Regiment was split up and attached to the *4th, 5th and 6th Infantry Divisions* as Divisional Cavalry squadrons. I don't know exactly which battles Pop was involved in but the Regiment went to France with the *British Expeditionary Force* and saw action in the *Battle of Le Cateau* in August 1914, *the Retreat from Mons* later that month, the *Battle of the Marne* in September 1914, the *Battle of the Aisne* later that month and the *Battle of Armentières* in October 1914. Whatever Divisions these cavalry soldiers served in they certainly did not have it easy.

The Regiment was brought together again in April 1915 and attached to the *9th Cavalry Brigade* with whom it served for the remainder of the *Great War.* It saw action at the *Second Battle of Ypres* in Spring 1915; the *Battle of St Julien* in April 1915; the *Battle of Frezenberg* in May 1915; the *Battle of Flers–Courcelette* in September 1916 which was part of the *Battle of the Somme;* the *Battle of Cambrai* in November 1917; the *Battle of Amiens* in August 1918; and at the *Pursuit to Mons* in Autumn 1918.

A million horses and mules served in the British Army and almost half died. 7,000 horses died in one day during the *Battle of Verdun* in 1916. The Cavalry and horses remained in active service throughout the long four years of the War.

Two million dogs and carrier pigeons were serving in the front lines throughout the war providing essential services. Heroes one and all!

Pop was injured by a German lance in the arm in a charge at the *Battle of Mons in France in 1914* which was the first major action of the *British Expeditionary*

Force (BEF) in the First World War. The Allies clashed with Germany on the French borders and at *Mons* the British Army attempted to hold the line of the *Mons–Condé Canal* against the advancing *German 1st Army*. Although the British were significantly outnumbered and out-gunned they fought hard, inflicting heavy casualties on the enemy but they were eventually forced to retreat due to the greater strength of the Germans and a sudden retreat of the *French Fifth Army* which exposed the British right flank.

The retreat from *Mons,* also called *The Great Retreat,* is the name given to the long withdrawal to the *River Marne* in August and September 1914 by the British Expeditionary Force and the *French Fifth Army.* A number of battles took place including the *First Battle of the Marne* which forced the German armies to retreat towards the *River Aisne.*

In 2016, due to his injuries, Pop was posted to the *Reserve Regiment of Cavalry,* and clearly wasted no time in marrying my Nan in July 1917 while serving in *Aldershot.* There were reserve Cavalry Regiments across the U.K. and *Aldershot* was one of the largest.

The *12th Reserve Regiment of Cavalry* was formed in 1914 at *Aldershot,* training men for the *11th and 13th Hussars, the Leicestershire, Lincolnshire* and *Staffordshire Yeomanry.* When absorbed into a new **3rd Reserve Regiment** *early in 1917* they trained men (I'm not aware that any women were trained for combat in the Cavalry?) for the *15th and 19th Hussars, the Buckinghamshire and Wiltshire Yeomanry* and *Sherwood Rangers.* Presumably, some years earlier the *Rangers* had chased *'Robin Hood and his Merry Men'* around *Sherwood Forest*?

Aldershot barracks and training grounds must have been a very busy, bustling, noisy, smelly place to work and train. I remember Pop in his latter years as a very quiet old man sitting in the corner of the living room in the family home he shared with Nan and their youngest child Ron. He did favour one arm, his war wound, but it hadn't prevented him from living a very full and physically demanding working life, mostly in and around *Docklands* in the East End.

Dad's ancestral family tree can be traced to an early existence in *County Donegal* in the Northwest of what is now *The Republic of Ireland* in the province of *Ulster.* 'Scribes' in Ireland during the Middle Ages recorded names as they sounded, and so family members could be recorded with different spellings. Family births in Ireland recorded from 1864-1913 show where the Fearon family spread and settled: *Dundalk, County Louth* (180 babies); *Kilkeel, County Down* (128); *Lurgan* (76), and *Newry* in *County Armagh* (218).

In June 2019, Joni, Buddy (the dog) and I set off on a holiday to Ireland and visited a library in *Letterkenny*, in *County Donegal* to the West of *Derry* to see if I could find any trace of my Dad's ancestors living in the County. There were no marked borders between Northern Ireland and the Republic so there was no notification of passing into a different Country, but a noticeable difference was the large number of pubs in the Republic compared to Northern Ireland. There must be an interesting book to be written on the history and culture of pubs across the length and breadth of the island of Ireland to be sure!

I found a small bunch of *Fearon's* in the library records in *Letterkenny* (The staff were very patient and Buddy was very popular) and here they are with their birth year and location: *Mathew*, 1721 from, *Lisburn; Launcelot*, 1760, from *Bailieborrow, County Cavan* - he was a farmer but I was obviously hoping he would have a direct connection to *King Arthur and the Knights of the Round Table* (Maybe the big table was actually based in the Emerald Isle?); *Daniel*, 1796, from Tullylis, Craigavon; *Catherine*, 1814, from *Derryhale*; and finally *John*, also 1814, from *Mulladry*, Craigavon - I wonder if he and Catherine were brother and sister?

There are three others with only their birthplace recorded: *Henry* from *Annaghmore, Craigavon; Michael* from *Corn*ascribe, *Portadown, Craigavon*; and finally, *Murtagh* from *Cargans, Craigavon*. What a splendid name *Murtagh* is! It's an Anglicised form of the Gaelic 'ó *Muircheartaigh*' - *Muir* means 'sea' and the name means 'skilled navigator.' The *County Kerry* surname of Murtagh is Anglicised as *Moriarty* but I can find no link to *Sherlock Holmes,* however, if I do, I may not live long enough to tell the tale?

All of these Irish folk are from an area to the south or south west of *Belfast*, so I conclude that my Irish descendants from at least the 1700s hailed mainly from 'Greater Belfast' and surrounding areas south of the great *Loch Neagh*.

~

I went to the *Republic of Ireland* on holiday with M&D in the late 1960's, we stayed in *Cork* and drove around to see the sights. I bought a local hat, a striking hand-knitted *'Tam o' shanter', and a Shillelagh*. I know that a *Tam o' shanter'* is best known as a Scottish hat but my pale blue with white fleck Irish version was just about the warmest thing I have ever put on my head. The Irish *Shillelagh* is a wooden walking stick, club or cudgel made from hard knotty wood with a large knob sawn flat like a mallet at the top. Mine was too short for a walking stick but it was a lovely, shiny piece of wood associated with Irish folklore so for young me it was quite magical, a bit like a clumsy pre-Harry Potter wand I suggest.

Our hotel in *Cork* had a bar in the cellar with resident musicians, two young men who played guitars and sang their own 'folky' style and guest requests. We went most nights and everyone in the bar loudly sang traditional songs about the murdering English soldiers in Ireland from back in the days. There was no animosity and we had a thoroughly good time, but together with the many roadside memorials to people who had: *"Died at the hands of the murdering English soldiers,"* it was an important part of my education as a child.

My June 2019 holiday with Joni and Buddy was at *Port Rush* on the northern coast of Northern Ireland and we arrived when preparations for the *2019 British Open Golf Tournament* were well underway. We had no idea the tournament was scheduled for *Royal Port Rush* in July, but the excitement and anticipation around the town were high. The scale of the construction and logistics of this event must be amongst the biggest of any sporting event in the world, it all appeared very well planned and under control and we have many fine pictures of the three of us on the periphery of the golf course with the beach and Atlantic Ocean as the backdrop.

We enjoyed much better weather than the tournament itself the following month, which was won by *Shane Lowry*, an Irishman. A perfect outcome to an Irish sporting festival of unbridled joy! Fans crammed into the bar of Shane's local golf club at *Esker Hills, County Offaly* and sang *"Ole, ole, ole, ole"* in celebration. I thought I could hear them back home in Kent? The Irish do love a good Spanish song?

We had a splendid week and saw some of the stunning Irish seascapes and landscapes including a *'Game of Thrones'* venue - the episode where bodies were floated out to sea in boats and cremated. There was absolutely no evidence that anyone apart from tourists had been there and certainly no Dragon scorch-marks or manure, which led me to wonder if they may not actually have been real?

~

Dad's surname is of French origin and it was an occupational name for a worker in iron i.e. a *'Smith'* and is derived from *'Le Feron,'* most commonly a Blacksmith or other iron worker who would work in the agricultural economies of the day and often travel with military campaigns at home and abroad. The family name was introduced in England by the *Normans* after the highly consequential *1066 Conquest* which kicked off on 14 October with the defeat of Anglo-Saxon *King Harold Godwinson* at the *Battle of Hastings*. The family name is still fairly common in Normandy.

In 1180, *N.Feron* of *Normandy* helped spawn a flock of colourfully named folk born from 1198 including Geoffry, John, Odo, Richard, Robert, Roger, Sulpice and William. I think there's a possible resonance of *'Lord of The Rings'* and the *Hobbits of the Shire* in that list of names?

Today, *Féron* is a small town of around 500 inhabitants in the *Nord* region in northern France which was created from the western halves of the ancient Counties of *Flanders, Hainaut* and *Cambrai* in which *Lille* is the main city. *Nord* is the most densely populated area in France and is where the French, Flemish dialect of Dutch is still spoken as a native language - it sounds very complicated to me?

The first recorded spelling of the present-day family name in London is that of a man called *Walter* in 1179 during the reign of *King Henry II*. '*The London Hundred Rolls*' of 1273 records three examples of the name, Alan, Stephen and Henry. Fearon appears in *London Church Registers* including a Christening in 1660 at *St. Botolph's, Bishopsgate* and a marriage at *St. Dunstan's, Stepney* in April 1712, so there has been a very long-standing family namesake presence in the East End and *Stepney*.

British records include an *Elinor Fearon* born 1647 and buried in *Pardshaw Cemetry,* a Quaker cemetery in *Cockermouth, Cumbria*. A *William* was born in 1804 and lived at *Hundith Hill Farm,* also in Cockermouth, so there may also be a longstanding family base in beautiful *Cumbria* not far from *Whitehaven,* a port on the west coast of England 'across the sea from *Ireland*.' I feel a song coming on!?

Those Who Sailed Away:

Settlers with Dad's surname are recorded arriving in the USA in *Philadelphia* in 1745, 31year-old *George* landed in *New York* in 1812; *Joseph* aged 36 arrived in *Missouri* in 1845; and *George* and *Henry* arrived in *Philadelphia* during the Irish potato famine in 1842 and 1848 respectively.

Dad would have been happy to think that some of his ancestors were cowboys in the American *Wild West*. He loved a cowboy movie and song and '*The Black Hills of Dakota*' (Ref *Doris Day* as *Calamity Jane,* 1953) and '*Home on The Range*' ("*Give me a home where the buffalo roam and the deer and the antelope play....*") are amongst my very favourites. *Home on the Range* was very well revived by *John Denver* and *The Muppets* in '*Rocky Mountain Holiday*' in 1982 - the original dates back to *Dr Martin Brewster Higley VI* an *Otolaryngologist** who in 1872 wrote the famous poem '*My Western Home*' which provided the lyrics for *Home on The Range* in 1876.

(*If like me you are thinking that an *Otolaryngologist* must be a Doctor who dispenses cowboy medicine containing snake oils, you'd be wrong, as they are doctors who treat ears, noses and throats as well as areas in the head and neck – '*ENT*' does it better for me)

Returning to the family ancestors who sailed away, *Ida May* was born in 1874 and lived in *Syracuse* near *Lake Ontario, New York State*. Others settled in Canada and New Zealand in the 19th Century including a farm labourer aged 34 who arrived in *Wellington,* New Zealand aboard the ship '*Wairoa*' in 1877.

Dad's namesake *Thomas,* aged 31, a labourer, arrived in *Saint John, New Brunswick,* Canada aboard the ship '*Cupid*' in 1834 along with his wife *Catherine* and daughter *Mary* aged 5 years. *Mary,* a 23year old servant from Ireland, embarked on the 923 ton *'Lord Raglan'* from London on 16th July 1854 to Plymouth, arriving 27th July, then on to *Port Adelaide,* South Australia arriving on 24th October. Mary was 99 days on board and there were 6 births and 4 deaths at sea. The *Sydney Shipping Gazette* reported that *"372 souls were landed in the Colony."*

A search of the family tree shows the spread of ancestors outside the UK as: 12% USA; 10% Jamaica; and 3% Canada. I wonder what the historical family name connection is with Jamaica? Transportation of African workers to the Caribbean to work in the sugar plantations is a possible connection. Not a pleasant thought.

Other notable people with the family name:

James Fearon was a sailor and quite important judging by the size of his hat in a portrait painting, he served in the time of *Admiral John Jervis,* 1735-1823, *1st Earl of St Vincent.* This was a buccaneering time at sea and Jimmy may have served later in his career with a young *Horatio Nelson?* I like to think so as coincidentally I have a direct connection with the famous Admiral in so far as I was boys games captain of *'Nelson'* house at *Squirrels Heath Primary School, Hornchurch* in 1965/66, our colour was red and I remain proud of my high office and link with Lord Nelson.

A *Catherine J Fearon* born in 1888 sang as *'Josie'* in the Music Halls of the day, and I have indeed maintained a little of the musical tradition of the family with my flair for the bongo drum and the ability to strum two or three (simple) chords on the guitar.

Captain Edward Fearon **'The King of Motueka,'** was the youngest son of Isaac Fearon, a London-based merchant and stockbroker and his wife Elizabeth. Edward was born in 1813 at the family home on *Shove Place, St John's, Hackney,* London. As a youth he ran away to sea, where he progressed to become a *Master Mariner* in the *British Mercantile Marine,* the equivalent of today's *Merchant Navy* and in his twenties captained ships trading to North and South America, Cape Colony in South Africa and Australia.

Having earned a relative fortune during his successful career, King Eddy as I like to call him in his absence, retired from the sea and at the age of 29 emigrated to New Zealand.

An un-titled historical report from New Zealand reports:

"Times were turbulent when one of Motueka's earliest Pakeha* pioneers (*Pākehā *is a Māori-language term for New Zealanders of European descent)* arrived to take up his newly-bought block of land. Edward Fearon had barely pitched his tent and made a start on clearing his section when the *Nelson District* was thrown into a state of panic, fearing an imminent Maori uprising following the *Wairau*

Affray of 17th June 1843.

Motueka was an isolated spot, covered in thick bush, with sea access only, a large resident Maori population and only a very few other widely scattered settlers in the vicinity. A former ship's captain well used to taking command and dealing with sudden crises, Fearon is credited with playing a significant part in calming local tensions. He went on to see the tiny settlement grow and prosper, and such was his influence and involvement in almost every aspect of the fledgling township's affairs that fellow residents jokingly dubbed him the *"King of Motueka."*

Joking or not, *"King Eddy"* is good enough for me!

Today the *Motueka* place names *"Fearon Street"* and *"Fearon's Bush"* remain as a reminder of Eddy and his family. I wonder what went on in the *Bush*?

John T (1869-1937), first editor of the *Sunday Mercury*, a newspaper published in Birmingham (UK). The first edition was published in December 1918, John left the Dublin-based *Freeman's Journal* to take up the position. John would have moved to Birmingham at the time the infamous *Peaky Blinders* gang were tooling up once again after the first World War. Let's hope the *Sunday Mercury* was renowned for its coverage of sport, gardening and the arts and not crime reporting?

Hugh P was a USA Democrat politician from *Kings County* and candidate for the *New York State Assembly* in 1920.

George R (1883-1976) was a USA Republican politician and Member of the *New York State Assembly* from *Onondaga County* and was acting *President of the New York State Senate* in 1931-1932.

Peter was an English *'Greaser'* (Engineer) from *Bootle, Lancashire* who worked aboard the *RMS Lusitania*, a British ocean liner which was awarded a *Blue Riband* for the fastest Atlantic crossing - it was clearly well-greased. The *Lusitania* was the world's largest passenger ship for a short time but shockingly was sunk on 7 May 1915 by a German U-boat off the south coast of Ireland. Many believe that the sinking encouraged the United States to declare war on Germany in 1917.

Blair was an *Otorhinolaryngologist* (I would be impressed with plain old *'Ologist'*) who established the *Hospital for Sick Children* in *Toronto, Canada* in the 1950's, caring for children with life threatening airway obstructions and helping to reduce the death rate in the hospital to the lowest in the world. He served in the World War II as a Captain in the *Royal Military Corps* from 1942-44, he rose to *Professor Emeritus* at the *Department of Otolaryngology* in Toronto and was a consultant at the *Women's College Hospital*. He passed away in 1996. Blair clearly had the characteristic family 'work ethic'. What a man!

~

Mother In-Law's Ancestors:

Jean's maiden name was *Douglas*, that of the historic and infamous *'Black Douglas'* clan who were fiercely loyal to the Scottish Crown. Some have claimed that the early *Black Douglas's* not only pillaged, raped and murdered their enemies but they ate (some of) them!? Jean has certainly possessed a good appetite throughout her life (But she doesn't like mashed potatoes). There were many clan skirmishes over the years including those between the *Black Douglas* and *MacDonald* clans and it's perfectly possible that the very first MacDonald takeaway was completed by ravenous Black Douglas warriors.

Sir James Douglas (1286-1330) was son of *Sir William Douglas* who was captured by the English and died, presumed murdered, in the Tower of London. James was *Lord* of the Douglas family and Champion of *Robert de Bruce (King Robert I* of Scotland). He was known as *"The Black Douglas"* to the English and *"Sir James the Good"* to the Scots. His grandfather was killed alongside *William Wallace (Ref Mel Gibson* in the 1995 movie *'Braveheart').*

James spent his childhood in safety in Paris before returning to Scotland aged 18. He arrived home to find an Englishman, *Robert de Clifford*, in possession of his estates. A coincidence, given the *'Clifford'* connection in Mum's family.

James attended *Robert de Bruce's* Coronation at *Scone* (March 1306) and was the first Scottish nobleman to pledge loyalty to the King. They wandered together in the *Highlands* after their defeat at the *Battle of Methven* (June 1306) and James fought with *Bruce* for the rest of his life. His ability to seemingly appear out of nowhere and rush a larger enemy gained him a "demonic" reputation with the English troops. Mothers warned their children to behave or *Black Douglas* would come for them and he became known as the '*The Bogey-Man.'* Fellow Scots considered him a hero.

The story of *The Black Larder* in *Walter Scott's "Tales of a Grandfather"* illustrates James's renowned stealth. In 1307 he asked *Bruce's* permission to launch an attack on his home, *Douglas Castle*, which was held by the English. Bruce couldn't provide troop support, so James crept to the castle with only two men. He waited until *Palm Sunday* when the English in the Garrison were attending church then he broke into the Castle and barricaded the English in the church. There, in keeping with *Bruce's* "S*corched Earth*" policy, he set fire to the church killing everyone inside.

In 1314 as *Bruce's* second-in-command at the battle of *Bannockburn,* James fought 'valiantly' and chased the English a considerable distance to *Berwick on Tweed*. In 1319 he invaded Yorkshire with *Thomas Randolph, Earl of Moray*, defeating an English army assembled at *Myton-upon-Swale,* and he nearly succeeded in capturing *King Edward III* in a daring night attack on the English camp in *Weardale, Durham* (August 1327).

James's last recorded act of loyalty was to agree to *Robert de Bruce's* death-bed request to take his heart on a Crusade. On *Bruce's* death James cut out the King's heart and placed it around his neck in a silver casket, he then left for Spain where his fame and reputation brought Knights from across Europe to rally round his banner and they travelled to *Grenada* in southern Spain to support *Alfonso XI's* Crusade against *'the heathen Moors.'*

In the village of *Teba* a fierce battle took place against the forces of *Mohammed IV.* James fought his way to safety and encountered *William Sinclair* of *Roslin* isolated and in danger. On his horse, James threw Bruce's heart in its casket into the battle and charged shouting *"A Bruce, a Bruce!"* He was immediately overwhelmed and knowing he was going to die, picked up the casket again and threw it at the enemy crying out: *"Now, go in front of us, as you had desired, and I'll follow you or I'll die."*

The Scots won the battle and James's body was found beside *Bruce's* heart. His men would not bury him on foreign soil so boiled his corpse in a cauldron of vinegar, *"Until the flesh fell from the bones,"* and they returned his bones to Scotland.

So, my mother in-law is to be respected and preferably socially distanced when showing any signs of the emergence of her ancient war-mongering *Black Douglas* ancestry.

~

Jean's 'Nana' on her Mum's side was a '*Malarkey*,' an Irish name, although she was born in India. The word '*malarkey*' is traditionally used to mean '*insincere or exaggerated talk, balderdash, baloney or bunkum*' and was originally used in Irish-American language from around the 1920's. Interestingly M&D used 'malarkey' quite often ,for example, when talking about politics and politicians, but hardly ever in relation to Jean I should add Jean's Grandad was *Jim Owen* who changed his surname from *Onion* which may originally have been *O'Nion,* the origins of which are French, meaning 'onion grower.' He obviously preferred Welsh leeks.

My dear old mum in-law has a rich and interesting ancestry to be sure!

~

Father in Law John's Ancestory:

John had a Great, Great, Great Uncle, *Louis Breeze*, a *Master Botonist* born in Norfolk in 1823. Louis oversaw *The Hygienic Institute Stratford* and was a medical philanthropist whose name in 1887 was known throughout England (An early 'celebrity').

In October 1887 'The Biographical Magazine' *wrote of Louis:*

"*The* smattering of herbalism picked up in early life enabled him to perform some extraordinary cures of cases pronounced incurable. Until he entered his teens he enjoyed vigorous health, was taken ill and Dr. Mills of Pulham, Norfolk pronounced his disease to be a determination of blood to the head and leeches were applied to his temples, blisters to his back, a seton in his neck and he was salivated, the result of which was to reduce him to a skeleton (One wonders if Louis' problem was ill-health or the treatment he received!?)

Several London physicians pronounced him to be a hopeless case and gave him over to die (There was no NHS in those days – three strikes and you were out on the street). Fortunately, at about this time Mr Breeze was reading 'The Theory of The Reformed Botanic Practice.' He states most earnestly that he owes his life to practical application of the theory contained in the works of Thomson, the great American Naturalist and others and totally abstained from mineral and vegetable poisons, tobacco and intoxicating drinks – none of which has he ever taken or prescribed since – also by the free use of a much abused specific, Lobelia Inflata which he frequently took as an emetic; this course permanently reinstated him to convalescence and vigour (Steady on old boy!), which state he has enjoyed ever since without any sign of relapse.

His ailments were subject to almost every conceivable form of disease – especially indigestion, chronic rheumatism, an enlargement of the joints, so that often he could not walk without artificial help (I doubt the pogo stick was available at the time?); some doctors declared his complaints to be consumption; others heart disease, and Dr. Richdale believed that his kidneys were decayed; he was generally debilitated, with haggard countenance and indications of premature old age, attended with agonies for fourteen years which language would fail to describe (Most supporters of professional football clubs will likely have endured some of the self-same sufferings); most of which he fully believes was induced by being overdosed with improper medicine.

His own case was so remarkable that he was asked to prescribe for others and the benefits of his remedies were received by hundreds. It was fully demonstrated by long and successful experience (above five and thirty years in the town of Stratford, London).

It is to Nature's own sanative productions, to the herbs of the field and the waters from the fountain we must look for the grand catholicon for the remedial wants of man." (What?)

A Testamonial to *Dr Louise Breeze* was written and signed by hundreds of patients from all across London and beyond including Norfolk, Brighton, Cambridge, Reading, Ipswich, and Whittlesea:

"We the undersigned under a deep sense of obligation to Mr Louis Breeze respectfully present to him this testimonial of our heartfelt gratitude for the benefits received through his skilful and judicious treatment whilst suffering under the most painful form of one or other of the following diseases:

indigestion, bilious fever, enlargement of liver, diseased bowels, chronic rheumatism, rheumatic fever, gout, tumours, St Vitus' Dance, Asthma, paralasys, Hydrophobia (Rabies), Scrofula (scurvy) and Leprosy as well as from various accidents of a serious nature." (This makes Louis sound like another *'Dr Good,'* selling his jollop* from his roving wagon out in the American Wild West.)

"We the undersigned were discharged from medical treatment as incurable and as a forlorn hope had recourse to Mr Breeze. He administered medicines he had prepared from herbs grown in the Green Lanes and Hedgerows of Old England, which together with his far-famed Medicated Vapour Baths, effected such marvellous cures that we stood amazed and wondered, until we felt desirous of expressing our gratitude for miraculous restoration to perfect health and strength."

~

'The Biographical Magazine' continues:
"In July 1883 a *Grand Complimentary Concert* was given at Stratford Town Hall, holding upwards of one thousand persons, in commemoration of the sixtieth birthday of Mr Breeze and in recognition of the excellency of his medical treatment and his persistent advocacy of temperance of more than a quarter of a century in Stratford.

The following demonstrates the bitterness of medical prejudice and jealousy. In February 1886 a man suffering from a bad form of hernia had a bath and an emetic at Mr Breeze's establishment. The hernia became aggravated by a struggle with a workman on the following Thursday which resulted in the man's death. A local doctor chanced to hear that the man had used Mr Breeze's treatment and was seized with the idea of casting a slur on the botanic treatment (more especially the Lobela emetic). The doctor hastily took possession of bottles bearing Mr Breeze's name and made a post mortum examination on the deceased. The result being a Coronor's Inquest. To this Mr Breeze went as a witness.

The great point of contention at the Inquiry was as to the poisonous or non-poisonous nature of the Lobelia, a drug which the medical faculty have tried to get on the poisons list for years. It is used by botanic practitioners very largely with the best of results.

The Hearings created something of a sensation in *Penge* (Not renownded for its sensations.) for a considerable concourse of people had gathered to see the principals in the case leave, and when Mr Breeze drove away three hearty cheers were given to him by the crowd and the cheering was kept up until his Brougham (Horse carriage) was out of sight." (I love a happy ending)

~

But Louis didn't drive off into the sunset just yet, soon after the Hearing he created a newsletter which he named *"The Winnowing Breeze,"* and in his opening address he said: "Compulsory vaccination is one of the governmental institutions to which this paper will be squarely antagonistic; whilst to every institution, and to every agent who espouses the rightful causes of the poor and defenceless, it will be a true and permanent ally."

'The Biographical Magazine' reports:

"Mr Breeze has used the Russian vapour bath in his work of healing for nearly thirty years. The only bath in this country which receives the support of the medical faculty was the Turkish Bath. Mr Breeze after mature consideration had become fully satisfied that as the action of dry heat upon human skin was to contract animal matter, the Turkish Bath was the enemy rather than a friend to the results which he desired to achieve. Acting upon this conviction Mr Breeze thought out for himself the principle of baths which are now so successfully used in conjunction with his practice. Every person using the bath enters first into a vapour and the vapour is medicated with such essences of herbs as in his opinion are likely to minister to the health and comfort of his patients. His patients according to their own judgement pass to and fro between this room and the shower, plunge, spinal spray, and needle baths – all of which are administered in cold water" (I prefer a nice Spa hotel thank you Louis).

"It will be readily seen that Mr Breeze has been the victim of a considerable amount of persecution but up to the present the discredit has rebounded upon themselves whilst Mr Breeze has made fresh friends and comes triumphantly out of each ordeal with greater honour and a more fixed determination.

In his politics Dr Breeze is a dedicated liberal and has a profound admiration for *William Ewart Gladstone.*"*

End

*Note: *Gladstone* was an influential Statesman and Liberal politician whose sixty year career included twelve years as *Prime Minister* spread over four terms between 1868 and 1894.

Well there it was, old Louis was a bit of a hero in his day and his legacy lived on with baths in the East End like *Poplar Baths* where M and her family and friends would go for a bath (And the vapours maybe?) during the 1930's and 40's, and Joni regularly swam for *Redbridge Swimming Club* in the swimming pool at the baths in *West Ham* in the 1970's and 80's.

~

Surely there is a little book to be written by most families on their ancestral links. I, however, will stop at this point with just the one chunky Chapter offering much to enjoy about the interesting and colourful lives of some of M&D's extended family, most of whom were not rich or famous.

~

Top: A loving young Mum.

Below: Mum & Dad with Billy and Tommy.

Top: Dad with DaveyCrocket (Tom) and Billy the Kid.

Below: Big brother on duty.

Top: Dad in Italy at the end of the Italian campaign.

Below: Brothers Arthur, Tommy and Vic at the beginning of the War.

Top: Sergeant Tommy serves chow.

Below: Brief respite after Monte Cassino

Top: A Desert Rat signaller in action.

Bottom: Dad had some fun in Egypt after the War.

Top: *A double wedding of sisters and best mates.*

Below: *Jean and Jess, teenage East End sisters during the War.*

PLACES OF SIGNIFICANCE

London:
To know Central London is to love it, or at least a lot of it, but a lifetime or two is not long enough to get to know all of it well.

Docklands by the River Thames:
M&D lived within a stone's throw of Docklands throughout their youth and never has there been a more dangerous place to live or work, particularly if you didn't know your way around. Policing in the residential areas around the Docks was limited but informal self-policing was in the history and culture.

The Docks demanded formal policing for many reasons but mainly theft and death – accidental and deliberate. Vast fortunes were made and lost, for example, Merchants in the 18th Century would lose an estimated £500,000 a year (About £51 million today) of stolen cargo plus lost tax duties. The Thames Police are the oldest professional police force in the world, they were formed in July 1798 and officers had to be tough individuals who could weald a cutlass and a musket. They merged with the Metropolitan Police in 1839 which originally had been established by *Robert Peel*. Its base was and continues to be in Wapping High Street and it has evolved into the *Metropolitan Police Marine Policing Unit.*

Stepney, East London:
A Brief History:
M&D lived with their families from the 1920's to the '40's experiencing typical East London working class childhoods. They lived in close proximity around *Stepney Green* without meeting until their late teens. They talked about the hardships but not of concerns about personal safety, largely because of the strong community spirit in their neighbourhoods and a strong culture of helping family, friends and neighbours, from the very young to the elderly. Local communities looked out for each other.

M's mum Ada had a reputation for moving the family around, mostly in the *Stepney* area, but the house in *Latimer Street* was the one the family occupied for longest and the eldest son Fred remained there with his family, Scottish wife Eva and four children until the 1960s when the streets in the locality were demolished and modern accommodation was built. *Latimer Street* has gone without trace, but *Latimer Church* still resides today in *Ernest Street* just a few hops and a skip east of *Stepney Green Underground Station.*

Dad's family lived and some of the children were born in *Charles Street* to the south of *Latimer Street* across *Stepney Gardens*. It became *Scurr Street* and was demolished after the War. During the war years they moved to *Carlton Square,* a couple of streets north of *Stepney Green* Station near *Mile End Hospital which* remains in good shape today. When Dad was demobbed after the War, he went home to the family house in *Rush Green Romford.*

The family were part of the *St Dunstan and All Saints Church* local community in *Stepney High Street, E1.* Today the church describes itself as being: *"At the heart of the community for over a thousand years. It is the mother church of London's East End and also its oldest, the foundation dating from the 10th Century."* Most of Dad's brothers and sisters were christened at the church and some like Dad would have enjoyed the Sunday *Scout/Guide* church parades with an interesting assortment of marching styles and flag bearing down the High Street and into the main aisle of the church.

The following was written by Sydney Maddocks in *'The Copartnership Herald' (November 1933)* and it provides some interesting snippets from the very rich history of Stepney and the surrounding area:

"Writing in 1578, the chronicler *Holinshed* said: "This common land was sometimes, yea, in the memorie of men yet living, a large mile long (from Whitechappell to Stepenheth church) and therefore called Mile-end Green; but now at the present, by greedie (and seemeth to me, unlawful) enclosures, and the building of houses, nowwithstanding hir maiesties proclamation to the contrarie, it remaineth 111 acares a halfe a mile in length." (*It seems to my untrained eye that the folk back in the day liked to stick the letter 'e' on any word that stayed still long enough)

Syd continues: Perhaps once upon a time many an ancient man in his latter years recalled, like Mr. Justice Shallow, the days of his youth, when archers held their meetings on the Green. King Henry the Eighth, who encouraged this noble exercise, gave his patronage to a company of bowmen who practised here. Coming one day to see their performance, he was so pleased with the display of skill that he instituted the " Famous Order of Knights of Prince Arthur's Round Table or Society." The scene was gay with pavilions and tents adorned with banners and pennons, and the spectacle attracted many onlookers from far and near. The entertainment concluded with a feast for which a buck of the season had been presented to him who was Prince Arthur to regale him and his companions after their exertions of the day.

When England was threatened by Spain in 1588, it was on this Green that the men of the City assembled to exercise themselves in martial array. Two hundred years before, in 1381, *Mile-end Green* had been the place of riot and tumult, for on it gathered the men of Kent and Essex who had taken part in what is called *'Wat Tyler's Rebellion'.* On the 14th June the insurgents from the two counties joined forces there. The young King, Richard II, who was only sixteen years of age, rode out of the Tower and listened to their tale of grievances (which were, indeed, bitter wrongs), and promised all they asked. The promises, however, were never realised. The following day they assembled in Smithfield, and the death of Wat Tyler there by the dagger of Sir William Walworth, and the action of the King who placed himself at the head of the insurgents, brought to a sudden and dramatic close the only spontaneous popular rising on a grand scale presented in our history.

All that is left of the old Common is the small remnant that survives as *Stepney Green*. The house of Henry le Waleys or Le Galeys is described as being on Stepney Green, which may be taken to mean anywhere in its modern vicinity. At this house Edward I, in 1292, held a Council, often improperly referred to as a Parliament, to deal with the dispute between the citizens of London and the merchants of Gascony concerning the importation of wine."

~

A glimpse at '*wiki.casebook.org*' sets the scene around *Commercial Road,* which later in the 1800's became the infamous *A13*:
"In 1802, the East India Company secured an Act of Parliament for the building of a new road beginning at the new West India Dock Gate and terminating at Church Lane, Whitechapel. The existing pathway ran through fields, and road construction began in 1803.
The residential neighbourhood began with the creation of sugar refineries in St. George's-in-the-East, which led to the building of small houses for the workers. The Stepney stretch saw the development of an attractive residential District for the 'well-to-do,' forming 'Terraces' and 'Places,' and for a period, Commercial Road had attractive shops and an air of real prosperity.
Heavy road traffic (*Horse and cart of course) and the introduction of a toll in the 1820s and 30s lead to the degradation of the road and surrounding areas, and prior to its paving in 1855, Charles Dickens described the Commercial Road thus:
Pleasantly wallowing in the abundant mud of that thoroughfare and greatly enjoying the huge piles of buildings belonging to the sugar refiners, the little masts and vanes in small back gardens in back streets, the neighbouring canals and docks, the India vans lumbering along their stone tramway, and the pawnbrokers' shops where hard-up mates had pawned so many sextants and quadrants that I should have bought a few cheap if I had the least notion how to use them."

~

Around 30 years later the Whitechapel, Aldgate and Stepney areas became infamous for the murder of (probably) eleven women by an unknown assailant called *Jack the Ripper*. The brutal murders have retained their notoriety to this day and a constant trickle of tv dramas and movies continue to be produced.

Here is a short account of 'the Ripper' from *'inspiringcity.com'*:
"It's easy to forget just how awful his crimes were. Five women, known as the *Canonical Five* (*The best description I can find of 'canonical' in this respect is *'authorized; recognized; accepted'*), are widely accepted to have died at the hands of Jack the Ripper with up to six more women seen as possible victims. As he was never caught there is much debate about just what number is correct and the truth is that nobody knows. The main judgement to whether a victim was 'official' or not, being the horrendous way the Ripper would dissect the bodies and slit the throat.

All the victims were prostitutes and many could well be described as alcoholics desperate to do what it took to get a bed for the night. One of the victims, Mary 'Polly' Nichols had been thrown out of her 'doss' house on the night she was murdered because she had no money. In order to get it, she walked the streets, yet had bragged to a friend earlier in the day that she had already made three times the money needed that day, but drank it away. The price for services rendered was a couple of pence, pretty much the same as a loaf of mouldy bread.

Gunthorpe Street/Georges Yard Buildings – Whitechapel.
If ever there was an alleyway which evoked memories of the dark old days of London's East End, it's Gunthorpe Street with an atmospheric archway and cobbled street next to the White Hart pub on Whitechapel High Street. The pub and the alley would have been very well known, being, as it was, at the heart of darkest Whitechapel. Prostitutes would have drunk there and the alley would have been a favoured location for a quick 'knee trembler.'

A corridor inside George's Yard Buildings was where the body of Martha Tabram was found on the morning of the 7th August 1888. Her killing was just over three weeks before the first 'official' victim recognised as the first of the 'canonical five' victims. In my mind, the viciousness of the attack is enough to firmly link it to the Ripper. On the day in question, she and her friend May Ann, 'Pearly Poll' Connelly had picked up a couple of guys in a nearby pub, Martha went into one alley and Pearly went into the other, Martha never came out."

~

The Chinese In East London:

The history of Chinese migration to London can be traced to the early 15th century when the *Ming* Emperors of China sent out fleets which consisted of the largest ships built anywhere in the world at the time. Chinese sailors had reached London on board *East India Company* ships by 1782 and this small group lived around *Pennyfields* and *Limehouse Causeway* near the Docks. The *East India Company* was the most important commercial organisation in the world at that time and China became a very important, profitable market. In the mid-18th century, imported Chinese products became fashionable including porcelain, and tea dominated Anglo-Chinese trade as it quickly became a favourite English habit.

The *East India Company* began to export opium from India to China, selling it to raise the money to buy shipments of tea, this was illegal and angered China's authorities. War broke out in 1839 over the opium trade and Britain defeated China, consequently, under the terms of the *Treaty of Nanking in 1842, Hong Kong* became a British Colony.

In 1857, following the cessation of the slave trade a second *opium war* led to the *Treaties of Tianjin* which included a clause allowing Britain and France to recruit Chinese to the British Colonies, North America, South America and Australia, as cheap labour known as '*Coolies*'. Forced to pay for defeat in these and other Colonial wars, the poverty-stricken Chinese people were driven abroad for work where they were often treated with hostility. The first Chinese immigrants arrived in London in the 1780s and most were employed as sailors and worked for the *East India Company* and the *Blue Funnel Line*, frequently as cooks.

In the early 19th Century, Chinese seamen began to develop small communities in the port areas of Liverpool and London. In London, the *Limehouse* area became the site of the first *European Chinatown*. The *East India Company* employed a Chinese seaman, *John Anthony*, who helped support Chinese sailors, and by 1805 *Anthony* had the wealth and influence to become the first Chinese man to be naturalised as a British citizen. An *Act of Parliament* was required to allow it to happen.

The first Chinese immigrants settled mostly in the *Poplar* and *Stepney* areas near the Docks. In the law courts, Chinese defendants affirmed the truthfulness of their testimony by breaking a round plate rather than swearing an oath on the Bible. Sounds like fun.

In the early 20th Century the Chinese community was still based around *Limehouse Causeway and Pennyfields*. In World War II, 10,000 Chinese men enrolled in the Merchant Navy while others defended *Hong Kong* and fought the Japanese in the Far East. After the War the Chinese began to move into *Soho* and bought up cheap property (Smart). Today, in the rebuilt Docklands, some of the street names are a reminder of the history of the Chinese community including *Canton Street, Mandarin Street, Peking Street, Ming Street and Nankin Street.*

The People's Republic of China has the World's biggest population with around 1.404 billion people living in approximately 9,600,000 square kilometres. China is one of the oldest Civilisations on earth and the *Xia Dynasty* of China (*From c. 2070 to c.1600 BC*) was the first Dynasty to be described in historical records.

*Please note: It is my ambitious hope that people in China and the Far East in general will stumble upon this little book, read it (Perhaps even have it translated into their own language?) and then make a small donation to a children's charity of their choice. A lot of small donations would raise a great deal of money for the benefit of children. Sometimes, highly unlikely things happen.

~

'Clifford's Inn' Central London:

My Nan, Aida, Maiden name *Clifford*, provides some historical family interest in the *City of London* (*The Financial services *'Square Mile'*). Presently there is a property on the original site of a small building called *Clifford's Inn* on the north side of *Fleet Street*. One of the original *Inns of Chancery*, *Clifford's Inn*, was one of three Inns attached to *Inner Temple*. *Inns of Chancery* were used to teach the 'rudiments' of law providing a college to one of the four *Inns of Court*. *Inns of Chancery* no longer exist but from the 1300s to the 1800s there were twelve such Inns. Today if a law student wants to become a Barrister, she/he must become a member of one of the four *Inns of Court* - *Middle Temple, Inner Temple, Gray's Inn or Lincolns Inn*.

If the word *Inn* brings 'pub' to your mind you are not alone, however, large houses owned by Christian Bishops in London were often called 'Inns,' such as *Exeter Inn, Bath and Wells Inn* and *Chichester Inn* near Fleet Street. Many Inns that were a hostelry/public house continue as popular 'watering holes' in London today.

Clifford's Inn was leased in 1345 by the widow of the Sixth *Baron de Clifford* to a group of lawyers. It was an independent *Inn of Chancery* with its own constitution and was governed by a *Principal* and twelve *'Rules'*. *'The Knights Templar'* who fought in the *Crusades* also had a set of *'Rules',* but they were very different. The Inn's affairs were finally wound up in 1918, and in 1935 the old building was demolished but some of its fine carved woodwork can be seen in the *Victoria and Albert Museum*.

Offices now stand on the site but the small alleyway off *Fleet Street* with its ancient lamp and gateway bearing the name are striking reminders of a significant, historic institution with its origins in the 14th Century. (*Source: knowyourlondon.wordpress.com).

In London, the '*West End'* is an area shown on many road signs but as far as I can determine there are none for the '*East End.*' Originally the *East End* was considered to cover the area from *Spitalfields* to *Whitechapel* but industrial and commercial expansion and new 'suburbs,' the areas of *Stepney, Mile End* and *Bethnal Green* became part of the East End. These days East-enders might feel that it extends to *Manor Park* but not *Ilford*, to *Leyton* but maybe not *Leytonstone* and opinions differ on *Hackney* and *Walthamstow*. Personally, I think it extends to *Romford* in the Far East.

One of Christopher Wren's most famous London City churches is *St Mary le Bow* in *Cheapside*, which traditionally determines anyone's claim to be a true *Cockney,* however, in 1994 the definition was questioned by *Dr Malcolm Hough* from the *Meteorological Office* when he concluded that in the days before motor cars the bells would have been audible all over London. Wow!

By contrast with today's traffic levels the peal of Bow bells are hard to hear from just a few streets away. *Dr Hough* estimated that in the days of horses and carts *Dick Whittington* could have heard the bells while standing on *Highgate Hill* six miles away. Regardless of all the cockney boundary shenanigans, I will continue to proudly claim to be the son of a proper Cockney Mum who hails from Stepney.

~

Here's a graphic description of the East End in 1895 from *'Arthur Morrison:'Tales of Mean Streets'*:

"Who knows the East End? It is down through *Cornhill* and out beyond *Leadenhall Street* and *Aldgate Pump* and one will say, a shocking place where he once went with a curate; an evil plexus of slums that hide human creeping things; where filthy men and women live on penn'orths of gin, where collars and clean shirts are decencies unknown, where every citizen wears a black eye and none ever combs his hair."

There are many very vivid accounts of Stepney in the turmoil and carnage of the 2nd World War to be found in a very good, large, heavy book called *'The East-End Then And Now.'* It's edited by *Winston G. Ramsey* and contains many eye-witness accounts a few of which I have adapted for this little, light-weight book, in order to give an insight into the suffering and fighting spirit of the East-Londoners who lived and worked for a very long time in the dead centre of a key target area for the bombs, rockets, mines and other deadly munitions of the German Luftwaffe. M&D and their families were living in the little frail dwellings hunted by the bombers.

Cable Street, Eat End of London:

On Sunday October 4th 1936, *Sir Oswald Ernald Mosley, 6th Baronet,* planned to celebrate the fourth anniversary of the birth of the *British Union of Fascists.* The assembly point for an anniversary rally was to be *Royal Mint Street* at 2.30p.m. where the fascist *'Blackshirts'* would be inspected by his Lordship. They would then march through the East End.

At 1.40 p.m., around five hundred demonstrators, a significant number of whom were Jewish, surged through *Aldgate* towards the *Minnories* along with around two thousand anti-fascists shouting: *"Box up the fascists."* At 2.00 p.m. the police attempted to separate the opposing factions, however, by 2.15 p.m. there were around 15,000 in the *Aldgate* area about half of who formed a human barrier across *Commercial Road* at *Gardners Corner* making a clenched fist salute and chanting: *"They shall not pass."* Meanwhile the Blackshirts continued to form up in *Royal Mint Street;* the police reported around 1.900 fascist cadets, women, four bands and around twenty flagbearers carrying *Union Jacks* and fascist colours.

By 3.00 p.m. all surrounding roads were packed with people and all traffic stopped. *The Battle of Cable Street* was about to commence. *Mosely* turned into *Royal Mint Street* in his Bentley limo, but police informed him that he couldn't proceed through the East End but would be allowed to parade westwards with the *Chief Constable* leading the march. Was that a wise decision I ask?

The true battle of *Cable Stre*et wasn't actually fought between fascists and communists but rather between fascists and a range of individuals and factions who had anti-fascist beliefs, a number of who I suspect were anarchists. The police reported: "At 2.00 p.m. anti-fascists congregated at the junction of Cable Street and Leman Street, later joined by a column of ex-serviceman, anti-fascist slogans were shouted and upon the crowd becoming unruly police were compelled to draw batons to clear the streets. Brickbats were thrown and fireworks discharged."

Dad was in the crowds opposing *Mosely* and his Blackshirts, and my Father-in-Law to be, John, was a 7 year-old 'toe-rag' (His description not mine) who watched the battle unfold from various precarious vantage points. Dad said: "*I was a brown shirt and the Boy Scouts didn't support fascists or communists.*"

The Blitz:
Blitz is short for "Blitzkrieg" meaning "lightning war" in German. On September 4th 1940, *Adolph Hitler shouted:* "And if the British Air Force drops two, three or four thousand kilos of bombs then we will now drop one hundred and fifty thousand, one hundred and eighty thousand and two hundred and thirty thousand, three hundred or four hundred thousand kilos in one night. If they declare that they will attack our cities on a large scale, we will erase theirs." (It doesn't seem Adolph was very good at sums?)

In September 1940, Hermann Goring said: "As a result of the provocative British attacks on Berlin in recent nights the Fuhrer has ordered a mighty blow to be struck in revenge against the capital of the British Empire.

Black Saturday:

In the middle of August 1940, The Battle of Britain took on a different phase when the Luftwaffe attacked RAF fighter aerodromes in the South-East and on the outskirts of London. On September 7th the first bomb fell at 8 seconds past Midnight on 43 Southwark Park Road, *Camberwell* in South East London, a Grocer's shop whose roof was damaged; the first bomb fell on the East End at 2.49 a.m. in Prince Edward Road damaging the road and three private houses; and at 3.45 a.m. the first bomb to hit *Stepney* fell on 12 Harford Street where a three-story building was blown up.

Less than 100 incidents were reported to the *Fire Brigade* before 5 p.m. but at 5.30pm while glorious sunshine shone in a blue sky over London, 348 German bombers escorted by 617 fighter planes pounded London until 6.00pm. Using the flames as beacons to guide their flight path a second group attacked with more incendiary bombs two hours later continuing into the next day.

Winston Ramsey's book contains a witness account written by a Fire Officer, *Cyril Demarne* in 1986 of his experience on that fateful day:

'I was in the yard and heard the drone of approaching aircraft rapidly rising to a roar and suddenly squadrons of bombers appeared all over our East End sky at West Ham Fire Control in Abbey Road flying high escorted by hundreds of fighter aircraft glinting in the sunlight as they weaved and turned over the bomber formations.
Rosettes of black smoke from anti-aircraft shells spread across the sky as the menacing roar of aircraft engines combined in the devilish symphony of the bark of anti-aircraft fire, the scream of falling bombs and the earth shaking thump as they exploded.

In the clear afternoon light it was easy for Nazi airman to identify their targets and the first bombs fell on the Ford Motor Company at Dagenham closely followed by a rain of high explosive and fire bombs on Beckton gasworks which was the largest in Europe. Then came an avalanche of bombs raining on the East End from an estimated three hundred bombers. Flames erupted from the many factories and warehouses along the River Thames from Tower Bridge to Woolwich. In the Docklands streets massive warehouses and tiny dwellings crashed down under the impact of high explosives, burying under debris the residents, workers and passers- by. Much of West Ham's dock area was ablaze, six hundred fire pumps from West Ham base alone raced to fires in ships and warehouses, sugar refineries, oil depots, paintworks, chemical works and the humble homes of the local population in addition there were hundreds of other fires, any one of which would have made headline news in peacetime.

In the Surrey commercial docks two hundred acres of timber stacks blazed out of control and the Rum Quay Buildings in West India Docks gushed flaming spirit. An army of rats ran from a burning Silvertown soap works and along North Woolwich Road molten pitch flooded from a tar distillery halting all emergency vehicles.

On the riverside blazing barges threatened wharves, and they were set adrift by well intentioned people only to be swept by the tide broadside downstream to the peril of fireboats attempting to pump water ashore to feed the land pumps. It was a scene of horror and chaos as Civil Defence workers shocked and terrified by their first experience of the blitzkrieg dug into demolished buildings in search of buried casualties. Others helped dazed men, women and children rendered homeless but thankful to have escaped with their lives to rest centres in schools and church halls.

The All Clear sounded at 6 o'clock but there was no relief for fireman striving against the odds to contain the great fires that blazed all around. Street water mains were totally inadequate and further depleted when some were fractured by bombs.

At 7.30 the bombers were back, about two hundred and fifty drove home the attack and squadrons of Heinkels and Dorniers queued to deliver their cargoes of destruction on a target still blazing from the afternoon raids. The closely packed streets succumbed to even the smallest German bombs and great gaps were torn in the terraced houses leaving piles of debris. Grotesque figures sprawling in the road, splayed against walls or tossed into corners like rag dolls were camouflaged by mortar dust, bricks, tiles, roofing timbers and shattered glass littered the road together with remnants of cherished items of furniture that once made a home. Many families were buried in the rubble of their homes and had to be dug out.

Those lightly buried freed themselves and immediately began digging frantically for their nearest and dearest. Scenes of heartrending grief were witnessed as survivors uncovered the torn and mutilated bodies of loved ones. First aid and rescue parties treated the injured covering the dead with a blanket or whatever came to hand, leaving the body stretched out on the rubble to await collection by a mortuary van.

Hour after hour the bombs rained down demolishing more buildings and starting fresh fires. Great blazing embers carried aloft in the terrific heat spread fire over the heads of the people and firemen. Powerful jets of water turned to steam, the effort appeared to be in vain and the task overwhelming.

As the sun slowly dipped below the western horizon thousands living to the west observed the phenomenon of a crimson sunset in the east! Strangely as night descended over the blazing city it brought no darkness but simply changed the colour of the sky from blue to varying shades of pink and red as the glare from hundreds and hundreds of fires reflected on clouds of smoke drifting across the East End.

Still the squadrons droned overhead, and the bombs screamed down. Water mains were fractured by the pounding, telephone cables and gas mains were also destroyed. These were days before the Services had radio contact and fire officers unable to telephone situation reports or call for assistance relied on motor cycle despatch riders or the heroic teenage messenger boys with their bicycles to maintain communication.

And so it continued throughout the night. Bombers delivered high explosives for fire-bombs on the eastern suburbs on both banks of the River Thames returning to their bases in Northern France to refuel and re-bomb for return trips. Fire pumps were mobilised from as far as Yarmouth, Brighton, Rugby and Swindon bringing crews of auxiliary fireman. The first glimpse of dawn tinged the eastern sky at about 5 o'clock when the Luftwaffe called it a day. The all clear sirens announced their departure leaving fireman in action at nine conflagrations (*Large areas of fire that were spreading and not under control).

Londoners emerged from their shelters to scenes of devastation coming face to face with great fires and the dismal sight of burned out buildings with wisps of smoke and steam rising from the charred embers of their homes. The first thought of many was for a cup of tea but they were disappointed because there was no water, gas or electricity. They were faced for the first time with the problems that would confront them for another fifty-seven mornings in succession.

During the first day and night of the attacks four hundred and thirty-six men, women and children were killed and sixteen hundred severely injured. It was a night that none who lived through it will ever forget.'

~

Cyril Demarne's account is the best/worst insight into the first day and night of carnage and horror of the Blitz on London that I have read. The Luftwaffe returned day and night to repeat and extend the carnage from September 1940 to May 1941, dropping a total of 18,000 tons of explosives on London.

As a child living in *Elm Park, Hornchurch* near to one of the 'Battle of Britain' RAF Airdromes and for many years after in the *Greater London* areas, unexploded bombs would cause roads to be closed and buildings evacuated while they were disposed of. The instances have dwindled but still occur up and down the UK from time to time.

A typical newspaper report in September 1940 in the **London Press** read:
"On Saturday night for over eight hours and on Sunday night for over nine hours the raiders rained bombs on the East End. Again on Monday night for eight hours there was more haphazard bombing."

Winston Ramsey records:
'Many hundreds of those who had fled from the Silvertown and Tidal Basin areas had been assembled in Agate Street School in Canning Town, still well within the danger area. Corridors, classrooms and halls were crowded, everyone awaiting the coaches promised for 3 o'clock. That was Sunday. At night more homeless arrived, but still no coaches, which had still not appeared as darkness fell on Monday. In the early hours at 3.45 a.m. a heavy bomb scored a direct hit on the school demolishing half the building and bringing down hundreds of tons of masonry.'

Richie Calder in **'Carry On London'** wrote about this particular tragedy:
'The next morning I saw the crater, I saw the rescue men descending perilously into it with ropes around them, saw them pause every now and then in a hushed painful silence listening for sounds of the living. I saw the tomb of whole families, by then two days after the coaches had been due the survivors were boarding buses. They were speechless and numbed by the horror of it all.

This tragedy was one of the first and grimmest lessons of London. About four hundred and fifty homeless people lost their lives in that school – a figure to be dismissed lightly by those who measure casualties in terms of Passchendaele or The Somme. It was the needlessness of the tragedy which made it so terrible'. There were communication problems and human errors that lead to the problem of the failure of the coaches to arrive.'

Winston Churchill 11th September 1940:

"These cruel, wanton, indiscriminate bombings of London are of course a part of Hitler's invasion plan…. what he has done is to kindle a fire in British hearts, here and all over the world, which will glow long after all traces of the conflagrations he has caused in London have been removed. He has lighted a fire which will burn with a steady and consuming flame until the last vestiges of Nazi tyranny have been burnt out of Europe and until the Old World and the New can join hands to rebuild the temples of mans' freedom and mans' honour on foundations which will not soon or easily be overthrown.

This is the time for everyone to stand together and hold firm, as they are doing. I expressed by admiration for the exemplary manner in which the air raid precaution services in London are being discharged, especially the Fire Brigades, whose work has been so heavy and also dangerous.

All the world that is still free marvels at the composure and fortitude with which the citizens of London are facing and surmounting the great ordeal to which they are subjected, the end of which, or the severity of which, cannot yet be foreseen. It is a message of good cheer to our fighting forces, on the seas, in the air and in our waiting armies in all their posts and stations, that we send them from this capital city. They know that they have behind them a people who will not flinch or weary of the struggle, hard and protracted though it will be, but that we shall rather draw from the heart of suffering the means of inspiration and survival, and of a victory won not only for ourselves, but for all – a victory won not only for our times, but for the long and better days that are to come."

Historians can look back and analyse *Churchill's* contributions to the War for good and ill, but I know that if I had been in Mum or Dad's shoes at that time I would have been reassured by his powerful, confident words which gave the British people the motivation 'to do their bit for King and country' and their Allies.

~

Random Chats With M About 'Places'

Born in the *East End*: Here's an impressive list of real life, proper 'celebrity' *Eastenders* who will have many different memories of the *War*.
Des O' Connor, *Stepney*; Barbara Windsor, *Shoreditch*; Jack Warner, *Bow*; Terence Stamp, *Bow*; Dame Anna Neagle, *Forest Gate*; Dame Vera Lynn, *East Ham*; Bert Weedon, *East Ham*; Kenny Lynch, *Stepney*; Honor Blackman, *Plaistow*; Jack 'Tesco'
Cohen, *Whitechapel*; Arch-Bishop George Carey, *Bow*; Joe Brown, *Plaistow*; Alfred Hitchcock, *Leytonstone*; Alf Garnett, *West Ham* (Where else); Greer Garson, *Manor Park*; Angela Lansbury, *Poplar;* David Essex, *Plaistow*; and Derek Jacobi, *Leyton,* to name but a few.

Home in *Romford*: After Dad died the family were relieved that M felt secure in her bungalow in   Romford, it was her safe-haven, and she enjoyed the support of some very good neighbours. *"An Englishman's home is his castle"* was a phrase coined by the English historian *Edward Augustus Freeman* (1823-92) in *The History of the Norman Conquest of England* (*Oxford,* 1868) but is it really? M's answer would have been 'yes!'

It has been a legal precept in *Common* law in England since the 17th Century that no-one may enter a home unless by invitation. The Institutes of the Laws of England,1628 stated: *"For a man's house is his castle, et domus sua cuique est tutissimum refugium [and each man's home is his safest refuge]."*

In 1763, the British Prime Minister, *William Pitt the Elder,* said: "The poorest man may in his cottage bid defiance to all the forces of the crown. It may be frail, its roof may shake, the wind may blow through it, the storm may enter, the rain may enter, but the King of England cannot enter."

M's little bungalow was not a castle, but it was our family HQ. Her large wider family and friends often visited and always felt welcome. It was styled in M's taste, most of the furniture was longstanding, I played behind and bounced on the settee in the 1960's and after she died in 2015 watched it carried out by two men to a charity collection van.

The walls were adorned with family photos, various paintings, mostly prints and a couple of works of art by friends, some of her own framed 'decoupage' creations and a pencil portrait of eleven year-old me on holiday in Majorca (Wearing a yellow corduroy shirt with a front zip – Groovy!). The kettle was the busiest item in the house.

She had a weekly cleaning regime which was military in its precision, the curtains would be washed for Christmas and early summer and with help, she would move her living room furniture from the front room in winter to the back room for a view of the garden in the Spring.

Today at Joni's house (Where I live), we have created a minor, less important HQ of our own and we have some of M's cherished knick-knacks including a small, pink, Bakelite* salt pot that was in M&D's little end of terrace house in *Fernbank Avenue, Elm Park* where I was bought home after being born. Sadly, the pepper pot perished at the turn of the Century.

Note: Bakelite or 'polyoxybenzylmethylenglycolanhydride' was the very first form of plastic made from synthetic materials. The big, heavy telephones of yester-year were Bakelite.

M worked tirelessly in the garden of her bungalow in Romford and created a small idyll, thriving just 200 yards from Romford marketplace as the crow flies. Two crows lived in the neighbourhood and would terrorise M&D for years, flying into the closed patio door intent on attacking their own image. Occasionally, on account of their strong territorial instinct they would attack anyone in the garden, so a broom handle had to be kept in readiness for defence purposes. I have a life-long memory of Dad wielding the broom in the garden while under attack. I laughed until I had to go quickly indoors to the toilet.

That memory leads me nicely to the next subject of 'holidays' as it reminds me of a photo of Dad in a field in Devon, he asked M to take a picture of him 'near' a large bull with long horns, she told him he was being stupid but he reassured her and she took the picture at the very moment the bull spun round and charged at Dad. The picture captures Dad with his arms raised like *Spiderman* and a terrified look on his face. He escaped without injury as presumably the bull took pity on him?

~

Romford was my place of birth, where I went to school and where I lived in or near for most of my life until the age of 54. In my lifetime, Romford has slowly become subsumed into the rambling extension of East London and is a very different, more multi-cultural town today compared to the one I visited with M and brother Tom on the bus (Red double-decker number 66 I think) from *Elm Park* in the 1950's. At that time, Romford's best-known features included the (Roman) cattle market in the cobbled marketplace, *Ind Coope* brewery and *Roneo Vickers* (Office machinery manufacturers).

Many successful people were born in Romford and it has its fair share of famous ones, examples allegedly include:

-*Michelle Dockery,* actress *(Ref Lady Mary* in *Downton Abbey - "I am going upstairs now to remove my hat."* Further detail follows later)

-*Tony Adams*, footballer - Captain of England and Arsenal. A friend of mine was an Arsenal apprentice in the late '70's/early 80's and drove him to his first game for Arsenal reserves against Manchester United at Old Trafford;

-*Steve Davies*, World Champion snooker player. Dad's youngest brother, Ron, played against him regularly in the *Lucania Snooker Club* in *Romford* in the '70s when Steve was a teenager - a "nice lad";

-*Millicent Martin*, singer, actress, and comedian, resident singer on the BBC tv show *That Was the Week That Was* (1962-1963). She received Tony Award nominations for *Side by Side by Sondheim* and *King of Hearts*; tv roles include *Gertrude Moon* in the NBC sitcom *Frasier.* She lived next door to my Aunty Kit and Uncle Gordon in Emerson Park, Hornchurch (Sharing a boundary with Romford);

-*Lady Elizabeth Russell*, English noblewoman - an influential member of *Queen Elizabeth I's* Court - known for her refined poetry and musical talent;

-Pam Sawyer, lyricist and songwriter from the mid-1960s, she co-wrote hit records for *Motown* including "*Love Child,*" "*If I Were Your Woman,*" "*My Whole World Ended*" and "*Love Hangover*";

-*Edward Falaise Upwood*, novelist and short story writer - prior to his death he was the UK's oldest living author - his career exceeded eighty years;

-*Martin Woodhouse*, author and scriptwriter, including the tv series *The Avengers;*

-*Billy Ocean MBE*, R&B singer, he moved to Romford from Trinidad with the 'Windrush' generation at the age of 5; born in 1950 *Leslie, Sebastian, Charles* had many hits in the 1970s and 80s. His 1985 hit "*When the Going Gets Tough, the Tough Get Going*" reached No. 1 in the UK and No. 2 in the US, and in 1985 he won the *Grammy Award* for Best Male R&B Vocal Performance for his record "*Caribbean Queen (No More Love on the Run)*";

-*Ian Dury (No Blockheads)*, pop singer, was born at his parents' home in *Harrow Weald*, Middlesex but he pretended that he had been born in *Upminster* (Sharing a border with Romford). All but one of his obituaries in the press claimed it as a fact. Odd, but Ian was enigmatic.

~

There are many professional sports people from Romford with football the most common, including *Ray Parlour, Arsenal* and England, known as *The Romford Pele;* and *Jonjo Shelvey,* England and (Currently) *Newcastle United.* Romford's most famous footballing son is *Frank Lampard* - all-time leading goal scorer for *Chelsea,* 106 appearances and 29 goals for England and 660 appearances for *West Ham United.*

Joni lived near Frank's Mum and Dad in Ilford and her dog *Cobber* would run into their front garden and into the house if the door was open. They didn't seem to mind. In 1977, I completed three weeks teaching practice at Frank junior's Primary school in *Gidea Park* before going to Loughborough University to do a teaching qualification. I read Greek mythology stories to the children and joined in some of the P.E. lessons.

I can't claim to have directly influenced young Frank's football career in my long three-week spell at the school, in fact I only knew he was at the school because I recognised his Dad, *Frank Senior** at the school gates. However, I did tell him in P.E. not to run with his arms down by his sides and to raise his hands higher to improve his balance. I told him that he would remember to keep his hands up if he made a 'thumbs up" with both thumbs when he ran, hence, his characteristic, high-handed, thumbs-up running style through his career (There could even be a shred of truth in this claim?)

*Note: When I was a youth, I stood in the front row on the half-way line at home games at *White Hart Lane (*Home of *Tottenham Hotspur FC)* and Frank Lampard Senior played at left back, so we were very close to each other over a number of years. He had particularly muscly thighs and was a very fit, athletic player who was relatively quiet compared to many other colourfully spoken full-backs and wingers in the First Division of the Football League at the time.

So, with just this small sample of the great and the good of *Romford,* the reader will understand my pride at being a boy from *Romford.* In 1965, the town's address was officially removed from the County of Essex to the new *Greater London Borough of Havering* but we all (Or most of us) happily remain *Essex boys* and *girls* in our hearts and hardly any of us *'go upstairs to take our hats off.'*

~

In 1975, one of my summer holiday jobs was in the *Ind Coope Romford Brewery.* I worked in the section where the beer barrels were returned from the pubs and clubs etc and the remaining contents were tipped away. Some of the old beer was re-processed in a big open tank and malt extract was created (Maybe for *Marmite?*) We worked in a cellar/dungeon-like area with large cockroaches and feral cats, and the smell remains with me today and can only be described as (*Look away now if you are squeamish) a mixture of stale beer and vomit. The aroma stayed within me for 24 hours a day for three months after I had left and gone back to College, and the serious outcome of this curse was that I was unable to drink beer because the smell jumped from the glass and streamed straight up my nose and down to my stomach. I served about a four-month sentence in estrangement from beer, but no lasting damage was done.

To add salt to my queasy wound, employees had a free weekly allocation of freshly brewed bottled beer (*Light Ale* as I recall) but my condition meant it had to be drunk by my brother and Dad. They were at pains to assure me that it was very delicious and refreshing.

Holiday Venues: M&D were quite well travelled, and their holidays usually numbered around three a year, from a long weekend to two weeks depending on funds. They loved England, Ireland, Scotland and Wales but Dad was a sun lover so our young family of four, M&D and two kids were part of the early British 'package holiday' exodus to the *Costas* of Spain.

Our first trip in 1960 was in a small World War II airplane with propellers from *Southend* airport to a fly-ridden *Pension* (Think scruffy hostel) that was accessed via a plank over a ditch at *Lloret De Mar* on the *Costa Brava*. We had a great time. Uncle Harry, Dad's old army friend from the War came with us and he played the piano in the bar/canteen with gusto. He was the *Chartered Secretary* at *Newham Council* in the East End for many years, had fought in the War with Dad and was the best of friends with M&D until he died. He usually took M's side when he thought Dad was being too argumentative, which was frequent as he also loved a good argument.

During the holiday, Harry named my brother '*El Choc*' for his love of chocolate ice cream and I was '*El Cid*,' I suspect this was because he didn't know what to call me but I obviously had to be 'El' something. The following year *Charlton Heston* starred in the truly epic movie '*El Cid*,' Harry was a generous man and treated the family to tickets in *Leicester Square*. I have lost count of the number of times I have watched it since on telly.

Charlton was equally fearless in '*Ben-Hur*' another classis 'Epic' the likes of which they don't make any more - thousands of real-life extras, wooden swords and shields, papier mâché helmets, painted backdrops and the occasional drop of ketchup for blood. I don't understand why Charlton Heston wasn't awarded an *Oscar* for these performances? Perhaps it was something to do with his acting?

Note: If you are a Casting Executive or have influence over one, I will be available as a non-speaking film extra should *El Cid* be re-made, I will work for free, bring my own lunch and make my own costume and replica weapon if necessary. I don't mind which side I'm on, Spanish or Moors but I would like to be in the final battle on the beach please. Being 'killed' is fine thank you but my ultimate ambition is to carry the flag into battle alongside (the already dead) *El Cid*. I have riding experience gained on a plump pony called *Cherry* from the age of 5 to 7 years at *The Barn Stables* at *Upminster Common*.

Joni and I had a short break in Rome a few years ago, the huge number of tourists was challenging and at one point a famous watery statue (The *Trevi Fountain*) disappeared behind a shield wall formed of circular lines of tourists with raised mobile phones. We slunk away in retreat. El Cid would not have been impressed.

"When in Rome….." do as they did some of the time but obviously not when they were being debauched, engaging in Gladiatorial events or burning the City down etc. Nevertheless, Joni and I had a lovely long weekend in Rome (Before I returned for a very unpleasant operation on my nose which took 3 months to stop bleeding).

~

When I was ten years old Dad hired a *Morris Traveller* and drove M and I to Germany for a Bavarian holiday in the *Black Forest*. Dad had been to conversational German evening classes and was busy with his phrasebook chatting with whosoever could tolerate his plucky efforts to converse in German. I was certain that they would have preferred to speak to him in English. I referred earlier to a holiday when we became friends with a German family, and for a week I journeyed in the back of their large *Mercedes* playing '*Hangman*' (More appropriate than '*Battleships*' I suppose?) with their daughter who was my age.

The father had been a bomber pilot in the *Blitz* over London in the War, and I had no idea how uncomfortable M felt about the holiday until she mentioned it years later. She said it was hard to meet a bomber pilot, but she respected Dad's desire to befriend the man and his family and we enjoyed each other's company within the limitations of having no common language.

When M&D finally hung up their overseas travelling shoes on account of old age, I asked them their favourite holiday venue and they agreed it was the Greek island of *Rhodes*, the main reason being the friendly local people.

M&D and I arrived for a holiday in Athens in April 1967, it was mostly grey, cold and windy but we saw the ancient sites and spent one sunny day on the coast at *Glyfada* beach. I was a keen tourist and bought a *Fez** with a gold braded tassel (**A felt headdress shaped like a short cylindrical hat, usually red. It's named after the City from which it originated, the Moroccan city Fez*). I also purchased a long brass trumpet that I blew on the balcony 8 floors above a busy Athenian City street my instrument was carefully scrutinised at the airport when we left.

We met a young Philosophy student in a small local bar near the *Acropolis* and had a drink and a meal with him a few times. He and Dad spoke quietly together in the bar which resembled a dark cave, the student was part of a left-wing group and he claimed that there may be trouble to follow in Athens with the military *Junta**. We exchanged addresses and phone numbers with our young friend, and he promised to visit us while staying in London in the near future. When we landed at Heathrow Airport on our return the Captain told us that we were fortunate to have been the last airplane to leave Athens on account of a military Coup. We never heard again from our philosophical student friend. Perhaps the Greeks had unknowingly lost their next great Philosopher?

The 1967 Coup and the seven years of military rule that followed were the outcome of 30 years of division in Greece between the followers of the left and right-wing political parties which date back to the time of the Greek *Resistance* movement in World War II which fought against the three *Axis* nations to prevent the occupation of Greece.

*Note: *Junta* - a military or political group that rules a country after taking power by force. The *Greek Military Junta* of 1967–1974 called '*The Regime of the Colonels*' was a series of extreme Right-Wing military *Juntas** that ruled in Greece following a *coup d'état* led by a bunch (gaggle/brass?) of Colonels in April 1967.

~

Kent: I worked in Kent for ten years and so M took a close interest in this large, proud historic County. Essex is sometimes referred to as 'The Dark Side' by cheeky people in Kent but my roots are set deep in Essex and so I can never truly become a *Man of Kent* (Or is it *A Kent Man*?)

Kent is the closest English County to the rest of the world, so close in fact that some people swim across for fun. It's just 18.2 nautical miles from *Shakespeare Beach, Dover* to *Cap Gris Nez*, France. When we moved to Kent, M would come and stay and enjoy a holiday in the countryside. She was a committed tourist who enjoyed the pubs and their home-grown produce, the castles and grand old Stately Homes, the rural villages, the beaches (From the Promenade) and garden centres, particularly the one with the best fruit scones with jam and cream (Or is it cream and jam?) The only complaint I heard her make was about the potholes in the roads which are not good for old bones and joints.

We never took M to *Romney Marsh,* a relatively unknown part of Kent which you might associate with *Dungeness* power station, the wild and windy *Camber Sands* and maybe the *Romney sheep* from which around 80% of the sheep in New Zealand have their heritage.

Here are some extracts from a short speech made in 2016 by the Mayor of Romney, *Councillor Patricia Rolfe* to a group of Kentish business folk which shows the pride and passion that the people of Kent have for their County:

"Welcome to 'The Fifth Continent'. Reverend Barham, the 18th Century Vicar of Snargate wrote: "*The World, according to the best geographers is divided into Europe, Asia, Africa, America and Romney Marsh.*"

The Romney Marsh is a special and unique area – a haven for rare and endangered wildlife with a rich cultural heritage. Its proximity to Europe has ensured that it has been at the forefront of defence of this country for many Centuries.

One of the original *Cinque Ports*, Romney Marsh has a proud history, and local historians with the BBC recently found evidence that Shakespeare visited the area with The King's Players in 1609 and 1612.

Many people consider the marsh to be the finest landscape of its type in the Country, and a campaign group are now proposing that Romney Marsh should be designated England's 11th National Park.

Our region boasts an amazing array of local produce, both sea and land based. If Kent is 'The Garden of England', then I would suggest that we are all now in that special corner of the garden, that quiet place where you can relax, take a deep breath of fresh air, and truly appreciate all that is good around you. Enjoy"!

~

Roads: M and I agreed our collective shortlist of the worst roads that we have suffered on are the M25; M1; North Circular (A406); A13 (Old and new); plus the *Peripherique* in Paris. Never have I been so lost (With a car full of my rumbustious family and dogs) than on numerous occasions on either or both sides of the great River Seine. Once I inadvertently drove up the *Champs-Élysées* and thought I was in just another traffic jam in Paris until the great archway cast its shadow over a puzzled English twit (Me).

I now carry an old-fashioned compass in my car so that I will know which side of the *River Seine* I am on if I ever venture into the wacky race that is the *Peripherique* again. Be warned, no satellite navigation system can get you in, round and spit you out at the correct exit - they go blank, silent or into a frenzy of contradictory commands.

~

Wedding Day Venues: My and Joni's February Wedding Day was memorable for all the typically lovely things that spring from a family wedding, and the 'Arctic' theme chosen by Mother Nature added a unique frisson which can be clearly seen in the photo album including slate grey skies, people with purple lips and much blurring around people's mouths where their teeth were rattling around. After the ceremony, the Priest collected seven sets of false teeth (Three full and four partial sets) and most were returned to their owners within three weeks of the wedding. I don't know where the missing ones finished up, perhaps they were shared around the local flock, but the Priest remained under suspicion until the day he went to heaven (One must assume that's where he went). The wedding cake was of course iced along with the guests.

The Church was in the form of a rectangular concrete shelter on a prominent bend in a busy main road in *Barking* East London. Joni's Mum was happy to have the wedding in her local church and that was good enough for us. The wedding 'breakfast', a buffet grabbed from trestle tables, was in a Community Centre in *Collier Row*, Romford. Where it lacked glamour, it contained a floor that was perfect for the kids to run and slide on the finely dusted surface. Several grown-ups were skittled, and food and drink spilled by smaller sliding guests.

The music was presented by an organist (*A man who played music from a small music box while sitting on a chair on a small raised stage*) who was extremely popular at *Gidea Park & Romford Golf Club* where Dad was a member. The wedding celebrations were done but not dusted by 4 p.m., the organist playing a key role in the prompt finish as he was performing that evening at the golf club.

Collier Row keeps a low profile in the world but can't hide from the fact that *Suzi Quatro (Born Susan Kay Quatrocchio in 1950 in Detroit, Michigan)* the world-famous Rock star, singer-songwriter and actress married her first husband, *Len Tuckey* there. Len was the guitarist for *The Chasers, The Riot Squad* and *The Nashville Teens* and became Suzi's lead guitarist in the early 1970s. He wrote a number of Suzi's hit records but not my personal favourite *'Devil Gate Drive'* - "*Hey! Yyou all want to go down to Devil Gate Drive? Well, Come On"!!*

The highlight of our wedding day came when the formal events were over. Joni and I went back to our little upstairs flat in Hornchurch around 6 o'clock and triggered stink bombs on the stairs that were strategically placed by a family member (Belated thanks Ms X). The smell was like sulphur (Farts) and stayed in the flat for weeks, extending our memories of the happy day. We changed our clothes and put on our disco roller skates (As one did in the early 1980s). They were trending at the time and while neither of us could skate much at all, let alone swing about in a disco, I thought they would be good fun on our forthcoming Honeymoon in *Bournemouth* along the sea front etc. We practiced in the relatively quiet side- streets around our flat and enjoyed some exercise. I stopped in the road at some roadworks with temporary traffic lights, and on reflection I should have used the pedestrian pavement like Joni. A giggle in the dark revealed a bunch of teenagers sitting on a wall looking at me, so I assessed the situation and made the sound of a noisy car (Or maybe a lawn mower?) idling at the traffic lights. I achieved a rousing cheer when I eventually pulled slowly away with a wobble or three.

We hadn't eaten much at the wedding buffet so sensibly proceeded to the Chinese takeaway and crammed inside without a spare seat available in the tiny restaurant (Is it technically a 'restaurant' if all the food is taken away and eaten elsewhere?) A rugged looking fellow *(*Geezer)* looked at me and my disco skates and said: *"You're a bit old for that aren't you !?"* I was 27 years old and he had a reasonable point.

The honeymoon in *Bournemouth* was splendid, we enjoyed our disco roller skates along the Promenade where no-one batted an eyelid. Not that there were many people around on the sea front in the freezing, grey, windy February weather.

~

India: I have written a little about people from India in the Chapter on World War II and some of the words that we use every day show the influence that the Sub-Continent has had on the English language over the last several hundred years. M was astonished at some of them:

Shampoo – derived from the Hindi word *champo*, meaning to squeeze, knead or massage.
- *Thug* - from the Hindi word *thag* meaning a thief or a cheat.
- *Bangle* - from the Hindi word *bangri* meaning a glass ring or bracelet (Not a surprise).
- *Bungalow* - from the Hindi word *bangla* meaning, *'in the style of or belonging to.'* The word bungalow dates back to the 17thCentury when it referred to a type of cottage built in *Bengal* for early European settlers.
- *Yoga* - a *Sanskrit*word meaning yoking or union.
- *Cheetah* - from the Hindi word cita, meaning speckled or variegated. Not a pussy cat.
- *Juggernaut* - an unstoppable force or movement and derives from the word *Jagannath,* a form of the Hindu Deity.
- *Jungle* - from the Hindi word *jangal* meaning a forest.
- *Loot* - from the Hindi verb *lut,* meaning to plunder or steal.
- Pyjamas - from the Hindi word *payjamah* meaning leg (*pay*) and clothing (*jamah*).
- *Civil Servants* were created and named by the all-powerful *East India Company* in the 16-19th Century.
- *Chutney* - derives from the Hindi word *chatni*, which means much the same as the English word.
- *Cot* - from the Hindi word *khat*, meaning a bedstead or hammock.

~

10 Downing Street:

During the course of my career, I was invited to *Downing Street* by two *Prime Ministers* for my '*Services to Education.*' Please note that this is not self-aggrandizement (**Boasting*) but rather a pair of experiences of which M was proud and would recount constantly, mostly to friends and family who had heard the tales before (Often). I was prouder that she was proud of me than I was in receiving the two generous invitations. But I am proud of the invitations as well of course.

The first occasion saw *Tony Blair* answering the door to welcome a large, robust crowd of Head Teachers, College Principals, and a range of notary Educationalists. It was a convivial soirée upstairs and his young son peddled up and down the corridors and weaved in and out of the legs on his little tricycle.

Mr Blair stood on a low stool and addressed the room, first pointing out that the house staff were comfortable to leave the silverware on display for us, apparently something that was determined by the nature of evening guests attending? So that was good to know? Then he fixed his pale blue eyes on me as I was a tall guest in the centre toward the rear of the room thereby providing a good fixed-point for his address. I decided to take the plentiful praise he gave the guests as a personal, tailored speech for me. Just me that is. Thank you, Mr Blair, for your kind words

The second visit to *Number 10* was hosted by *Prime Minister Gordon Brown*. It was both a similar and different experience but I don't recall a stirring speech. I stood with someone I knew in an arched area providing access between two large rooms and we watched as Gordon chatted and made his way in our direction. When he reached us, he encountered two bouncing lady Head Teachers who engaged him in lively conversation (Although I didn't hear him say much?) I was well placed to listen as I was pressed up against the archway wall and Gordon's back was pressed fairly firmly up against me. I didn't recognise the PM's choice of cologne? He moved on when able to do so, hence, we didn't formally ever meet. I suppose I could boastfully say that 'I had the Prime Minister's back' (And head) for a few short minutes.

While I'm feeling boastful, have I mentioned my strong link with *Admiral Lord Nelson*?

~

PEOPLE WORTHY OF NOTE AND OTHER PEOPLE

A short account of an exceptional woman who lived in Stepney in the East End of London:

The most celebrated public figure in M and D's wide circle of friends was a woman called *Edith Ramsey MBE*. She came from a well-to-do middle-class family, arrived in the East End in the 1920's and never left. Today a care home for the elderly in Whitechapel is a legacy to Edith who was a mighty social campaigner who amongst many other things, stood up for Jewish families in Stepney against violent threats from Fascists and organised the evacuation of thousands of children of all religious denomination from the bombing raids in the War.

After the War she campaigned to take prostitutes off the streets in East London. The *1957 Sexual Offences Act* meant that women were driven off the streets, so they moved to cafes and illicit clubs in *Whitechapel* which became brothels by other names. Edith was the Head of the '*Stepney Women's Evening Institute*' and the women were encouraged to attend the Institute in *Myrdle Street* where they were taught dressmaking skills. *Lord Stoneham* described Edith Ramsey in Parliament as *"The Florence Nightingale of the Brothels."* I usually know a compliment when I see one?

Edith was the daughter of a Presbyterian church Minister and she moved to the East End where she graduated from *London University* and taught at *Old Castle Street School*. She said that she chose to live in an East End working class area to better understand the people she wanted to help. Her campaigning helped improve the lives of the poor including deprived children, the unemployed and alcoholics and she was a successful pioneer of education for working women.

In the First world war *The Times* newspaper carried the following obituary of Edith's brother Alex:

"Lt Alexander Ramsey was killed leading his men on a charge at St Julien, Ypres on 24th April 1915. He was a Classical Scholar of Gonville and Caius College, Cambridge, ex-President of the Union and later Scout Master at Hoxton and Captain of the Boys Brigade, Holloway."

Alex wrote home in 1914 that he had witnessed: "English and German soldiers leaving their trenches to fraternise, share drinks and join in the singing of Christ's birth." He lived in *Holloway* in London with three friends including *Rupert Brooke*, an English poet known for his war sonnets written during the First World War including '*The Soldier.*'

Another friend was *Hugh/Baron Dalton*, a *Labour Party* economist and politician who served as *Chancellor of the Exchequer* from 1945 to 1947. The third house member was *James Elroy Flecker*, a novelist, playwright and poet who at his death at the age of thirty was described as: "Unquestionably the greatest premature loss that English literature has suffered since the death of Keats." Pretty impressive flat mates I would say.

Edith took charge of 'non-school' evacuees on the day war was declared with Germany. She was at the assembly point at *Farrance Street School* in Stepney close to where the care home named after her now stands, and she organised buses to take evacuees to *Paddington Station* for escape to the countryside in Somerset.

Edith was in *Stepney* throughout the War and experienced the days and nights in 1940 when the Docks burned, the night in December when the City of London burned, and May 1941 when the *Luftwafe* launched an all-out attack on London (The Blitz).

At the end of the War, one of the last German V2 rockets fell on *Hughes Mansions* in Vallance Road and *Edith wrote:*
" The last bomb fell at 7.30am and it killed 131 individuals, and of the many others maimed, 40 were seriously injured. One soldier who arrived back from Burma that very day, found his wife and six children, all 'wiped out'. Statistics of raid casualties are alarming but let us never forget that behind each fatal casualty lies a poignant story of a life often prematurely ended, loved, mourned, and missed by many."

M&D lived and went to school on the *Stepney* streets that Edith worked in and a local resident at the time, *Bertha Sokoloff,* wrote:
"Stoicism and determination was the keynote of the War. You just got on with it. A combination of heroism together with 'uncomplainingness' was the way Edith put it. At *Dempsey Street Rest Centre,* where you went if your house was destroyed, Edith spoke to Mrs Baker who had lived in Latimer Street,* everything she owned was gone, all her possessions bombed into the ground, but possessions were unimportant - "There's thousands worse off than us" was her response." (* M's family lived in Latimer Street)

The much feared German *V2 rockets* fired at London killed 2,754 people and 6,523 were badly injured. *Stepney* 'copped' the first flying bomb and the last rocket. The rockets travelled fast with no sound so gave no warning. Bertha writes: "If you heard an explosion and a rumble you hadn't been hit. Not only Stepney suffered of course, in one incident 130 people were killed when the *Woolworth's* store in *New Cross* (South London) was hit."

After the War Edith was elected to *Stepney Borough Council* at the time of the 1945 'landslide' *Labour Party* victory which deposed the Prime Minister *Winston Churchill.* From 1959-62 she stood as an *Independent* candidate and then as a

Liberal in 1962-65. She was a strong local politician and the peoples' Champion.

Bertha Sokoloff wrote a book entitled '*Edith and Stepney,*' and I proudly now own a copy with an inscription to M&D from the author. Bertha asks: '*What makes Edith worth writing about?*' and her answer is:

"She stayed the course in Stepney, and the people knew it. Many of Stepney's most able sons and daughters moved on - if you got on you got out - but Edith stayed, her door open to those who needed her. She acted as village scribe when people needed letters written, she listened as a friend and adviser, and fearlessly interceded with authority when this was required.

To walk out with Edith meant stopping to talk to very different people, a Grandmother wheeling a baby in a pram, a social worker on an errand connected with a delinquent boy, the bank manager etc."

It's interesting to see that Bertha described *Stepney* as a village in those days. I don't know when the village life disappeared, but it's been a while now. Only weeks before her death at the age of 88 in 1983, Edith attended the opening of Gateway Housing's '*Edith Ramsay House.*'

M&D called Edith 'Tilly' and treated her with the respect reserved for Royalty when she visited us for tea on a Sunday. It was always a time to get washed, including behind the ears, wear my smartest clean clothes and try to behave as if I was a polite, mature boy. It was a little stressful.

The best tea service, knives and forks came out of the cupboard with the 'special occasion' tablecloth. We would have sandwiches and salad with beetroot and cakes from the '*Far Famed*' and later the '*Hale Trent*'* cake manufacturers where my Uncle Gordon was a very senior manager. Gordon would supply a large cardboard box of assorted cakes most Fridays of the year including a chocolate sandwich (Very good), big round coconut biscuits with chocolate on one side (I was only allowed two at a time), swiss rolls (Jam and cream) and '*Grannies Farmhouse*' fruit cake (The best).

*Notes **The Hale Trent Cake Group* were acquired in April 1974 by *Lyons* who bought them from *Fitch Lovell*. *Hale-Trent Cakes Ltd* Head Office and factory were in *Clevedon, Somerset* and the *Far Famed Cake Company Ltd* were based at *Poplar,* East London. The *Far Famed Cake Company* opened in 1881 and became part of *Fitch Lovell* in 1950.

I recently came upon an antique auction brochure offering: '*An early 20th century Far Famed hexagonal biscuit tin, printed with stylised leaves on sinuous stems, on a red and pale-yellow ground, 12cm high, 20cm diameter, lithographed to base, , lithographed to base, c.1912.*' The cost was prohibitively expensive otherwise I may have been tempted.

I remember Edith as a posh old lady with characteristic poise who usually wore a hat (Ref *Downton Abbey's* Lady Mary) and was genuinely interested in our little family having known M&D and their families most of their lives. Her lifetime memories were like listening to someone read an adventure book (An early *Lara Croft* maybe?).

M and I decided that if you can make a *'Citizen's Arrest'* for bad behaviour we would make a *'Citizen's Award'* to Edith and we posthumously named her *Dame Edith Ramsey of Stepney*. Our Decree was that of a *'Community Dame'* in recognition of her commitment to the Stepney community.

Readers should feel free to confer with your own people at home or work and bestow a *Citizen's Award* on a person you all believe is deserving. If your awardee is still alive, I recommend you tell them what's going on, tap them on both shoulders with a firm object approximately 12-18" long, for example, a wooden ruler or stick of celery etc. (No swords or sabres please), choose a 'Title' you like and say **"Arise Sir/Lady/Lord/Dame/Baroness"** etc. It will probably be fun, and they don't even have to get out of their chair if they find it difficult or prefer to continue watching the telly or use their smart phone. There need be no 'pomp or circumstance' (*An elaborate display of ceremonial grandeur)* and no need for kneeling or wearing a big hat and your best suit, just a moments recognition and respect for a lifetime well spent.

I came upon the obituary of an *Edith Ramsay* who died before Christmas in 2016 at the age of 92. She was from *Sunderland* and was clearly much loved and respected by a large number of family and friends across three generations.

These two Ediths both lived to old age in the 20th and 21st Centuries, shared the same name and achieved a great deal for the people they cared for, they lived very different lives almost the length of England apart. Thank you, Dames Edith and Edith.

Edith's *Wikipedia* entry serves as an appropriate obituary:

"Edith Ramsay, (1895–1983) was an educator and community activist who served on the Colonial Office Advisory Committee. Ramsay worked to improve conditions for immigrants arriving in Stepney, London in the mid-1900s and was known as "the Florence Nightingale of the Brothels "for her work in London slums. Ramsay successfully campaigned for the re-opening of the Colonial House, a recreation center that had been closed. From 1922-1925, Edith worked as the Stepney Children's Care Organizer and was responsible for distributing free meals, clothing and milk.
In 1928, she became the manager of Heckford Street Evening Institute that offered classes for mothers, workers and the unemployed. Ramsay has been featured in documentaries, and had a book written about her by a colleague, Bertha Sokoloff, titled *Edith and Stepney: 60 Years of Education, Politics and*

Social Change: The Life of Edith Ramsey. Ramsay was celebrated as a black British achiever in a workshop series that explored her writings during Black History Month. Gateway Housing Association in London contains a housing complex named after her and a tree was planted in her honour by Member of Parliament, Rushanara Ali."

~

People Who Lived Alongside Mum and Dad in Their Early Years

Following are some short extracts of profiles of people of M&D's generation who lived in and around the East End of London *Docklands* area before and during the War. Their accounts are written in a book called *'There Go the Ships. East End Lives In Words and Pictures' (By Chris Kelly).* Thanks to Chris for capturing these important, interesting, sometimes shocking historical accounts of the time and place:

Edith Hughes was born in *Canning Town* and moved to *Plaistow* as a baby. At fourteen she went to work at *Rathbone Market* on her own and was looked after by the people at the fish stall next door: "One day when the siren went I was at the stall and ran into the butchers to shelter in his fridge. We suffered almost a direct hit by a rocket. It blew the windows out of the nearby pub. Afterwards me and a friend just stood hugging each other."

Florence Waller was born in *Canning Town* in 1923 and was one of eight children. During the bombing years, the family were in the shelter every night: "We slept sitting on a plank with our arms folded, eight of us like birds on a perch. The family was bombed out three times, once when I was there. The first time was on 7th September 1940 and afterwards my uncle in Dagenham took us all in, Mum, Dad, Grandfather, five girls and a brother-in-law, my brothers had been evacuated. My uncle had a drum set and during the raids he'd say, "what's it to be: drums or guns?" and we all shouted "drums!"

Lillian Clark was born in April 1923, the second of nine children: "We lived in Plaistow until we were given a three bedroomed flat in East Ham. Dad worked in Silvertown chopping up soda. He'd come home at night and tear strips of material to put round his fingers. He used sacking to protect his legs.

He cut our hair and mended the boys' boots. He'd say "go up the road and get a sixpenny piece of leather" then he'd use a heel ball to put black wax on our boots. Most men mended their children's shoes in those days.

I left school at fourteen and worked at *RC Mills* the bakers in Plaistow for twelve shillings and sixpence per week (about 62p). Me and Lilly Middleditch would pack thirteen cakes, a baker's dozen on trays and the unsold cakes came back to the bakehouse and I would sell them at the door for a penny each. One day during an air raid I was with our neighbour and her daughter Rose and son

Bobby, we got a bus to Great Dunmow in Essex, we had no spare clothes and slept in a condemned cottage with evacuees. It was the first time I'd seen anyone wearing a dressing gown, I've got three now. If we were at home when the sirens went my brother used to sit between my sister and me in the shelter. We'd put our heads on his shoulder and he'd have an arm around each of us and a finger in our ears."

Ivy Francis was born in Blake Road, *Canning Town* in 1920: "Mum had two marriages and twelve children, eight girls and four boys. You always had a bag ready with personal things for the shelter. One night the Germans dropped landmines by parachute. I came home to see a big white sheet covering the front of the house and all my wedding presents scattered around. The back of the house was gone. We hadn't been married long. In 1944 (Husband) Joni's Mum's house in *Manor Park* was bombed by a landmine on a parachute. All the windows in the house next door were blown out, and at the time soldiers were encamped in an area of allotments at the bottom of the back garden. They were mustering for embarkation as part of the D-Day landing forces."

~

These stories were common across East London and many other places in the U.K. and are familiar to me as a next generation son. My Mum-in-law Jean and her family lived in *Manor Park* and so were the neighbours of *Ivy Francis's* husband and mother in-law.

The personal accounts that I have found from people of M&D's generation are an important part of this little book. They lived cheek by jowl with M&D and will have shared their young lives together in schools and churches, pubs, public baths, local parks, Brownies, Girl Guides, Cubs, Boy Scouts, youth clubs and on pavements and streets which at the time were for walking, talking, singing, playing, riding a horse and driving. Together these stories paint a vivid picture of East End working-class life of the generation born in the 1920's and 30's.

Here are a few more from Jewish folk living in Stepney (*Source: 'Growing up in Stepney'* - A local community publication):

Albert Glazerman – 'I lived in Stepney in Cephas Avenue, adjacent to *Charrington's* brewery from 1926 until 1942. I now live in Las Vegas. My wife and I were married in *Hendon* Synagogue in 1949 and migrated to the US in 1954. I am 86 years old.
Growing up, *Whitechapel, Mile End Road* and *Stepney* were my centres of gravity. I attended Stepney Jewish School from about 1926 to 1936. I passed the *London Jewish Hospital*, the Orthodox 'shul'* and on to school, four times a day and twice on Sundays to Hebrew classes' (*Orthodox Jews often use the Yiddish word shul to refer to their synagogue).

Miss Levine was my Standard One teacher. I remember lying on a cot after a glass of warm milk for our afternoon nap. *Hyman Lipshitz* was our leading Hebrew teacher. Although all the teachers taught Hebrew, Lipshitz was more educated in Hebraic teachings. He was the Standard Two teacher.

I so clearly remember the blacksmith near the *United* Synagogue which we attended along with *Redman Road* Synagogue and the *Majestic* cinema where we would run to get in before 3 o'clock so that it would only cost 3d 'thruppence'. After 3.00 it was 4d. There were the *Tom Mix* cowboy films and horror films with Lon Chaney (*Dad loved the *Tom Mix* cowboy films as well and the memory stayed with him for life - "*Ride em cowboy*"!).

The Troxy and the *Mile End Empire*, where I saw *Larry Adler* as well as Borah Minevitch, the harmonica player, among so many other artists of the time are vivid in my memories. There was the *Pavilion*, the *Jewish theatre* in Whitechapel by Valance and New roads. I have a very vague remembrance of seeing *The Dibuck* there at the age of four. I fainted.

And yes, I well remember October 4 1936, when *Oswald Mosley* tried to march through the East End. I was 14 and my brother 19. At Gardner's Corner, we were both in the melee. My brother was hit with a truncheon wielded by a policeman on horseback. A pleasant memory? Not really. Just a memory. But most other memories are pleasant and filled with nostalgia. Somehow, I wish I could remember with greater detail. Ah well!'

J Perkin – 'As far as getting milk was concerned, well we lived next door to *Caves the Dairy.* They had a small herd of cows at the back and we took our jugs to the front counter which opened on to the street. At Pesach time *(*Passover or Pesach is a major Jewish holiday)* they had a Rabbi at the back who supervised and we had to go to the back of the yard which was in *Charles Street* and get the milk which was kept separate from that which was sold at the front. Every now and again they took the cows for some exercise up *Jubilee Street*. They also kept chickens at the back so fresh eggs were always available. We were woken up by a combination of cock crowing, and cows mooing.'

Shayndel Epstein (Maiden name) 'I was born in Rutland Street which later became Ashfield Street. We were two houses from the corner of *Jubilee Street* and I remember it well. On the right corner there was a greengrocer's called *Isaacs.* On the opposite corner was a grocery shop called *Davis.* Next to Isaacs were, if I remember rightly a few houses and then a sweetshop *Shineholz* - Mrs Shinholz was a very good friend to my mother.

There was a shop next to this which refilled accumulators for Wireless sets. These accumulators had to be recharged or refilled, and I well remember as maybe an eight or nine year-old carrying these two acid filled accumulators home. How my parents let me carry them I will never know! Had I dropped one, I would most probably have been splashed with acid.

Next to *Davis's* was a house which had a cobbler working in the 'front' room. There may have been another few houses, but I remember *Mrs Horowitz*, another sweetshop. She used to have her hair swept up and a black velvet ribbon round her neck. I think there was a barber's shop behind the sweetshop.

Before this there was *Miller's* which was a shop selling all dairy foods. I found on the internet a picture of one of the milk carts with *Miller's Dairy* on the side and it was in a hotel in *Los Vegas* and was filled with flowers. How it had made its way there I will never know?

At the corner of *Oxford Street*, afterwards called *Stepney Way* was a baker. I used to have to collect the cholent* from there on a Saturday (*Cholent or hamin is a traditional Jewish stew). On Thursday my mother used to prepare an enormous tin of 'kichels*', biscuits or cookies depending which side of the Atlantic one lives (*Kichels are made with egg and sugar, rolled out flat and cut into bowtie shapes). These were taken to the baker to be cooked as our gas oven was too small.

Further along Jubilee Street was *Jubilee Street shul*. I remember on *Simchat Torah* parading around it with all the other children with a flag with an apple on the top and a lighted candle stuck in the apple (*Simchat Torah is a celebratory Jewish holiday that marks the completion of the annual Torah reading cycle. Simchat Torah literally means "Rejoicing in the Law" in Hebrew) The whole shul could have caught fire, but nobody even thought of these hazards then.

On the opposite side of Jubilee street was *Dempsey Street School* (I think Dad went there). It had a mixed infants department, and the senior part of the school specialised in children who had eye problems. Next door to the school was a house and in the window with his back to it sat a scribe. He had no artificial light and sat there hunched over his work every daylight hour. On the other side of the school there was a block of flats and then houses and a few shops - one of which was a shoe shop, and then came *Cave's Dairy*. My mother used to take myself and my sister there every day after school and buy us a glass of milk and a penny sponge cake.

I could write much more but think this is enough. I wonder if anyone remembers my grandparents *Kayla* and *Michael Pelovski*. He was a *Rabbi* (I believe) a *melamud** (teacher) and a herbalist (*Melamed-in Biblical times denoted a religious teacher or instructor in general). He was also an entrepeneur and apparently he had a small shul in the house in *Rutland Street*, also a *cheder** (*A traditional elementary school teaching the basics of Judaism and the Hebrew language) but for the High Holydays he used to rent the *Pavilion Theatre* and hold services there, and people bought seats.

I hope this reminiscence pleases someone and brings more memories to light.

~

Thank you Shayndel, these are important memories for the people of East London, present and future and to those with an interest in this culturally rich part of the world. I wonder if her family were related to the 'Beatles' manager Brian Epstein?

Michael Davey writes - '*Reuben Weintrob,* aka *Bud Flanagan,* was born at *12 Hanbury Street* above *Rosa's Café.* My late grandmother *Kate Musaphia* always told me she lived next door to Reuben Weintrob. Her father was a Fish & Chip shop owner. I believe the shop was called *Johnny Martin's* and was in the *Mile End Road.* Years ago I used to meet Bud Flanagan at lunchtime in *Isows Restaurant, Brewer Street,* Soho and he remembered my grandmother well from when they were kids. He told me that his parents did so many midnight flits to avoid the rent man that they could put blue plaques up at about 45 houses round the East End!

I've many stories of *Bud* and the *Crazy Gang,* but one of the best happened up North. *The Gang* were staying at a boarding house and had a bottle of sherry in the room. They suddenly noticed it was going down whilst they were out. So Bud decided to top it up with urine- each day it went down a little and each day one of the gang topped it up. They used to laugh about it until on the last day as they were leaving the Landlady said " *I hope you don't mind but I used your sherry each night to enhance your trifle"*!

~

Writer unknown?: 'At the North end of *Middlesex Street* E1 is a picturesque little quarter of cobbled streets, 18th century shop fronts and narrow alleyways with names like *Sandy's Row* (Home to the second oldest Ashkenazi synagogue in the UK, founded in 1854), *Gun Street, Artillery Lane, Brushfield Street* and *Widegate Street.*

(*The *Ashkenazi* Jewish population originated in the Middle East. Ashkenaz is a Medieval Hebrew name for Germany. European Jews were called "Ashkenaz" because the main centres of Jewish learning were located in Germany).

In Widegate Street is a curious reminder of what was once the oldest shop in London: *Levy Brothers, Matzo* Bakers* of number 31 (*Unleavened flatbread) In August 1928 *Ellis* the booksellers of *Bond Street,* established in 1728 laid claim to the title of London's oldest shop. The Jewish Chronicle disagreed because Levy Bros, Matzo Bakers on the corner of *White Rose Court* could beat this by 18 years, having been established in 1710. The article said: "*Antiquarians* *who love old pieces of architecture will find pleasure in studying the curious old carvings in the front of the quaint pointed roofs of the premises of this well known matzo baker."*

~

Brian Willey wrote: 'I write a monthly article for a nostalgia magazine about veteran songwriters of the 20s,30, 40s, and have researched a songwriter named Harry Leon. He wrote a thousand songs, but one of his most famous songs is 'Kiss Me Goodnight Sergeant Major.'

Harry was born in Spitalfields in 1901 at 139 Lolesworth Buildings, sadly none of it exists any longer so he can't have a plaque, but his real name was Aaron Sugarman, and his father, Abraham, was a cigarette maker. Like Bud Flanagan, young Aaron went to the Jew's Free School in Bell Lane. When he left he went to work at a hat factory and then joined the Merchant Navy. He began writing songs in 1930 when he left the sea and his first success was 'Sally' which Gracie Fields adopted as her signature tune. Harry became rich, spent it all, went bankrupt and died in 1968 in virtual poverty. So endeth the lesson.'

Mavis Steele: More on Harry Leon: 'Harry was living in a transport cafe in Kentish Town in 1966. I worked in the cafe and we chatted a lot and he told me his life story. He was very down and out and everyone knew him. He played piano in local pubs for drinks. He used to come down in the mornings when he heard me start work and often he would say "put my tea and toast on the book," and I often let it go. He told me lots of things. He said he had written for Gracie Fields and he said that if he had all the money that was owing to him he would be a rich man. I left the cafe when my baby was due to be born and I never heard any more of him, but I shall always remember him.'

~

Random Chats With Mum On The Subject Of 'People'

A First Daughter: Our first child was a boy and before he was born I didn't give much thought to how you bring up a baby, like everyone else, we just got on with it and when I dropped him or he rolled down the stairs we would pick him up, keep calm and carry on. He had a hard head which was obviously helpful. By contrast, when Joni was expecting our first daughter Noo, I was a bit apprehensive and asked M for some advice on how a (Rugged) man like me with no experience of little girls should adapt his behaviour, and could she give me some good tips about looking after a baby girl.

M said that 'Mother Nature would show me how' and I thought her reply could have been a bit more expansive/helpful. So once again I learned as I went along making Fatherly errors, but was surprised to find out that girls are every bit as tough as boys and sometimes more resourceful. Nature's way.

Good Friends: My brother Tom and I have old friends whose parents were the same generation as M&D and their lives were similar in many ways despite the fact that their childhoods were spent in very different parts of the world with different cultures, customs and ways of living.

Marco and I met when we were little boys at school in 1966, we were 11 years old, had passed the '11Plus' test to go to *Romford Technical County High School* (Romford Tech) and England had just won the football *World Cup*. We lived a few miles apart and travelled different ways to school, but we were in the same class and became good friends over the next 5 years at school and the nearly 50 years since.

No-one at school including me had any idea that Marco was bi-lingual in Italian/English as he rarely talked about Italy and never about his talent for languages. If Italian had been an option in school all would have been revealed! He 'came out' about it when we left school and it continues to be jolly useful to friends in restaurants and holidays in Italy.

Here is a short, potted history from Marco on some of his family:

In the 1920's his grandfather *Settimo* came to England to find work with a wife and two children and subsequently five more were born, one of who was Marco's Dad, Sergio *Vasco Palmiro Eliseo Biagioni* (Known as John or Johnny). John was born in *Cerretoli Castelnuovo di Garfagnana* (My English equivalent translation is *Newcastle*), a beautiful mountain village in the Province of *Lucca* north east of *Pisa*.

From 1920, Settimo bought, ran and sold cafes across London in *Shoreditch, Manor Park, Tooting* and *Woodford*. At the start of War in 1939 his daughters were sent back to Italy because *Settimo* thought they would be safer but this proved not to be the case as Italy changed sides in the War in October 1943, surrendering to the Allies and declaring war on Nazi Germany. Consequently, the family had serious challenges back home in coping with a powerful, aggressive, retreating German army who had support from loyal Italian Fascists who were fighting hard to halt the Allies.

*Note: The *Allied* invasion of Sicily in July 1943 led to the collapse of the Fascist Italian regime, and in July *Mussolini* was deposed and arrested by order of *King Victor Emmanuel III*. A new government signed an *Armistice* with the *Allies* in September 1943 but soon after German forces took control of northern and central Italy and *Mussolini*, who had been rescued by German paratroopers created a *'puppet state'*, the *'Italian Social Republic'* to collaborate with Germany in occupied territory causing the Italian nation to be split in two.

Settimo and his sons *Johnny, Guiseppe* and *Fausto* remained in England and Settimo and *Fausto* were interned on the *Isle of Man* as 'aliens.' *Settimo* was only held for a short period but *Fausto* remained there until Italy changed sides in the War. *Guiseppe* was called up as he was born in England but was excused service as a 'conscientious objector' due to his Italian family. Marco's Dad was in his early teens when the war began and at 14 years of age he volunteered as a *Fire Watcher* in the East End where he would find vantage points like fire escapes and roof tops.

In Italy, John's family lived in a village near *Castelnuovo,* and from 1943 the Germans were the enemy in occupation. The family lived amidst fighting between the Germans and mostly US troops, during which time John's siblings saw their first 'black man,' an American GI. (*Why do we refer to people as black or white when the majority are many shades of colour but not black or white?)

The biggest battle in the region was in December 1944 and is known as *The Battle of Garfagnana*, the Germans called it *Operation Winter Storm* and it was a successful *Axis* offensive against US forces on the western sector of the *Gothic Line* in the north *Tuscan Apennines*, near *Massa* and *Lucca*.

The German 14th Army and the *'Italian Social Republic'* forces launched an attack on the U.S. *Fifth Army* in the *Serchio* valley near *Lucca*. The allies had anticipated the attack and two brigades from the *Indian 8th Infantry* Division were moved rapidly across the *Apennines* to reinforce the *US 92nd Infantry Division* who were known as *The Buffalo soldiers*. By the time the (Asian) Indians had arrived the enemy had broken through to capture *Barga* and the US Division had been forced to retreat but 'decisive action' by the Indian Division's *Major-General Dudley Russell* stabilised the situation, the allied forces regrouped and *Barga* was recaptured one week later.

(*Note: The *Italian Social Republic (Repubblica Sociale Italiana)* was a provisional government allied with Nazi Germany. It was led by *Benito Mussolini* and his *Republican Fascist Party*. Notionally, it controlled northern Italy but, in reality the area was under German military control.)

Large numbers of Italian *Partisans* fought with the Allies during this period and Brazilian forces provided air support in *The Battle of Garfagnana*. Around 1,000 soldiers were killed or wounded on both sides in the battle. Civilian casualty statistics are not available.

During the German occupation, John's young brother *Lino* was instructed to use a donkey to carry supplies to the soldiers and to take the dead soldiers away for burial. Marco explains that the Italian people did not give up their Jewish neighbours and hid them in their homes throughout the War. The local people received little support from the Germans and consequently were hungry most of the time, the staple diet included local fruit and chestnuts. Lino was caught stealing by a German soldier who asked him why and Lino said it was because he was starving, the soldier gave him some food and moved on. The family believe that little Lino was required to carry the body of the same German soldier away for burial soon after their meeting.

Marco has a Certificate awarded to his aunt Dora from *Field Marshal Harold Rupert Leofric George Alexander, 1st Earl Alexander of Tunis, Supreme Allied Commander, Mediterranean Theatre* (He must have extra-large cheques to write that lot on or very small handwriting?) It reads:
"This Certificate is awarded to Dora Fiori as a token of gratitude for and in appreciation of the help given to the Sailors, Soldiers and Airmen of the British Commonwealth of Nations, which enabled them to escape from, or evade capture by the enemy. 1939-1945."
Well done, courageous Dora!

Allied bombers caused significant destruction in *Castelnuovo* in the War but when Joni and I visited in 2018 the town had been beautifully restored and many of the original iconic buildings remain.

~

Shortly after the War the entire family settled in England and Marco's Grandad *Settimo* opened a family ice cream business in 1947 called *Fella Brothers* in *Hornchurch* by *Emerson Park* Station. They made the ice cream, choc-ices and lollies on the premises and sold them in their shop on the main road. It was high quality Italian style and the atmosphere in the shop was typically family friendly - a veritable Mediterranean island in a busy Greater London commuter suburb. When I was a child we would go to *Fella Brothers* for a special treat and then take-home a 'brick' of ice cream in a cardboard wrapper for Sunday lunch with apple pie/crumble/strudel - Dad was an ice-cream lover and we had apple trees in our garden.

Settimo Died in 1961 and the family ran the business for another 40 years. The entire family worked in the business but *Fausto* (Fred) ran the business with his son for most of the last 20 years before it was finally sold. John met Marco's Mum *Sandrina*, on a holiday in *Castelnuovo* in the early 1950s, they were married in Italy in 1953 and returned to settle in England. My youthful memories of John are of a big, friendly, Italian Londoner and Sandra a quiet, reserved mother with a strong Italian accent who was the heart of the family.

The *Biagioni* family were in birth order: *Settimo*, born in 1894, *Fausto* (Fred) the eldest born in 1919, *Esta*, *Guiseppe* (Jim), *Sergio* (Johnny), *Palmira* (Lina), *Bruno* (Lino) and *Romano* (Lido) who was the youngest born in 1935.

~

My brother Tom has a close friend **Bill** who is from a *Sikh* family, they met at *Hornchurch College of Further Education* in 1966 when they were both 16 and they remain close friends more than 50 years later.

The *Punjab* is the historic homeland of the *Sikhs* and Bill's family are from *Bilga* a small town in the North West. When his Father died Bill had to work from the age of nine, his Father, *Jaswant Singh Gahir*, arrived in *Rainham* in Essex in 1953 and his wife and three children followed in 1957. The family house in Romford was bought by the residents of the village back home for £1,900. In the late 1950's Bill's Dad started his own building contractor's business, one of the first established by an Indian immigrant at the time, and he spent many years helping immigrants to settle and establishing Sikh temples, '*Gurdwara*', across different parts of England.

Bill was born in Delhi in 1949 and he wears a turban, his first name is *Kunwarjit* but we called him 'Bill the hat' for a number of years from the college days in the 1960s. It was obviously politically incorrect and unintentionally rude, but Bill is one of those friends who has effectively become part of our family and fortunately he is able to forgive us for our not infrequent foolish behaviour.

~

The English On Holiday:
M was unimpressed by British adult male dress-sense while on holiday e.g. replica football shirts. She would refer to the times when people wore their best clothes to go on holiday, men would wear a suit and turn up their trousers to paddle in the sea and put a handkerchief with a knot in each corner on their head as protection against the sun. It seems ridiculous looking back but the family photo album bears witness.

Ironically, I think people of my generation who were young pioneers of the foreign package holiday in the 1960's probably laid a foundation for what has developed over the years and *'Brylcreemed'* hair, turned up trousers with braces and knotted head-hankies have been replaced with shaved heads, football shirts and a fair share of big bellies - *"Ingerland, Ingerland, Ingerland"!* etc.

The French:
In travelling by road from France to Spain and back again many times, I have noticed that there is a determination not to understand each other's language across the border lines. I wrongly assumed that as they share long land borders and lived in such close proximity that their respective languages would be mutually familiar but this is not the case, for example, while the word 'tea' seems to be commonly recognised, it's easy to feel foolish when asking for a coffee in the 'wrong' language. You will not receive sympathy if you ask for a *café au lait* in Spain or a *café con leche* in France, a bière in Spain or a cerveza in France, and if you ask for a brandy in a *Cognac* region in France they will not (want to) understand what you're asking for - repeating the word Cognac slowly several times has absolutely no effect.

In my limited experience, the Spanish can sometimes try a little harder to comprehend wrong-speaking English people but the French seem comfortable to wait until you ask for coffee correctly in French, or alternatively, disappear down a hole in the ground or walk away in embarrassment.

Jewish People:
M&D lived with their parents in an East End neighbourhood where there were a lot of Jewish people many of who them had left their homes in Eastern Europe to escape the Nazis in the 1930's. The children integrated well at school and outside and M&D's families retained through their lives some of the humour they had experienced with Jewish friends and neighbours.

Some people thought Dad was Jewish because of the shape of his nose which was shaped while boxing as a youth and in the Army. He didn't mind.

The BBC: M's several radios in her bungalow gave her companionship and she enjoyed the company of BBC Radio 2 most of the time. M's favourite broadcaster was *Sir Terry Wogan, 'The Grand Togmeister'* - we were both *'Tog's* (**Terry's old gits)* as all age groups qualified to be a *'Tog'* which seemed a bit Irish to me?

M explained that the BBC are very good at pairing men and women on the radio and while the man thinks it's his show, he is in fact being expertly managed by a woman to minimise poor taste and inappropriate behaviour. We agreed that one of the best examples of expert woman/man chaperoning was in the morning on the *Ken Bruce* show on Radio 2. Ken considered it his show and he had been allowed to do so for many years, his first *Radio 2* presentation was '*Ballroom*' from Scotland in 1980 but his long-standing minder, *Lynn Bowles*, diplomatically and skilfully minimised Ken's foolishness and brought the best out of him.

Technically Lynne was a traffic reporter but for 5 days a week she was much more than that on the '*Ken Bruce (Lynne Bowles) Show*'. She was born in *Splott* near *Cardiff* and in June 2009 the *South Wales Echo* referred to Lynn with the headline: "*Talking traffic with the Totty from Splotty.*" After 18 years with the BBC everyone worried for Ken when Lynn suddenly announced she was leaving and moving to her native *BBC Radio Wales*. Ken was obviously in a state of shock for several months but he pulled through and now has a small army of travel, weather and other broadcast specialists keeping a close eye on him – they operate a complex daily schedule to ensure he is never alone on air and he remains blissfully unaware.

Broadcasters:

M and I observed that radio and tv broadcasters will often titter* amongst themselves (*To *laugh in a restrained, self-conscious, or affected way as from nervousness or in ill-suppressed amusement*) about their personal lives in the knowledge that thousands/millions of people are listening or watching. Short conversations are often about the weather, their plans for the rest of the day or evening, their gardening activities or what they are having for tea when they get home, for example, beans on toast with a couple of cups of tea etc. The obvious question is 'why?'

Favourite Sports People and Teams:

M and I made a list of our favourite sports people and teams, M didn't know much about football or sport in general, but she would support the people and teams that her sons and husband liked:

Footballer – Jimmy Greaves (Spurs and England) born February 1940, *Manor Park,* London. Jim and I both missed the *World Cup Final* in 1966. He was injured and I didn't have a ticket. When I was a boy, I thought every goal he scored was marvellous, even little tap-ins while standing on the goal line after someone else had done all the hard work.

Jimmy is the highest scorer in the history of English top-level football, between 1957 and 1972 he scored 516 goals in 357 matches, a strike rate of 0.69, which means he would score a goal on average every 62 minutes of a game. He was the highest scorer in English football in six seasons, the highest ever to date. He was not popular with goal keepers.

I met Jimmy briefly at the funeral of *Alan Sealy* in 1996. Alan scored both goals in *West Ham's* 2-0 win against *TSV 1860 Munich* in the 1965 *European Cup Winners' Cup* final at Wembley. I was lucky enough to play cricket with Alan and his son Anthony for *Rontays* cricket team. Alan's football career was virtually ended by a broken leg sustained while playing cricket when he fell over a park bench while fielding on the boundary (He wasn't playing with us at the time).

The funeral at *Manor Park Cemetery* was conducted during a heavy, grey rain storm and after the service I saw Jimmy who was sitting behind me looking for somewhere to put his hymn book, so I offered to take it for him and put it away. He gave me a nod and thanked me kindly and I felt ten feet tall. It was a nod that under very different circumstances could have scored another great goal for Spurs or England such as a deft glancing header off his ear from 2 yards out. A mutual friend said that this brief meeting with my football hero was 'Alan's gift' to me.

Footballer and Manager - Harry Redknapp. Harry is my wife's favourite football person. She tends to support whichever team Harry is managing. When he was managing *West Ham* in 1995, he was driving his black Mercedes in *Emerson Park, Hornchurch* and while in a queue of traffic he should have let me turn right at a junction, but instead he rolled forward and blocked my access. He knew what he had done and immediately put his hands up and shook his head to apologise for his discourtesy. I thought 'what a nice man' as indeed he is.

English football team - Tottenham Hotspur F.C. Dad and his younger brother Ron were season ticket holders in the East Stand behind the tv gantry for many years. I would stand in front of them below on the terraces near the half-way line with my wooden rattle through the iron railings (Rattles were banned from grounds many years ago. They would have made a dangerous weapon in the hands of a football hooligan (I was always a lover not a fighter.) M enjoyed chanting *"Come on You Spurs!"* when we watched them on the telly, and she knitted many good bobble hats and scarves for me and Tom and a grandson or five over the years.

Scottish football team - Motherwell. In October 1970 Spurs played them at home in the *'Texaco Cup,* a type of *'British Isles'* cup competition that no longer exists. A tall elderly Scotsman stood near me on the terraces and kept shouting: *"We can beat this million* pound team"!* (*Million was pronounced *'miwyon')*. He was loud and proud, and his team played very well and were unlucky to lose 3-2 in the first leg. "T*he wee Well"* won the second leg and knocked Spurs out 5-4 beating a team with international stars like Martin Peters, Martin Chivers and Alan Gilzean.

Spanish football team - Torrevieja (The Torre Army!). We have enjoyed many family holidays in this part of the *Costa Blanca* over the years.

German football team - Bochum (Currently Bundesliga Division 2). *Bochum* is an industrial town in the *Ruhr* region. When I was a spindly youth, I won an arm wrestle in a seedy bar against a local man (Youth), it was an unofficial international England v Germany match, but national honour was at stake and the pressure was on me to put up a good show. There was a lot of mutual grunting, our chairs slid around on the floor and some spittle was exchanged without intent. The winner was (Pause for effect....) me! I beat him fair and square, but he demanded a rematch and placed his elbow on a pile of beer mats because he said I had an advantage with longer arms. I beat him again and then my friend Big Al and brother Tom joined me to form a human wall like a rugby union front row to sing victorious English songs fuelled by beer. This sparked a singing competition which we lost heavily in terms of volume and tone to a large group of Germans equally fuelled by beer. If I remember correctly, it was a most enjoyable evening. *Come on you Bochum!'*

Cricket team - Essex County Cricket Club. 'Boy and man' in that order.

Athlete - Usain Bolt. M liked to do his lightning-bolt pose but I had to put a stop to it because she would groan with her bad back whenever she did it. In her later years she would do it from the relative safety of her armchair with just the arm actions - this also eventually became a painful experience.

Netball team. My two daughters Noo and Small played for *New Cambell (Dagenham)* for a number of years from little girls to grown young adults and Joni coached one of the junior teams for a while. We travelled the length of the country for netball rallies and M, who was always interested in how her three netball girls were doing made a *Citizen's Award* to *Pat Watson*, a magnificent woman, Coach and manager of almost everything associated with running *New Cambell, a large*, successful club and community for a great many years. *Arise Lady Pat!* She deserves a proper Knighthood in my view.

Swimming club - Romford Town Sports. All five of us in my little family trained and swam in galas for the club at some time. I swam twice for the *'Veterans'* and my medals (For attendance not winning) were lost in the four other much larger winner's piles in the house. We took the kids to training up to five times a week including a 5.30 a.m. wake up call, after school, and at weekends. It was hard work for all concerned and for me, a bit like banging your head on a brick wall, it was quite nice when it stopped. We have, however, enjoyed watching some of the youngsters that our kids swam against grow up to win medals in every level of competition including the Olympics.

I was known at the swimming club as *'the man with the in-tray'* as I would take my work with me in a metal desk basket to the many and various swimming pools we visited. In the good old days before smart phones, lap-tops and tablets my work correspondence was often soggy and smudged with 'roof drip' condensation.

Favourite Tennis player - Andy Murray. Is there another tennis player?

Favourite Athlete - My daughter Small went to Kingston University and played netball with the *Team GB* sprinter *Asher Philip* who is "very nice and great fun."

My second choice is the triple-jumper *Pedro Pablo Pichardo,* who is Cuban-born and has competed for Portugal since December 2017. He was the 2012 World Junior Champion and the 2013 World Championship silver medallist. Impressive indeed, but the main reason I like him is because his name in English is *Peter Paul Pilchard.*

NFL (American football)- Chicago Bears. In 1977 when I was a student I travelled across the USA on Greyhound buses with my girlfriend and felt particularly at home in Chicago? The day before we flew home from San Francisco we went to watch the *Oakland Raiders*, it was a major event and we queued without refreshment as we were down to our last few bucks. When we got to the turnstile we were just over one (Single) Dollar short on the ticket price so had to push our way out and walk back with our tails between our legs through the crowd which flooded towards us. *"Come On You Bears!"*

Fools:

M and I also invented *'The Order of The Fool' which* is another free and easy *Citizen's Award* which need not cause any offence so long as you don't tell the person concerned.

An example of a fool deserving this award is the man who a few years ago shot and killed a famous and much-loved lion for fun. Afterwards he said that if he had known it was that particular lion he would not have shot it (But presumably would have killed a different one for fun). Fools are very often good at missing the point. My advice to this fool would be 'if you want to shoot something that is alive try one of your own feet.'

Celebrities: *Note: Dictionary Definition: One who is widely known and of great popular interest. Billy Ping's Definition: See above, or alternatively, a description of someone's perceived status created by media attention, possibly for no good reason.'*
M said that true celebrities were people to be celebrated not people who celebrated themselves. It's not a favourite term of mine but M didn't particularly share my negative view of 'all things celebrity.' She couldn't see why I moaned about so many people being desperate for 'celebrity'. My view is that these days too many young folk are driven by a desire for fame and fortune at the expense of seeking a good career which provides little or no celebrity. When I was a lad, I wanted to be a bus conductor because I loved the little metal ticket machine that made a lovely clicking noise and produced a nice little ticket. Not massively ambitious I know but to my credit celebrity was not on my mind. Today, people stain their skin orange and willingly suffer cosmetic surgery to create an impression of celebrity, and *Super-Hero* costumes abound for the

under 5's? Sadly, the bus conductor and their little metal ticket machine are a wonderful thing of the past.

M was not a publicly acclaimed celebrity, she did nothing to mark her as a 'star' or a hero, she had no exceptional talents and never received a special award for her services to society, community, country, mankind or her garden, but she was one of the very many '*uncelebrated celebrities*' known only to a relatively few people. The very best type.

Women:

M and I perceived British *Dames* from Politics, Business and the Arts etc becoming a little grumpy and intimidating once they have been honoured by *Her Majesty*. I don't dare to name anyone in particular for fear of '*The Tower*' (Re *Beefeaters, Ravens and head chopping-blocks* etc). Have they really changed or is it a '*Damely*' façade? We agreed that we need more *Dames* who can show that it's ok to be relaxed, amusing and maybe a touch silly in public. Why not!? We proposed the comedian *Sarah Millican,* who would make a very good un-intimidating, jolly *Dame*. In February 2013, *Sarah Jane Millican* was listed as one of the 100 most powerful women in the UK by BBC Radio 4's *Woman's Hour*. Arise *Dame Sarah of South Shields.*

Note To Folk From Overseas On 'Dames':

In the USA, '*dame*' traditionally refers to a woman, as do *chic, broad, baby, honey- child* etc. It's advisable not to confuse the two definitions.

Since there is no female equivalent to a *Knight Bachelor*, women are appointed to 'A*n Order of Chivalry.*' The title of *Dame* is the equivalent of *Knight* and was introduced in 1917 with the introduction of the *Order of the British Empire* (OBE) and was subsequently extended to the *Royal Victorian Order* in 1936, the *Order of St Michael and St George* and the *Order of the Bath* (Not bathroom) in 1971.

Prior to this, female Knights existed for centuries in many parts of the world, like men they were identified by the flying of coloured banners and generally had their own *Coat of Arms*.

~

Miss Collard: She was my Head Teacher at *Squirrels Heath Primary School, Hornchurch* and I liked her. She was a well-spoken kindly lady with posh glasses and was very good at her job. Her hometown was *Oxford* and so I support Oxford in the annual University boat race on the River Thames.

I was four and three-quarter years old when I received my first ever official school report. My teacher *Mrs Simmons* wrote in the 'Concluding Statement': "*Billy is a good boy, and he eats his dinners."* I remain proud.

Pupils queued in the corridor for lunch which was delivered in large steaming metal containers from a *Havering Council* lorry. The two dinner ladies were *Mrs. Bacon* and *Mrs. Zip*, they called me *Billy Fury** after the pop star of the day who was a bit like a fair-haired Elvis but not quite as good.

*Note: Billy's hits included *'Halfway to Paradise'*; *'Jealousy'*; and *'It's Only Make Believe'*. He equalled *The Beatles'* pop chart record of 24 hits in the 1960s. I could have been called much worse by Mrs Bacon and Mrs Zip.

Posh* People: *(*Refers to the quality of being stylish, elegant and often upper class)*. M always said 'don't assume because someone speaks in an upper-class manner that they are superior, they are just as likely to be talking *codswallop'* (**Nonsense or rubbish*, possibly named after *Hiram Codd* who in 1875 invented a fizzy drinks bottle?)

Santa Clause: I did point out to M that technically Santa Clause could possibly be described as a '*Viking'* but she didn't want to discuss it?

Kindred Spirits*: (** A person whose interests or attitudes are similar to your own.*) M's kindred spirits included *Sir Michael Terence Wogan, KBE DLA* who was born in *Limerick* in 1938 and passed away in 2016, a year to the day after M died.

She would also have chosen *Sir William Connolly/Billy Connolly/The Big Yin,* comedian, musician, presenter, actor and artist. She spent most of the time watching him on the tv snorting with her hand over her mouth because he was so rude.

M sat next to **Brian Clough** (English International footballer and highly successful manager/coach of *Nottingham Forest* and *Derby County FC*) on a flight home from the *Canary Islands* in the 1970's. M knew nothing about him or his team but she said: *"He was a very nice, interesting man"* and she enjoyed sharing Brian's Champagne with him throughout the flight.

Film Stars: M loved films and never called them 'movies,' she would watch one or two at almost any time of the day once her daily chores were done. She preferred older films even if she'd seen them multiple times, musicals were her favourites, and she didn't like violence or horror. Black and white was fine and 'special effects' not necessary.

We both held *Meryl Streep* in high regard and agreed that the modern day actors like *Tom Cruise, Tom Hanks* and *Russell Crowe* provide enjoyable action entertainment despite criticism from film/movie critics who generally prefer complicated, miserable films that often have no ending let alone a happy one. 'They all lived happily ever after' was our ending of choice.

Another "very nice man": M attended a University Degree Ceremony at *Chelmsford Cathedral* for our son David and *Alan Titchmarsh* was presiding over affairs in his honorary role as *Patron of Writtle College* at *Essex University* (*Alan Fred Titchmarsh, MBE is a gardener, broadcaster, poet, and novelist).* We have a photo of M and Mum-in-law Jean with Alan; he was the thorn between two roses and M dubbed him with her favourite commendation: "*He was a very nice man.*"

He bounded around the Cathedral throughout the ceremony helping people find a seat and he made an entertaining speech showing a love of his vocation and genuine respect for the students who were about to set out on their professional careers.

Nice one Alan! Thank you for your hospitality and a super family photo.

Napoléon: On arriving at M's house one Saturday morning she announced that "*Napoléon Bonaparte's* family was Italian and he was made *Emperor* of the French twice"! It was duly noted.

Alastair Cook: Alastair is a cricketer for *Essex County Cricket Club* and England and M saw him on tv when he first played for England in 2006. She never took much notice of the cricket on the tv and would usually knit something while I watched. If I got excited about something in a match she would say "*That's good Bill*" and return to the knitting but she surprised when she announced that she thought Alastair Cook was "*A nice, smart young man, he's a farmer and lives with his family on the farm you know. I'm sure he'll do well.*"

In his early career he looked ok to me, a steady, slightly boring batsman and I forgot M's comments until Alastair was given a *Knighthood* in the *New Year's Honours* list in 2019. He became one of the most successful batsmen ever to play for England and is one of the highest scoring batsmen of the modern era. He is the fifth highest Test run scorer of all time, England's most-capped player and captained England in a record number of Test matches and One-Day internationals. He is the leading run-scorer in Test matches for England, he scored a record 33 Test centuries for England and is the first England player to take part in 50 Test victories. He often fielded as a catcher in the 'slips' and guess what? He took lots of catches!

M spotted his potential from the beginning and clearly had a good eye for a talented cricketer, but I suspect the fact that he was a farmer and family man had more to do with it than his cricketing potential?

Attractive People: M said that good looking people who think they are attractive can often be dull.

Politicians: The economist *John Galbraith* said: "*Politics is not the art of the possible.*"

It consists of choosing between the disastrous and the unpalatable." (*Brexit* springs to mind*)*

M wasn't particularly interested in politics or politicians and she said that because a lot of politicians have never done much else other than be a politician, they know a little bit about a lot of things so can only really operate at 'beginners' level. *Ed Milliband*, Leader of the *Labour Party* and the Opposition between 2010 and 2015 seems a decent chap but he allegedly had some trouble a while back eating a bacon roll?

Sebastian Newbold Coe, Baron Coe, CH KBE, often called Seb, was elected as the Conservative Party MP for *Falmouth and Camborne* in 1992 and lost his seat in the 1997 General Election. He became *Leader of the Opposition* and *William Hague's Chief of Staff* having been made a Life Peer in 2000. He was a middle-distance runner who won four Olympic medals including the 1500 metres Gold medals at the Olympic Games in 1980 and 1984. He set three indoor and eight outdoor world records and he was at University in Loughborough at the same time as me in 1977- 78 (Or rather I was there at the same time as him) and he was still there when I returned in the early 80's to complete a part-time Master's Degree. Come to think of it, he was there a long time?

We never met but he was successful enough at his young age to be easily recognised and I often saw him training and competing on the University's athletics track. I was required to make a presentation to a group of students and staff as part of my final Degree assessment and was chuffed when my tutor told me that Seb Coe was interested in my research topic and that he would be coming to the presentation. As I was driving into the Uni for my presentation, he ran past me in the other direction and so was a 'no show.' He decided that a training jog was more important than my presentation that I had toiled long and hard to create, however, I'm forced to admit that missing it doesn't seem to have held *Lord Coe* back in his athletics, political or sports diplomat/administrator careers.

Sir Patrick Barnabas Burke Mayhew, The Lord Mayhew of Twysden served as an officer in the *Royal Dragoon Guards*, studied law at *Balliol College, Oxford*, and was president of *the Oxford University Conservative Association* and of *The Oxford Union*. He was called to *The Bar* (Legal not pub) in 1955 and held a number of senior positions in his career including *Attorney General* of England, Wales and Ireland and was *Secretary of State for Northern Ireland* from 1992 to 1997, the longest anyone has served in this office.

Sir Patrick was a Patron and supporter of a college where I worked, and he regularly attended the annual awards ceremony for students receiving higher education qualifications. It was a grand affair in the local ancient *Saxon* Parish church. On one occasion he took his usual seat with the VIPs on a raised platform by the pulpit, he was seated at the end of a semi-circle near the audience and he adjusted his chair to make way for a passing guest and fell off the platform in his chair. It seemed to happen in slow motion, but he broke his fall expertly with an outstretched arm like a black belt Judo player. Hundreds of people gasped and held their breath and I reached for my phone to dial 999 for an ambulance. *Sir Patrick*, who was approaching 80 years of age lay still briefly then sat up and then miraculously slowly stood and made his way back up on the platform, apparently none the worse for his dramatic fall.

I asked him after the ceremony if he was ok and told him how impressive his cat-like escape had been, he laughed and said in his characteristic English Gentleman's accent: "*I am fine thank you, my jungle training from the Army enabled me to break my fall.*"

~

Dad was a moderate socialist who voted *Labour* and occasionally for the *Liberal party* and he was more interested in politics and politicians than M. When I was a teenager, we lived next door to the Mayor of Havering who used the front of his house and lawn that faced a busy main road to display a striking number of blue 'Vote Conservative' posters at election times. My bedroom had the only upstairs window that could be seen from the road so with Dad's encouragement it was used to display a red (and yellow) 'Go Labour' poster to keep the red flag flying in a Tory stronghold in *Gidea Park*, Romford. The Mayor, whose name was Bill (Often the sign of a good man) was a nice, retired gentleman with a good sense of humour and I am sure he saw the funny side of our cheeky poster.

One evening in the 1970's a man canvassing for the right-wing *National Front* was unfortunate enough to choose our front door to knock on while seeking votes. He had begun his introductory sentence when Dad snorted: "*In two minutes I will be disinfecting this doorstep and if you are still on it you will be washed clean away.*" And then he abruptly shut the door.

Note For Folk From Overseas On 'Politics':
If you encounter the expression '*floating voter*' it refers to a person who has no allegiance to one specific party and may change their voting preference at elections. They will never float while in the act of voting unless swept away by a freak torrent of water. 'Political party' refers to an organized group of people who share the same political ideology, they may also organise parties to have fun or to celebrate a special event but this is a different meaning of the word 'party'.

~

The Royal Family: Having boasted briefly about my Prime Ministerial experiences at *Downing Street* I feel the need to continue with the theme. M and I were proud of me in receiving an invitation to join the Royal Family for a tea party on the lawn at *Buckingham Palace* with Joni. It was a very hot July summer's day in 2006, and there were hundreds of people from all over the world in attendance.

The buffet tea was every bit as grand and delicious as you could imagine and while the plates were clearly appropriate for '*Ladies in Waiting,*' they were a little petite for a boy who had pushed a barrow through *Romford Market*. Fortunately, it was permissible to return for as much food as you could unreasonably eat and because I was on my best behaviour, I made less than circa 12 return trips to the refreshment marquee. My favourite single item was a small, round, multi-layered chocolate *petit four** which had an edible Royal Crest affixed to a chocolate button on the top. If you are keen to know how many I consumed, unfortunately it's impolite to ask.

*Note: *Petit Four - A small bite-sized confectionery or savoury appetizer* also known as '*mignardises.*' *In 18th and 19th century France, large brick ovens took a long time to cool down and bakers used the ovens during the cooling periods for baking pastry-this was referred to as baking 'à petit four' ie. "at small oven."*

Joni and I were among the early arrivals at the Palace and I had to curb a strong instinct to run about on the magnificent lawn doing cartwheels and head-over-heels in childish, joyous excitement. We were both in our Sunday best clothes and on our best behaviour which was a terrible strain on the marriage. We had a wonderful afternoon and were mightily impressed by the friendly engagement and substantial stamina of all members of the large Royal Family group who spent over two hours meeting and chatting with guests in the hot sun.

Spike Milligan: Our family often laugh at Spike's humour and one of brother Tom's favourite comments is on his gravestone: *"I told you I was ill."*

My Geography Teacher: *Jim Palmer* taught Geography to me and many other itchy youths at Romford Tech. It was much tougher for him than me. I passed the A level in the 6th form and have retained an interest in parts of the subject ever since, cloud formations are a favourite but my 'boat has never been floated' by Capital Cities, the main manufacturing activities of countries or rock formations.

Question: Which European country boasts rich deposits of iron ore, abundant waterpower resources, extensive forest reserves, paper and pulp and steel manufacturing? My schoolboy memories are dated from the 1970's but some things you don't forget. The clue is, 'this country's brand of car starts with a 'V' and ends in 'O'? It's still pretty boring Geography knowledge 50 years later.

Jim Palmer was simply a very nice man, so nice in fact that he earned respect from all the testosterone-rattling, fidgeting, sleeping teenagers in his daily care. His classes were often moderately raucous, but he usually managed to deliver his key learning objectives and maintain sufficient interest from a small critical mass of pupils in his classes.

One of my classmates was a very large, sexually advanced girl who once shut me and her in the book cupboard at the back of the class and advanced upon me with evil intent. I was able to jump out of the window as we were on the ground floor. We remained just good friends.

Another geographical incident involving this particular-classmate was when she sat at the back of the class, un-buttoned her blouse and rested her large bosoms on the desk, hidden by a large blue school atlas of the World (Including the old British Commonwealth marked in pink). While chatting with a friend she failed to hear Jim asking her to be quiet and pay attention so he walked with intent down the aisle of desks from the blackboard at the front of the classroom and slapped the atlas down on the desk saying: "*Please will you get on with your work*"! and on noticing her bare bosoms, without pause said: "*Yes and put those away*"!

Never have I laughed in such extended pain again in my life. Thank you, Jim Palmer.

Neighbours: I have always been lucky with my next-door neighbours who have proved to be good folk and often our friends. With one exception. When we lived in a semi-detached house in Cranham with three small children and a dog we shared a driveway with elderly neighbours. They didn't have a garage because they didn't have a car and we replaced our old garage with a shiny new one and the people next door (Mostly him) suddenly became very grumpy. He said we were criminals because we had stolen his land and put the new garage base over the boundary line. It was professionally constructed comfortably inside the boundary line and fence so there was no truth or logic in his accusation.

We also shared a sewer drain which periodically would smell and signal that it was blocked, so I would lift the rusty old drain cover and shove in my expensively purchased drain rods (They are a marvellous thing, do an essential 'job' and make an excellent Birthday gift for your handyman/woman).

One day while rodding the drain (Like 'medalling' in the Olympic Games but different) I was removing a wayward sticky problem with a trowel and rubber gloves when the lady of the house next door appeared and cast a shadow over me that she had borrowed from *The Grim Reaper* and demanded to know what I was doing with the drain and to stop interfering with it.

My initial reaction was to grab her and throw her into the drain, but the feeling passed quickly, and I pointed with my rubber-gloved hand to a smelly miniature pyramid of turds while others bobbed along accompanied by other toiletry accessories. I said: *"You may recognise some of these turds as your own or your husbands but out of the goodness of my heart I am removing the blockage and the stink for our mutual benefit."* She immediately became the first person I had ever witnessed who was not an actor in a *'Carry On (Rodding)'* film to suffer a jaw drop and loss of the ability to speak. After what seemed like the time it takes for a long toilet flush she shuffled off in the direction of her front door.

Her husband clearly plotted revenge which emerged on a sunny day soon after the drain incident while I was painting the kitchen window frames in the driveway. I was listening to cricket commentary on *'BBC Test Match Special'* on the radio and the commentator *Jonathan Agnew (Aggers)* was describing how the famous English cricketer *Ian Botham,* while batting had been dismissed by hitting his own wicket (By mistake). As Botham spun round to hit the ball *Aggers* famously said: *"Botham wasn't able to get his leg over and has struck his own wicket."* Millions of radio listeners including me laughed along with and at the commentators who weren't able to speak in their state of mirth and at that very moment Mr Misery from next door came through his garden gate and shouted at me: *"Turn that bloody noise off or I'll throw a bucket of soapy water over you and your radio."*

Turning the radio off while listening to *Test Match Special* in my world requires an 'act of a god' and otherwise is not an option I would ever consider and so shortly after a bucket of soapy water was sloshed under the old git's gate and although it was a spirited effort the flow stopped inches short of my favourite *Roberts* radio.

'All's well that ends well' (Apart from Ian Botham losing his wicket and not getting his leg over), the radio stayed on, the window frames were painted, England amassed a decent score, and a small area of the shared driveway had a little wash.

In truth, surely there can be no winner in a poor, bickering relationship between neighbours.

~

Notes For Folk From Overseas On 'People':

'The Man On The Clapham Omnibus': This is not a reference to a real person, it means: *'An ordinary, reasonable man going peacefully about his business, not necessarily on the Clapham or any other omnibus or other form of transport.'*

The route of the original Clapham Omnibus is not known but *'London Buses, Route 88'* was briefly branded *"The Clapham Omnibus"* in the 1990s. Please don't wait for an omnibus in Clapham.

Aussies:

Australian people would generally not like to admit it but they are like the British *'Pommie'* in many respects. 'Pom' is a shortened version of 'pomegranate' which became a slang name for British immigrants to Australia. Around 1850, British settlers were referred to as *'Jimmy Grants'* a name that rhymed with *immigrant'*. In 1912 'Jimmy Grant' changed to 'Pommy Grant' then to *pomegranate.*

It is never easy or comfortable to compete in sport against an Aussie, for example, if you are playing against one in a game of tiddly winks never look away or turn your back as they are likely to wink your tiddle (Or is it the other way round?) quicker than you can say *"Jack Robinson. (*Between 1660 and 1679 the officer commanding the Tower of London was Sir John Robinson. Jack is a diminutive form of John and it is thought to refer to the speed at which he beheaded people with an axe).*

Like the Brits/Poms, the Aussies love sport and most of all they love beating the *Poms** and we love beating them of course. If you should go to a sporting event involving *Poms v Aussies* expect noise, beer, passion and colourful language.

~

LANGUAGE

In the *Preface* I mentioned the *East End* language which was central to the culture of the people who lived and worked there and while it remains in the multi-cultural *East End* to this day it has found its way out around the UK in a form that has evolved into a more general 'Lundun' way of speaking which is sometimes loosely described as an '*Estuary*' accent. The Thames I presume.

The spread and dilution of the East End language came about partly through the substantial migration of M's East End generation after the War often to housing in the *Greater London* areas and beyond such as the North Kent coast. Also, the London 'accent' has spread (A trickle not a torrent -maybe a dribble?) way beyond London through the popularity of its indigenous musicians, actors and media celebrities. The '*East Enders*' tv series has surely made a mark of sorts on the spoken word since 1985 e.g.*"Get owt of my pub"!!* The portrayal of '*Henry VIII*' with an *East End* accent by actor *Ray Winston* seemed very odd to me, it just sounded wrong? The tv series won an *International Emmy Award* for *TV Movie/Mini-Series in 2004,* so obviously I have not missed the chance of a successful career as a tv critique.

The Indigenous 'Cockney':
A proper '*Cockney*' is someone born within the sound of *Bow Bells (St Mary-le-Bow Church* in *Cheapside*, London). M was born in the *London Hospital* in the *Mile End Road* and was, therefore, an official *Cockney*, but Dad was born a way up the road in *Walthamstow* Hospital and I can't imagine the *Bow Bells* were audible from there even on a quiet day in 1922 with the wind blowing in the right direction (More thoughts on this to follow).

'*Cockney rhyming-slang*' was a part of the working man's language when M&D were children when people lived and worked together in close proximity in the small *Stepney* 'village' community, with *Docklands* at the centre of much of local employment and culture. Cockney rhyming-slang has become a thing of international interest - ref *Dick Van Dyke* as the Chimney sweep in '*Mary Poppins*' or '*Merry Porpins*' as Dick says in his very own American-Cockney *('Americock'?)* accent. We forgive you Dick.

The East End verbal dictionary of rhyming slang gives it large with popular favourites like '*mince pies*' *(E*yes); '*plates of meat*' (Feet); '*apples and pears*' (Stairs); '*dog and bone*' (Phone); and '*bottle-and-glass*' (Ar-e).

M&D didn't routinely speak rhyming slang but there were a bunch of expressions that we used at home particularly while Dad was alive like '*Joanna*'-piano/pianna; '*ackers*'- money/loose change; '*rosy lee*'- tea; '*me old china*' *(plate)* - mate; '*tea leaf*'- thief; '*currant bun*'- sun; '*daisy roots*'- boots; '*whistle and flute*'- suit; and '*jam jar*'- car. To name but a few.

M said that when she was young, she was a *Cockney sparra* (Sparrow), small and skinny, but her Mum wouldn't let her own kids talk like that because it was: "*Only for common people.*" At times, my Nan was a working-class snob, but she wasn't alone amongst the proud, aspiring Mums of East London.

Author *Paul Baker*, a Professor of English who uses expressions like '*performativitytheory*' and '*sociolinguistic coding orientation*' (Academic slang) has identified 18th Century criminals (*Vagabonds*) as the source of some of the slang we recognise today, such as '*cove*' and '*cull*' which is to do with picking locks and evading magistrates; '*Bevy*' was a drink; '*kip*' was lodgings where they slept; and '*the Smoke*' was London. He identifies Fairground words such as '*scarper*', to run, and notes the influence of the *Romany* language used by the gypsies from Eastern Europe, for example, '*cushty*' (Ref '*Del Boy*') from *kushtipen and* '*chavi*' means girl.

American GIs/servicemen introduced their own language into the UK during the War including '*butch, fruit* and *naff*' amongst many other expressions. GI stands for *Government Issue, General Issue* or *Ground Infantry* but it originally referred to 'galvanized iron' which was used by the Logistics services of the US Armed Forces.

M&D's Jewish immigrant neighbours in *Stepney* had an influence on local language, one of the most enduring expressions is '*Mazel Tof,*' a term for 'congratulations or good luck' which for many years was used in our family when a glass was raised in the pub, club or at home. A drink at home was often referred to as a "*noggin*" which is a small drinking vessel or measure of alcohol, *origin unknown.*

M rarely swore and if she did, they were the less offensive words like *bloody, sod, cow and bitch,* and I think *bugger* was maybe her strongest curse. Dad was similarly mild in his vernacular, but strangely his instinctive 'go-to' curse was '*git*' (More detail to follow).

M's generation unknowingly built the initial foundations for what has become the infamous '*Essix*' culture which is typified in the tv show *Towie* (*The only way is Essex*). While Essex born and bred in the *Far East End (Romford)* I remain un-converted by the *Towie* movement, preferring to strike a pose in my beloved *Crocs* (With and without socks), vest (For undergarment warmth or gardening in hot weather - muscle flexing is no longer possible for me) and all manner of spirited headgear such as the common *Beanie*, no chin strap, which remains a firm favourite.

To some extent our children were of the early "*Essix*" fraternity. *Overseas folk* should please soften the letter 'e' and accentuate the letter 'i' when speaking in the Essix dialect, for example, '*engine*' becomes '*injin*'; '*Colchester*' (*The Roman Capital City of England*) becomes '*Colchista*'; and '*isn't it*' becomes '*init*'. In her early teenage years our middle child *Noo* was in the pre-*Towie* genre, she intermittently became orange in colour through a combination of sun beds, fake tanning cream and '*Wotsit*' cheesy puffs. She soon became a fine young woman regardless.

Dad had died before this generation of orange-tinted party-pros (*Professionals*) became a fact of life but he would not have approved of the *Towie* style of life. I am confident of this because of his view of *Top of the Pops* on the BBC for most of the years I lived at home. He would never miss it on a Thursday night from his armchair, although he often disappeared behind a large newspaper. He would mutter the same thing every week regardless of who was performing: "*This isn't proper music*" - Why not Dad? - "*I can't stand the boomp, boomp, boomp*"! Shortly before I left home in 1981, we had our last ever *TotP* '*Groundhog Day*' experience: "*This isn't proper music*" - Why not Dad, is it the boomp, boomp, boomp? - "*No it's the bang, bang, bang I can't stand.*"

M wasn't impressed by the way the young *Essix* generation spoke, but she was rarely critical, she didn't like the short skirt and high heel dress code worn by our two daughters in their early teenage years and would say: "*They look like prostitutes.*" I agreed with her but as their Dad my view was of little consequence.

~

M often recalled her own Mother Ada's expressions which included:
"*Here she comes, the bum's to follow.*"
"*Here's your hat what's your hurry*"?
"*It's all bloody bunkem*"! "*It's grown like Topsy.*"
"*That's a bugger's muddle.*"
"*That woman's got a bread and dripping voice.*"
"*She's another Totty Fay.*"*

My other Nan shared some of these expressions and had one of her very own:
"*Look at him, Von Auptmann Bonce.*"**

Notes: *Totty Fay: Ref: 'A London Police Magistrate' The North American Review, March 1897: "Another notorious woman, whose name is scarcely less known than Jane Cakebread's, generally chose to call herself Totty Fay, though she had a number of more high-sounding aliases. My first acquaintance with her arose out of a most scandalous escapade, which was succeeded by others more or less serious, all having their origin in drink. She became a confirmed drunkard and lost any good looks she ever possessed, and when last I saw her in court had a dirty, bedraggled look, her feathers and other finery being in a woeful condition."

**Von Auptmann* Bonce: *Gerhart Johann Robert Hauptmann* (1862-1946) was a German dramatist and novelist, he is considered one of the most important promoters of '*literary naturalism*' (Sounds boring?) and received the *Nobel Prize in Literature* in 1912. He was no fool.

My Nan's only real interest in him was that he had a large, dome-like head, she used his name rather unkindly if commenting on someone who she considered had a large head, physically or in relation to their behaviour. She pronounced his name in a derisory tone with a silent 'H' and *'Bonce'* referred to his head.

~

Random Chats With Mum About 'Language'

Like so many people when they are older and live alone, the 'telly' was a household companion for M and she liked all manner of programmes, not least those that made her laugh. She would be embarrassed and hide her face when she was caught laughing at *'Catherine Tait's 'Nan'* who was: "Very vulgar and rude". It was more acceptable to laugh at *Hyacinth Bouquet/Bucket* in *'Keeping Up Appearances"* than at *Nan* from South London, but in truth M had a poorly hidden soft spot for *Nan*. You can take the girl out of Stepney, but you can't take Stepney out of the girl.

When our three children were first learning to speak, they would un-knowingly mimic Joni's (South) *Ilford* East London accent which is akin to the *Essix gel* brogue, for example, we all continue to enjoy the Joni word *'sallniceinit'* (*It's all nice isn't it). M's accent was more neutral (Suburban?) so brother Tom and I didn't have such a colourful accent to 'parrot' in the same way when we were small.

We would sit our son *David* on the floor in front of the telly before he could crawl as it kept him quiet for short periods (Technically poor parenting). He never did crawl which was a worry until at 8 months old he got up off the floor and ran everywhere, a bit like *Forest Gump,* until he had the strength and balance to control his body and walk. He enjoyed shouting: *"Barrr Funkhouse"* (Bob Monkhouse) at the beginning of the entertainer's shows, and his two favourite presenters who are still going strong 30 years later were *'Fip Skofield'* (Philip Schofield) and *"More Moira"!* (Moira Stewart). He was always interested in people with brown skin and wanted to marry Moira at the age of 3, he also told anyone who knocked on the front door to: *"Come in man/lady, shoes off, coat off, would you like a nice cup of tea."* It was a mystery to us where he had got such good manners from?

Words that M and I agreed we liked included:
'Soporific' - a word that can give the illusion that you are intelligent by virtue of using it. It means *'tending to induce sleep or drowsiness'.*

M liked *'commonorgarden'* - *bog standard, ordinary.*

'Sanctimonious.' Making a show of being morally superior to other people.

'Gruntled.' Pleased, satisfied or contented. Its more commonly used cousin is

the word *disgruntled - angry or dissatisfied.* I don't know why it's more popular, let's all try to be more gruntled.

'Discombobulated'. A favourite word of my brother Tom, it means *'disconcerted and confused'* and he applies it when people in his company are over-refreshed on alcoholic drinks.

As a child I thought the best long word was *'Antidisestablishmentarianism'* - *Opposition to the disestablishment of the Church of England.* I had no idea what the word meant but I wrote it on the back cover of my school notebook. Our teachers didn't mark your notebook, but it had to be covered and brown paper was a common choice. Some pupils called *'Boffins'* - *studious pupils who want to impress teachers* - would cover them in wallpaper which gave me my first glimpse of people seeking higher status in life as some of the wallpaper was indeed very grand.

The longest word in Britain is the Welsh place name: 'Llanfairpwllgwyngyllgogerychwyrndrobwllllantysiliogogogoch.' M and I felt this name was a little indulgent, and agreed that the first eight and last eight letters joined together would have been more than sufficient.

For information, other long words include 'Floccinaucinihilipilification' and 'Pneumonoultramicroscopicsilicovolcanoconiosis,' I don't know what either of them mean and I don't really care.

Question: What phobia is *'Hippopotomonstrosesquipedallophobia'*?

Answer: The fear of Hippos? No, a fear of long words (Someone's *avinalarf!*)

~

M had her own spoken 'affectation' (*Quirky thing) where she would add: "As I call it" to something she was saying e.g. "A deck- chair, as I call it"; "a bunch of bananas, as I call them"; "Sir Terry Wogan, as I call him" etc. It was strange because usually there wasn't another obvious way of describing what she was referring to?

M liked people who spoke well ie. posh. We agreed that the broadcaster Anika Rice has a very pleasant speaking voice (*Note - Folk from overseas may wish to impersonate Anika if they wish to speak English well). We both enjoyed Downton Abbey on the telly and liked the speaking voice of Lady Edith (Laura Carmichael) but we felt that Lady Mary was too posh which is an irony because the actress Michelle Dockery who plays the role went to school in Romford which is not known for people wot talk posh.

In one episode of Downton Abbey Lady Mary says: "I am going upstairs to take off my hat." People in Romford generally don't do that, most hats will go in a coat pocket, on a hook or nail, on the bannisters or maybe wherever they land when they have come through the front door.

American Actors: When we watched telly together M and I would often struggle to hear what American actors were saying, M said they spoke too quickly and didn't open their mouths enough i.e. they mumble quickly. She said it was ridiculous *'to spend all that money on a film but not bother to make sure that people can hear what's being said.'* We also preferred *Gwyneth Paltrow's* English accent to her real (Native) American one.

Lazy Phrases: Dennis Potter said: *"The trouble with words is you don't know whose mouth they've been in."*

The English language evolves, and trendy phrases and vocal mannerisms emerge and die off again constantly. Talking quickly in short bursts without opening your mouth beyond the size of a small frozen pea is presently popular with younger people (Under 57 years of age). An American influence maybe?

M and I discussed this and hoped it would become unfashionable but recognised it was probably our advancing ages causing us to be left behind in the development of our native tongue. We also noted that *The Queen* doesn't speak nearly as posh now as she did when she was a younger woman and agreed that if she has moved with the times then we should also make the effort. Init.

The phrase *'can I get'* spoken in a shop or pub etc is a modern term that means *'please can I have'* e.g. *Can I get a pint of beer; can I get a regular latte with skinny milk, maple syrup and marshmallows to take away please.* M and I felt that the salesperson in a shop or pub should always reply: *"No you can't, I will get it and you can pay for it."* That said, there may be a business opportunity for an experience where people clamber over the bar in the pub or a counter in a shop and serve themselves and then pay the money into the till or hand it to an employee? Further work is required on this seed of an idea before it can progress to *Dragon's Den.*

Here is a *dog's breakfast* (Messy mixture) of some other expressions that M and I would like to see banished:

At the end of the day; it's not over 'til the fat lady sings (How rude); to be honest (Why wouldn't you be?); apropos of nothing (What?); you're not wrong (i.e. You're right!); I'm reverting back (Can you revert forward?); at the end of the day (Bla, bla, bla); when all is said and done (Well stop talking then!); no news is good news (Rot!); I'm gutted! (I can see that you are not?); OMG!' (Wannabe celebrity talk); "an Englishman's home is his castle" (Define castle?); LOL (Unsettling to people called Lol); 'x' (Can mean 'kiss' or 'multiplication'- one may of course lead to the other); he is hard hearted (He would be dead if he was?); go the extra mile (What's that in kilometres?); etcetera, etcetera, etcetera (One is sufficient, three is verbal posturing); wake up and smell the coffee (We preferred tea first thing).

M never experienced *Brexit* but I am certain she would have shared my dislike of the boringly over-used expression *"Kick the can down the road"* (Why? Is it empty? If not what's in it - dynamite?) I can also surmise that she would have objected to the ex-Prime Minister *Theresa May's* expression: *"Brexit means Brexit"* which she would have dismissed as *'meaningless tosh'*!

M and I recoiled from the expression: "I was like...": *I was like yeh!; I was like wot? I was like uh!* and we preferred the alternative "I said..."

Showing-off Words: M and I agreed on some commonly used words that can be classified as *'show off'* words or phrases, one such phrase is *'apropos of nothing'* (*With reference to nothing*). People who use this expression may like listening to themselves speak which for folk from overseas is called *'liking the sound of your own voice.'* If you feel the need to declare: *'With reference to nothing'* I advise you say nothing at all.

'Ipso facto'- *'By that very fact'*. I recommend not using this posturing word either.

Note: 'Ipso Facto' were also an English, *"melodramatic, gothic, psychedelic"* Rock band founded in 2007. An appropriate name, I think.

'Show-off' words and phrases include those that can be categorised as unnecessarily 'posh.' M particularly disliked the pronunciation of the word 'anything' as *"unything,"* she said it was a showing-off word used by people who wished to sound posh but were in fact *"A little up themselves"* (Having a big ego -nothing physical). That's as rude as M ever got.

One of my choices of a show-off word was *'buk'* when used to mean *'book.'* You can ride a buck horse (To *Banbury Cross* if you like) or spend a buck (*Money in the USA*) but you can't read or write one. In fact, *'Buk'* is Polish for *'King or a person of great power'* and *Buk-buk* means *'A type of Filipino person who accentuates an embarrassing level of Filipino pride'"*?

Some people clearly like to use certain words that they believe are impressive to enhance their image and one such word is *'existential.'* A popular dictionary defines it as: *'Of or relating to existence, especially human existence.'* M and I didn't find that a helpful definition as you would not expect a definition of *'custard'* to read: *'Of or relating to custard'* because custard is a real and useful substance and so can be described in a clear and helpful way. The same dictionary defines custard as: *'A dessert or sweet sauce made with milk and eggs.'* Existentially, I think it's best served hot and thick, apropos of banana, apple pie or jam roly-poly etc.

I tried to better understand the word 'existential' by exploring what an *Existentialist* is or does? A popular Thesaurus declares: *"An Existentialist could either be a religious moralist, agnostic relativist, or an amoral atheist."* What? Assuming anyone knows what that lot mean, who decides which one it is?

It concludes: *"Existentialism is the search and journey for true self and true personal meaning in life."* So, I conclude it is: *"Striving for maximum self-indulgency while contemplating one's naval."*

Yet another show-off word that M and I grumbled about was '*genre*': '*A style or category of art, music or literature.*' It's a much more useful word than '*existential,*' however, it tends to be over-used by people who are 'artistic' or who are in an 'artistic' frame of mind at the time they choose to use the word. Heavy use of the word '*genre*' often occurs when self-proclaimed artistic people hang out together and collectively use the word like a 'badge of honour.'

*Note: '*Artistic*' is a self-defined persona *(*A person's perceived personality or personal image)* so help yourself to the title if you like it.

**Another Note - *For folk from overseas:* If you wish to appear artistic in the UK you would blend well with other like-minded artistic folk if you wear mostly black clothing and wear a hat of your choice (Indoors and outdoors). If you like to grow facial hair, a minimal 'goaty' beard and pencil-thick moustache would enhance your look (*Goaty* refers to the beard of a goat).

M and I decided that showing-off words and speak are only acceptable if used by actors who are officially proclaimed '*Luvvies*' - '*Someone in the acting profession with a tendency to affectation and behaviour, speech or writing that is pretentious and intended to impress.*' Why not name your favourite/least favourite luvvies while contemplating your naval, existentially.

Beware 'Word Devaluation':

M and I agreed back in 2014 that some words like *genre* were in a state of over-usage and required regulation to avoid devaluation, one such word was the previously high impact word '*Amazing*' (*The 'A' word*). It continues to be so over-used that it now has little value and registers virtually zero when its impact is measured.

I suspect the word *amazing* has become the most commonly used English word in the world easily beating words like '*the, a, and, I.* Examples commonly used include: *When I got out of bed this morning I put my socks on one after the other, it was amazing;* "*I cleaned my teeth this morning and the toothpaste tasted amazing*"; "*I waited on the platform and the train arrived on time, it was amazing*"; "*we were in the café and my friend had a cup of tea with two sugars, it was amazing.*" And so on throughout the day and night.

People who are interviewed on tv and the radio about a personal experience often instinctively gush the word amazing, which unintentionally has the effect of reducing the range of creative, interesting words that are available in the English language. From winning a Formula 1 race in Dubai or lifting the FA Cup at Wembley, and from headlining at Glastonbury to winning *Strictly Come Dancing*, the interviewee who has won will often tell us that *"It was an amazing experience,"* but surely it was more unique, interesting and exciting than that?

The result is that the word 'amazing' no longer means *'Great wonder or astonishment'* but now represents *'Ordinary, normal or every-day mundane occurrences.'* It's a word that is close to extinction, so dear reader, please avoid further devaluation and only use it when you are truly in a state of astonishment or great wonder. Let us bring *'amazing'* back to full value and fine health. It would be *quite nice* if we could. Did you see what I did there?

From this day forward, in sickness and in health, please try hard not to over-use the 'A' word and use alternative words such as *surprising* or *unusual* and the phrase *'a little out of the ordinary.'*

*Note: If you are hooked on the word 'Amazing' here are some guidance notes to help you come off it. Don't rush the therapy, there's no need to experience *cold turkey* (*The abrupt and complete cessation of taking a drug to which one is addicted).*

Week 1 - If '*amazing*' starts to ooze out in conversation stuff your fist in your mouth and make a note in your journal each time you say it. At the end of the week plot your *amazing* hits on a graph and determine if a pattern is emerging e.g. the first one never occurs before 6.17 am; bunching is evident at certain times such as lunch time or in the pub or gym etc.

Week 2 - set a target to reduce the *Amazing* hit each day e.g. Mon-Thurs x 9 each day; Fri x 6; Sat x 4; Sunday- rest. If at this stage in your rehab you feel the damn word coming out just let it rip.

Week 3 - now it gets tough, set one target for each day that is at least 75% less than your usual hits before therapy began e.g. if you were 100 a day your target should be 25maximum.

Week 4 - picture yourself as a chilled out, interesting person who now only an occasionally uses *Amazing!* Yes, you can get through a week with clean days and a total hit of no more than say 5 *Amazings!*

Warning: If you follow these guidelines for kicking the habit and you continue to fail, consider an extended break away from people and apply for a job with animals e.g. a Shepherd or Zookeeper's assistant, as sheep or penguins won't know or care how many times you say A - - zing.

~

Finally, on the topic of word emasculation, M and I agreed that another seriously over-used word is *'surreal'* (*Ref *Cambridge Dictionary: Strange; not seeming real; like a dream*). If used appropriately it can add colour to the description of an experience but if applied to a mundane situation it loses its muscle and flops to the floor to be trampled by people who think they are having an amazing time, but in reality are only having a normal, bog-standard experience.

We felt that *surreal* is a word that should not be used perhaps more than once or twice a month. If you feel the need to use it more frequently, substitute it with words like *bizarre, strange or unusual*. If it transpires that you really do keep having 'surreal' experiences, review your weekly alcohol intake and have your medication checked by a doctor as soon as possible.

Be very vigilant in avoiding the *'Double-Doings'*: "The sausage was amazing and the mash potato surreal"; "my socks were clean which was surreal, and I put one on each foot which looked amazing" etc.

Dodgy Broadcasting: I would often complain to M about the media broadcasters who constantly exaggerated their language using standard phrases like *'devastated'* when something is disappointing, *'unbelievable'* when they really mean 'believable' or 'to be expected,' and *"Welcome to the Show"* when there is no 'show' but rather a programme on the radio with news and/or discussion. There is always a danger that members of the public will pick up this exaggerated language from media people and use it frequently, leading to word extinction and corruption of the English language.

Joni and I had a couple of cold drinks in a local pub last New Year's Eve then went home to watch *Big Ben* and the fireworks on tv. We are not hard to please these days. The regional news channel had filmed people during the evening walking around in a local town and sitting in pubs and restaurants and described them as *"Revellers."* They were effectively describing Joni and I! In truth, our days of 'revelling' under almost all circumstances are sadly behind us (Or at least one long pace behind), so this kind of exaggerated 'cut and paste' language is mildly ridiculous.

Beware the *'slow motion'* radio broadcasters, they are probably not hampered by medication or alcohol but for no good reason choose to slow down and stretch the words at the end of their sentences. *Slow-mowing* probably evolved in sports tv and radio programmes where before today's instant on-screen updates, live broadcasters received a continuous flow of information on ticker-tape and in their ear piece. Nowadays slow-mowing has spread into news-based and all manner of other programmes, which may be because some broadcasters simply like the way they sound when doing it? A more sinister reason maybe as a control technique similar to that used by magicians who hypnotise their victim saying: *"Look into my eyes, look into my eyes,"* instead, however, the *slow-mowers* are using our ears and not our eyes to control us?

Here is an example of *slow-mowing*: <u>Normal language</u>: *"And now we cross to Wembley Stadium where the half time whistle has just gone."*
<u>Slow-mowing</u>:*" And now we cross to Wembley Stadium where the half time whistle (Pause) haaasss juuussst gonnne."*

M and I agreed that radio slurring was an irritating fad or phase that would hopefully pass but alas I believe it has become more common. A favourite channel of mine is BBC Radio 5 Live which currently employs some of the worst/best slow-mowers. Sit comfortably with your radio and they will begin (And end slowly).

Reversing Words: There is no real purpose in swapping the first letter of two words, but it can be good fun. M and I sometimes took turns with famous names e.g. *Wolly Hilloughby* (Holly Willoughby); *Hom Tanks* (Tom Hanks); *Tonald Drump* (Businessman, golfer and President).

Reversing can also work well with commonly used phrases and can stimulate interesting discussions, for example, '*Wealth and Hellbeing*' (Health and Wellbeing) prompted M and I to discuss why very wealthy people are often miserable?

Human Resources (HR): '*HR*' is a term which refers to the management of employees in an organisation, it used to be called '*Personnel Management*' and' M said 'HR' was like describing the management of people as if they are livestock e.g. goats and sheep.

Politely Impersonating People's Accents: M and I used to like to impersonate accents (badly) from different countries or regions and a favourite of M's was from an old tv series about Scottish vets called *Doctor Finlay's Casebook*. I would play the part of *Janet MacPherson* who had a very high-pitched voice, and M specialised in *Dr Angus Cameron* who had a very low-pitched one: *"Sit down Janet"!* was never far from her lips.

Sporty People-Speak: Professional sporty people and the associated media that follow them around have words and phrases they like to use like. *"Over the moon"* and *"Sick as a parrot"* have both become out-dated but are remembered fondly.

Serious sports people refer frequently to *"The Group,"* an expression which replaces '*the team*' or '*the squad*.' I explained to M that in football *The Group* could include the manager, coaches, medical and marketing people, groundsman and his/her dog, the club mascot, laundry, catering and turnstile staff etc i.e. almost anyone associated with the club or activity. The blame for failure is more widely spread in a large 'group,' which is good if you are clearly to blame, but I advised M that the traditional 'team' or 'squad' references remain preferable because in the event that a game is lost the goalie or centre forward can easily be blamed and if its less obvious who to point the finger of failure at then blame the manager and carry on or sack him/her.

"*Box to box*" is another football expression which means 'running about a lot.' M said, "well why don't they say that?"

Australian sporting folk (Very competitive but always supportive in the après-match social activities) frequently use the expression "*Under the pump*" which means 'under pressure,' for example: "*We put the Pommie batsmen under the pump by bowling the ball at 97 miles an hour at their teeth.*"

Note for folk from overseas: British media presenters covering sports events now often say: "We'll be all over it." This means they will be covering particular sports action for the duration of their programme. This is based loosely on established 'press' (Journalistic and photographer/paparazzi) practice of getting as close as possible to their source or target (Like a pack of hyenas) rather than the act of climbing 'all over' something like a wall or a tree or the Eiffel Tower etc.

Pronunciation: One of M's favourite stories that always caused her to cover her face while laughing was when my children were young, they would go to the local Chinese take-away restaurant and the lady owner had a strong accent and she would ask if a customer would like chips, but it sounded like she was asking: "*You want shit?*"; and then she would ask if a customer would like a fork and it would sound like: "*You want fuk*"?

Children obviously often mis-pronounce or misinterpret words and expressions while learning to speak. Our son David spoke from a very early age, and some of his errors have become part of our family dictionary. Dogs were called "*get downs*"; 'Daddy' was "Dayee" until he decided to call me by my first name "Beel," and then I became "Dayee Beel." It was unusual for such a young child to call his Dad by his first name and I was asked more than once if David had more than one Dad?

My Nan (Catherine) was renowned for her mispronunciations and one of my favourites was the word '*hereditary*' which became "*hairy-dittery.*"

~

Notes For Folk From Overseas On 'Language':

Slang: Some of the language identified in this Chapter can be described loosely as 'slang': *A kind of language occurring in casual and playful speech, typically made up of figures of speech that are used in place of standard terms for added raciness, humour, irreverence, or other effect. Source: Free Dictionary of Slang.*

London-style slang has evolved over hundreds of years and the following are some examples:

-'*Done a runner* - to run away, it usually has a negative connotation eg. a thief or burglar may "do a runner."

-'*Youravinalarf*' - You must be joking.

-"*Tits up*"- things have gone badly, it's similar in meaning to '*Belly Up*' (Dead).

-'*It's all gone Pete Tong*' - tits-up (Pete is a professional DJ with a troubled, sometimes calamitous past who has turned his life around and is back in business).

-'*You're taking the Mickey*' - an older form of '*youravinalarf.*' One definition from '*The Urban Dictionary*' claims that '*Mickey*' is a "*Mick*," a racist nickname for an Irishman because many Irish surnames begin with Mc or Mac. I think that's tosh (*Rubbish*) because there are just as many Scottish Mc's and Mac's, but either way I advise that you don't call an Irish or Scottish person a 'Mick' unless it's his/her name.

-'*Sling your hook*'! (Pronounced *Slingyerook!*) This means get lost; go away i.e. it's nothing to do with a sling or a hook. A lot of East London phrases have come from seamen and dock workers, a ship's anchor was called a '*hook*' and the '*sling*' was a cradle that held the anchor, so '*sling your hook*' meant '*lift the anchor, stow it and set sail.*' The rest is Naval history.

Recommendation: Choose your slang words to suit your own personal style like selecting clothes on display for sale in a shop. For example, M and I found '*Lard Arse* '(Fat bottom) offensive but we liked '*Gismo*' (A gadget or device), we didn't like '*Geezer*' (A man) and were neutral with '*Gaff*" (House) which we found preferable to '*Spread*' or '*Manor.*'

Please note that you don't have to be in London to talk in slang.

Avoid Confusing Your Words: Beware, the word '*Wannabe*' can crop up unexpectedly at any time (*Cambridge Dictionary definition: *A person who is trying to become famous*'). It means 'want to be,' e.g., I wannabe a footballer; pop star; bus conductor etc.

This relatively new word should not be confused with the word '*Wasabi*' (*A plant of theBrassicaceae family which includes cabbages, horse radish and mustard*).

Other words that are similar and can be confusing with potential to cause embarrassment are:

'*Forgot*' (*To fail to remember*) and '*Fagot*' which means '*meatballs*' but is sometimes used offensively as an insult. For example, in 2001 on his way to winning the *Wimbledon Men's Singles* title, Goran Ivanišević beat Britain's Tim Henman in the semi-final during which a line-judge made a poor call and Ivan lost the rally. When interviewed afterwards he was asked what he thought of the line judge's decision and he said: *"I think he is fagot little bit."*

There's an old expression which is still used often: *"It's not over until the fat lady sings."* Do not take this literally, it doesn't mean there is or will be a fat lady singing, it means that we should avoid the presumption that we know the outcome of an event which hasn't yet finished.

*Note: The origin of the *'fat lady'* expression is disputed, some believe it relates to *'Brunhilda'* who was a powerful female figure from Germanic legend, however, the alternative source is thought to be from Baseball in the USA where the expression was coined by *Yogi Berra*. Others claim it came from *Kate Smith* a singer best known for her version of *'God Bless America'* which the *Philadelphia Flyers* hockey team broadcast before a game in 1969. They won and consequently played it regularly thereafter. My personal preference is for good old *Brunhilda*.

Random Words and Expressions: M and I discussed random words and expressions that people learning the English language may wish to add to their vocabulary, including:

'Turn-ups' typically refers to trouser material folded up at the bottom of each leg. Don't confuse them with people who arrive un-invited to a party or wedding reception etc.

'Conk' means 'nose' or mechanical breakdown e.g. 'my old car has conked out'. The word probably originated from a 'conch' (*Large seashell*). 'Conk' is also a procedure in which the hair of an African American boy is straightened by using potatoes, soap, Vaseline and lye.

'Do-gooders,' taken literally it means people who undertake good deeds for other people, however, it tends to be used with a sarcastic intent suggesting the people concerned should mind their own business. My Father in Law John didn't like *"do-gooders,"* which seemed to include Social Workers and volunteers like M (Arranging flowers in the hospital Maternity ward or delivering *'Meals on Wheels'* to older folk). John was often a miserable sod.

'Old Fart' is a slang expression often used in sport for an older person, commonly of some previous or current repute who is considered to hold old-fashioned views and methods. They are characterised as typically wearing a formal blazer, often with brass buttons and sometimes with an embroidered badge or pocket handkerchief, and a sports club, Federation or Association tie. There is a tendency for hair to grow out of their nose and ears.

'Stand-up comics/comedians' are people who tell jokes and funny stories. They commonly stand up, although may sit, lie, run, jump, juggle, hoola-hoop or do somersaults during their performance. Apart from *Billy Connolly* (*The Big Yin*), M didn't generally watch comedians on the telly although her twitching shoulders sometimes gave her away as she tried not to laugh. She said a lot of comedians use their on-stage performance as a personal counselling session, talking about

themselves and their troubles while the audience pays to listen. An unusually cynical view for M.

"*Give him an inch and he'll take a mile*" is a selfish person who thinks mainly of themselves. Similar to a '*git.*'

She/he is a "sight for sore eyes" is a pleasant looking person.

"*He has a face like the back of a bus*" refers to an unattractive person, although the backs of buses can be made to look attractive e.g. with a picture of the countryside, seaside or a nice Sunday roast dinner with thick, steaming gravy.

'*Budgie Smugglers*' are tight swimming trunks for men. No birds or other animals should be involved in the trunk area.

"*A penny for your thoughts*" is not a literal offer of money in exchange for an explanation of what someone is thinking but rather a polite enquiry encouraging someone to talk about what they are thinking about.

'*Pavement pizza*' describes the floor on which someone has vomited the contents of their stomach.

Miscellaneous Swear Words: Olde English swearing was referred to as '*cussing,*' another word for 'curse.' You may hear it described as the '*vernacular*' - *Using the native language of a country or place.* Some swear words are considered mild and others 'strong' i.e. very rude.

In times of great challenge or stress, my son David has an expression which I think helps considerably when you can't understand why something bad has occurred. He will look into your eyes and say with sincerity: "*It's all bollocks*"! (*Testicles*). Try it in the mirror and if it has a therapeutic effect use it to support others in distress.

It was very rare for M to swear and she chose mild words when she did. Dad used the word '*git*' as his swear-word of choice but if very annoyed he would say it through gritted teeth which increased the impact. I always considered 'git' to be a mild curse, however, the *Collins Dictionary* indicates otherwise stating that referring to someone as a git means '*you dislike them and find them annoying,*' or it can denote '*a child of unmarried parents.*'

Wikipedia define 'git' as "a 'mild oath' which "*Is roughly on a par with prat and marginally less pejorative than berk. Git is more severe than twit or idiot but less severe than twat.*" Interestingly, '*git*' is one of the 30,000 most commonly used words in *The Collins Dictionary* and was most frequently used in the year 1708. How did they measure that!?

In some parts of northern England, Northern Ireland and Scotland '*get*' is used instead of '*git.*' '*Get*' is used in the *Beatles* song "*I'm So Tired,*" and the *Speaker of the House of Commons* has ruled '*git/get*' to be '*Un-Parliamentary language*.' Consequently, I think Dad's favourite swear word certainly packed a punch. A very good value three letter word thanks Dad!

My advice to readers from overseas who are looking for a swear word that will have an impact but will not cause too much offence is the firm statement, "Sod off"! (*A sod is a layer of earth with grass growing on it, or a person who is difficult or causes problems. Source: Oxford Dictionary*).

Beware the two finger 'V' sign: If you make a 'V'-shaped sign at someone with your first and middle finger while showing them the back of your hand you are indicating that you wish that person to '*fuck off*' i.e. go away, but not in a sexual way. The following report serves as a warning:

"'V' Sign' Costs Rider Victory" (*Source: BBC Archives, 1971*):

"Controversial horse rider Harvey Smith has been stripped of his £2,000 winnings and a major show jumping title for allegedly making a rude gesture. Mr Smith was seen to make a two-fingered 'V-sign' in the direction of the judges after winning the British Show Jumping Derby. The rider has protested his innocence, claiming the judges mistook his gesture, he said: "*It was a straightforward V for victory. Churchill used it throughout the war.*"

Both signs are made using an upwards motion with the first two fingers extended, however, the victory sign is made with the palm outwards.

Enhance Your Image: If you want people to think you are refined and intelligent then use quotes from historically famous writers and poets like *Shakespeare; Dickens, Edgar Po, Churchill and Chaucer* (Who is very boring in my and M's view). You will create an illusion of being well-read and knowledgeable when in fact you may not be. All you need to do is remember a few lines from a few old writers, speak clearly but don't shout. Here is an appropriate phrase from *Edgar Allan Po:* "*In time the wind will blow in the sunken field of golden callous heather and awareness will tighten and life flow freely….*"

Your quote need not be word-perfect because most people won't know what the correct wording is. Also, it doesn't matter if you don't understand what you are saying because poetry obviously allows people to make their own personal interpretation. Sound confident when quoting your chosen poetic extract and have a dramatic look on your face – imagine that someone has just shut two of your fingers in a car door.

Children's' Names: If considering a British name for your child beware those that may be considered old-fashioned eg. *Malcom or Trixie*. If in doubt choose the name of someone who is currently famous and popular eg. *Adele; William; Beyoncé; Harry* or *Stormzy*.

If you are naming a child and wish to have a British one, be cautious with the choice of name to avoid embarrassing them when they are older. M and I felt the following boys' names may attract unwanted comment: *Spartacus, El Cid, Ponsonby, Geronimo* and *Ermintrude* (Often used for cows and donkeys). Apologies if you bear any of these very fine names.

The same concerns don't apply to naming your pets as almost any name can be safely given without fear of criticism, examples known to M and I were a goldfish called *Frank* and a tortoise called *Rhianna*. On no account name a person or pet *Hitler*.

'Aussie-speak': Understanding the Australian language can be tricky, for example, they often prefix a sentence with the word "*look*" but what they mean is 'listen.' Be careful to avoid looking for something when they say 'look' because they say it frequently and you may become dizzy or appear to be odd in your manner.

An Aussie will probably call you 'mate' which is a friendly acknowledgement, and they are likely to use the expression *'under the pump'* which means under pressure. Aussies can be blunt and may appear rude when speaking to you when in fact they are not intending to be, fortunately when an Aussie is being rude you will almost certainly have no doubt about it.

Ping and Pong: My second name is *Ping* which can be defined as: *'A pulse of sound in active sonar,'* and it is often used to describe something moving swiftly e.g. '*I will ping you a text.'* The typical *Ping* noise is a brief, high-pitched bell sound.

Ping is listed as the 95th most used name in the '*Song Dynasty*' Chinese dictionary, *'A Hundred Family Surnames,'* but it's not one of the 300 most common surnames in China. Lard chose it as my 'writer's name' in this book because he likes it. His phone 'pings' when receiving a message which he says is less irritating than other options like a trumpeting elephant, off-key Opera singing or the mating call of the *Giant Sloth* which sadly became extinct around 8,500 BC?

Pong is used to describe a hollow ringing sound or an improvisation by an actor on the stage to cover up a mistake, but most commonly is used to indicate an unpleasant odour. *'Ping-Pong'* is another name for a game of *table tennis* - listen to the sounds of ball on bat during a game and you will understand why.

Final Tips On Language For Folk From Overseas:
If you are greeted by a 'proper' East Ender they will almost certainly say: "All *white, ars it goin?"*- the literal translation is: '*Are you all right, how are you doing?'* and the meaning is '*Hello, how are you'?* A variation to this may be: "All *white, ars it angin?"*- the literal translation is: *'Are you all right, how is it hanging?'* - the actual meaning is again: *'Hello, how are you'?*

It's become common, particularly on radio music request shows to hear listeners describe their spouse, partner or best friend as their *'Soul mate* or *Rock.'* Don't confuse them with *'cell mate'* or *'rot.'* I encourage you to be bold, use fresh terminology and don't follow the usual trend, for example, if addressing a loved one choose something you know they really like and use it in a loving phrase, for example, I might say to my wife: *"Dearest, I want you to know that to me you are like a warm egg-custard tart."* Nice.

You may hear people refer to *'Every corner of the globe,'* however, this is a contradiction and mathematical impossibility but does not mean they believe the world is flat. It's an example of an expression which some people simply enjoy saying. Other popular phrases that should not be taken literally are: *"Every cloud has a silver lining"* and *"Brexit is/was Brexit."*

Avoid 'double negatives' e.g.: *"Thank you, that was not unhelpful"* - simply say *"Thank you, that is helpful."*

If someone asks you: *"Is there anything else I can do for you today?"* answer simply yes or no thank you ie. don't ask them for a pay rise, a lift home or a cooked breakfast as they almost certainly won't be able or want to do that for you.

When greeted by someone who says *"Hello, how are you,"* you could say how you are feeling e.g.: *'I feel miserable'* or *'I am feeling perky thank you,'* however, they will probably expect you to say: *"Fine thanks how are you"?* While this may be an inaccurate answer it is a British tradition to give a friendly, polite response despite your true feelings. Strange but true.

When having a sociable drink, *'cheers'** is commonly used in the UK *(Raise glass and clink once gently with all those in your group).* Our family have inherited the expression: *'Cheers our table'* from friends from *Manchester*, this is perfectly acceptable but preferably you should be seated at a table when making the *toast* (**A ritual in which a drink is held aloft as an expression of goodwill.*)

If you are in an audience in a theatre or at a conference etc and the host shouts at the audience: *"And now please give it up one more time for...."* eg. John Smith, it means that you should clap your hands to applaud John.

In conversation, if someone refers to *'Juno Wot,'* it's not a person but rather a question which means 'Do *you know what*'? If you find this confusing, then answer 'no I don't.'

~

MUSIC

This little book requires a Chapter on music as it was such an important part of M's life, she gave me a lifelong education in musical appreciation, and it was a favourite topic for our chats.

M was eclectic in her musical tastes and her generation should be remembered for sustaining the East Enders' love of a 'sing song' and a 'knees up' which was gifted to them by their parents and back on through the ancestral musical time machine. My kids like a singsong and a knees-up although they are not called that anymore - *Bop, boogie, party, rave, clubbing* and *making shapes* are among the many options, so the legacy somehow remains strong, I think?

M and I enjoyed a lot of the same kinds of music, she appreciated classical music more than me and we disagreed over *Gloria Estefan,* she said her voice was "manufactured and anyone can be made to sound good." She changed her mind later in life. In the 1970's I had a youthful appreciation of 'heavy rock' bands and was banished to my room with the door shut and headphones on while I got it out of my system. *King Crimson* and *'The Court of The Crimson King'* album remains a favourite to this day, but the heavy stuff was only a short symphony for me.

M&D had a very large vinyl record collection (*Long Player/LP: A vinyl record that revolves on a turntable at a speed of 33 ⅓ rpm, with a 10 or 12 inch diameter, and use of the "microgroove" groove specification*) and songs from the musicals in cinema and theatre from the 1940's onwards were among her very favourites as were Ella Fitgerald, Matt Monro, Val Doonican, Nat King Cole, Edward Woodward (Not universally well known), Dean Martin, Howard Keel, Paul Robeson, Andy Williams, Doris Day, Perry Como, Bing, Lena Horne and the Three Tenors, Plácido Domingo, José Carreras and Luciano Pavarotti. She was a big fan of Sammy Davis Jnr and Tommy Steel but not so much on Bruce Forsyth or Cilla Black (Harsh).

At Christmas M loved the *King's College* carol service and Andre Riéu's Christmas Special from Vienna. We both liked Naomi Cohen, Cass Elliot and Mama Cass (All the same person) and the *Mamas & Papas - "California Dreamin'," "Monday, Monday," "Dedicated to the One I Love"* etc. Cass died aged 32 in 1974 and was married to Jimi Hendrix from 1963-69. Two of the very many musicians who died too young.

M and I liked to share an old CD of *'Traditional Scottish Songs'* and would take custody of it for a few months each and sing our socks off when no-one else was listening. Favourites were Kenneth McKeller's *Loch Lomand*; Andy Stewart *A Scottish Soldier*; and Jimmie Macgregor's version of *Mairi's Wedding - "Step we gaily on we go, heel for heel and toe for toe"* etc. We agreed that it must have been our Scottish ancestral genes.

When I first became a grandad, I celebrated by inventing a dance called the *'Grandwister'* which M said was 'like *The Twist* with knobs on.' I explained to her that many Grandads like to dance but are very self-conscious so tend to dance privately eg. in garden sheds, basements and sufficiently spacious cupboards - phone box size is adequate (Don't use an actual public phone box as you may be arrested on suspicion of something you didn't intend). The dance needs to be done standing reasonably upright, but a little stoop can be tolerated. It requires no major foot movement, but elbows must be tucked in as flailing can cause injury or damage. The *Grandtwister* can be danced to any piece of music with a lively beat but shy performers are advised to wear headphones to avoid attracting attention. Health & Safety instructions are not available on request.

One central element of the dance is in M's honour and is a brief *'hand jive,'* she was an outstanding hand-jiver and would burst into a flurry at any opportunity, she had a nice voice, good rhythm and enjoyed the chance to sing, dance and 'party.'

M didn't like the *Eurovision Song Contest,* she thought it was 'like a circus' and didn't understand why there are countries in it who are not from Europe? Why did people with no talent win it? And why did no one vote for the UK anymore? M thought it should be scrapped and replaced by a *'World Cup' Song Contest* every four years. Despite all of that she watched it for years because Terry Wogan was the commentator, and he made the whole event comical (He took the piss).

While on holiday in Spain in 2013 I glimpsed a copycat entertainment programme on tv called *Arab's Got Talent* (Ref *Britain's Got Talent*). M refused to believe there was such a thing when I told her that it was won by a man who juggled vegetables from Australia (I don't know where the vegetables were from), and I qualified for my favourite *"Oh Billy don't be silly."* She didn't often watch *The X Factor* because too many of the singers were "shouting," she preferred *The Voice* but that was substantially due to the *'Tom Jones Factor.'*

Stardom with Val Doonican: A lifetime highlight for M was an evening at *'The Talk of The Town'* by Piccadilly Circus, she was a big Val Doonican fan and was seated at a table near the stage, he required someone to honk the hooter while he sang *'O'Rafferty's Motorcar'* and Val invited M to perform from her seat. She performed admirably without missing a single honk, the applause was generous, and it was a story often told.

I followed in her stage shoes back in the 1970's at one of nine Public Houses in *Burnham On Crouch* in Essex. It was a Folk singing night and guest performers were welcome, three school friends and I again sang *'O'Rafferty's Motorcar',* two played the 'squeeze box', I was on the hooter, and we all sang. The room above the pub rang loud with laughter and I'm almost certain that they were laughing with us and not at us. All together now: *"Now Dinny O'Rafferty's motor car is the greatest I declare, It's made of bits and pieces that he's picked up here and there...honk, honk etc..."*

The Rubettes: The *Rubettes* were a pop/glam-rock band whose biggest hit *"Sugar Baby Love"* was their first recording and was number one in the UK for four weeks in May 1974. *Johnny Richardson* formed the group from session musicians and played the drums and coincidentally, my cousin Clifford helped Johnny learn to play the drums before the *Rubettes* had their first gig in a local pub in the East End.

The vocalist booked for the studio recording of *"Sugar Baby Love"* didn't turn up, so Johnny sang the lead vocals and is the high-pitched voice prominent on the record. They are remembered for this iconic hit record and their white cloth caps.

We lived next door to Johnny in the 1970's in *Gidea Park*, Romford. There would be a *Winnebago* motorhome parked on the driveway next door when they were going on tour. I don't know what sort of rock-star existence the band lived on tour but at home Johnny was first and foremost a family man and a particularly nice fella. M&D were occasionally taken out in the band's limo, which was a special treat and M always mentioned the on-board drinks cabinet when telling the story of the evening out. Johnny became a well-informed dietician and gave advice on health and wellbeing, surely behaviour as rare as hen's teeth for a Rock & Roller!

M&D asked him to choose (an inexpensive) guitar for me for my 18th Birthday, I didn't play it until I became a Dad over 10 years later and sang nursery rhymes to my kids. *'Puff the Magic Dragon'* remains my biggest un-recorded cover hit. Thank you, John.

My cousin Clifford also helped *Kenny Jones* of the *Faces* to practice in his early days as there wasn't room for his drum kit at home, so he would play it upstairs at Cliff's terraced house in Stepney. *Faces* members included *Rod Stewart, Ronnie Lane* and *Ronnie Wood,* so Kenny's drumming couldn't have been too shabby. Clifford played in a number of local East End bands and was a *Master Bricklayer* by trade.

The Kings Head, Romford (Deceased): The pub dates back to 1678, and was rebuilt in 1898, later in the 1970's it was closed down and today a small section of the original front can just be seen above a chemist shop in Romford marketplace. The *Kings Hall & Lounge* were at the back of the pub and it was a venue for almost any form of entertainment, social event and probably funeral/wake over many years. It was one of five pubs in or adjacent to Romford Market and in the 1960's and 70's it was a tough working man's pub which served the market traders and customers during the day and music fans through the arch and round the back in the hall of an evening.

I first got down and groovy in the hall in the late 60's after the *'Teddy Boys'* era had been replaced by scruffier long-haired heavy-metal/rock fans who stood, jumped or sat on the old wooden floor *shaking their thing* - mostly their heads. We did stand up at various points of the evening to jump about, but it was not any form of 'dancing.'

One evening in the week and sometimes on a Saturday different bands would play, I would go with a mate or two and we would imbibe nothing stronger than *Ind Coope Best Bitter* (3.4% alcohol) from the Romford brewery and never once was there any *agro* (*Punch-ups*). It was always very loud in a relatively small, scruffy hall with all furniture removed and the surprising thing was the quality of some of the bands. Between 1969 and 1972, *The Kings Head* pub in Romford hosted the following bands, some on more than one occasion:

Deep Purple – November 1969; February 1970.

Matthews Southern Comfort (Of *Woodstock* fame) – April 1970.

Quintessence – September 1970; September 1971.

Uriah Heep (Supported by *'Nosher Brown'*) – January 1971.

Chicken Shack – July 1970; November 1970.

Yes – October 1970.

Pink Fairies – Active on the London underground (Not the trains) and *'psychedelic'* scene and they appeared in the first *Glastonbury Festival* in 1971. *Black Sabbath* – May 1970.

Free – May 1970.

In April 1970 at the *Kings Head* there was an *"All Nighter"* with (not so well known) *Writing on the Wall; Patto; Morning;* and *Emily,* I was never man enough for the all-nighters and was almost certainly in bed by 1.30 a.m. at the latest and up for Sunday morning football by 8.00. I would never have made a rock star or a roadie. Bed's best.

Edgar Broughton was at *The Kings Head* in December 1969 and at the *Buxton Pop Festival* (July 1973) with *Chuck Berry; Wizard; Nazareth; Medicine Head; Thin Lizzy; Hacken Shack* and *John Peel*. If time travel becomes possible in my lifetime, I will be first in the queue for tickets or a steward's vacancy for that Festival.

Meanwhile back at the *Kings Head*, *Jimmy McGriff* strutted his stuff in November 1969, he was an American *hard-bop* and *soul-jazz* organist and bandleader (*Hard-bop is a 'subgenre' of jazz). Jimmy's pedigree extended to appearances at *The Apollo, New York* in 1963 with *Mary Wells* and *The Chantels,* and with the *Isley Brothers* and *Gladys Knight and the Pips* in Chicago in January 1963.

Finally, *Led Zeppelin* belted out their early sound in the late sixties in the *Kings*

Hall & Lounge moving onwards and upwards to become music royalty. I saw a good number of these bands and looking back it's hard to believe that it was possible to rock-up midweek in *Romford Market* in my back yard to a scruffy pub, and for half a handful of loose change experience top class bands who were in the process of becoming legendry. Most of the bands were outwith M's musical genre but she liked *Matthews Southern Comfort's* single *Woodstock* written by Joni Mitchell.

A Favourite Musical Person: Charlie Pride is an African American whose family were cotton pickers in the deep south of North America, he's one of my favourites as much for his fighting spirit as his music and he became one of M's when I read her some extracts from his biography. BBC Radio 2 was M's constant music supplier, and it has never played much of Charlie's music, but M liked *Behind Closed Doors; Green Green Grass of Home;* and *There Goes My Everything*. She liked a good singalong song and I was permitted to play a select few sometimes on my cassette tapes on my *Philips N2233 Tape Cassette Player Recorder* (Available today on Ebay for £12.95 - portable and complete with microphone).

Charlie was the first black person to be accepted into American *Country* music and was the best-selling performer for *RCA Records* since *Elvis Presley,* who was a fan of Charlie's. When RCA released his first record, they didn't include a picture of Charlie which was their normal promotional practice, so when he first appeared on stage people were shocked that he was a black man.

During his peak years which were mainly the 1970's, he had 52 top 10 hits on the *Billboard Hot Country Songs* chart, 30 of which made it to number one. Hit songs included *Crystal Chandeliers; Kiss an Angel Good Morning;* and *Just Between You and Me.*

Notes For Folk From Overseas On 'Music':
Music is a great way to learn a language but beware of repeating phrases in songs as they may not be all they appear to be. Elvis is world famous and is often described as *'The King of Rock and Roll.'* Despite his great fame I would advise caution in using some of his lyrics in a normal conversation, for example, in his hit record *Shook Up* he sings: *Ah well I bless my soul,* What's wrong with me? *I'm itching like a man on a fuzzy tree......*

Avoid referring in conversation to *'itching like a man on a fuzzy tree'* as it may give the impression that you have a nasty skin rash. Also, some people like to sing like Elvis, but I recommend you don't as you are likely to sound ridiculous.

Mark Ronson's *'UpTown Funk You Up'* should be sung privately e.g. in the shower, as you may attract unwelcome attention if heard in public places like a busy train or a library. A popular hit record called *'Who's Zoomin Who?'* was released in 1995, it was the30th album by American singer Aretha Franklin, one of the World's greatest ever singers. Who's Zoomin' Who? was influenced by a range of mid 1980s 'genres' including dance-pop, synth-pop and R&B (*Rhythm and Blues). There is no clear, agreed definition of the word Zoomin, however, my research revealed a possible definition is: 'Pulling the wool over someone's eyes' i.e. deceiving them.

However, the plot thickens as in the practice of 'Chaldean Numerology' the numerical value of Zoomin' is 4, and in 'Pythagorean Numerology' it's only 2. Numerology is of course the belief in the mystical or divine relationship between a specific number and one or more coinciding events. In addition, it is also the study of the numerical value of the letters in names, ideas and words and is usually associated with the paranormal, astrology and similar 'arts.' I suggest you choose your preferred definition or make something up if someone asks you what it means.

There is an old 'pop' song from the 1970s by Johnnie Taylor called 'Whose Making Love,' and the lyrics include the question: "Whose making love to your old lady while you're out making love"? This is a perfectly reasonable question but almost certainly refers to a person's wife rather than an 'old woman' and so is not a respectful way of addressing someone's wife.

Singing Carols at Christmas - 'Carolling': The British love to sing carols at Christmas and anyone is welcome to join in regardless of their religion. Lots of people who sing carols are not religious, they just enjoy singing them. M was like this and so am I.

If you decide to join in the singing it is best to learn the carol first i.e. the tune and the words/lyrics. Most carols are quite old so the language can be strange e.g. 'Hark the Herald Angels sing'; and 'Lo, he abhors not the Virgin's womb' (Ref 'O Come All Ye Faithful' composed by Englishman John Reading in the early 1700s).

~

MISCELLANEOUS THINGS

This Chapter is all about random topics that M and I discussed, some only once and others often. It is a veritable rummage through a dustbin of conversation topics that we shared in M's front room in the winter, curtains washed and pressed for the beginning of each new season; in her back/dining room which was her favourite place as she could see the garden; in the kitchen while she whizzed around making a cuppa and in her lovely little garden when the weather allowed. We mostly talked about relatively trivial things that were tickling our fancy at the time which is why some of them are a little dated in this modern world.

Food: Mum had a healthy appetite and much enjoyed a meal with family and friends, she was a good cook without being an enthusiastic one and she had the ability to knock up a meal in the blink of an eye. She used many of the same kitchen utensils for most of my life, like a small kitchen knife, a stainless-steel tea strainer and a pink *Bakelite** salt and pepper set, and she rarely broke a cup, plate or tea pot. She would talk continuously while in the kitchen, tidying up as she went along, but could still present a hot meal in record time. Her younger sister Ivy used to call her "*Mrs whip- it-quick*"!

*Note: *Bakelite* or *polyoxybenzylmethylenglycolanhydride* was the first form of plastic and was developed by the Belgian-American chemist *Leo Baekeland* in *Yonkers, New York*, in 1907.

In the early 60's we were probably one of the first families in our street to have Spaghetti Bolognaise and I couldn't find any boys at school who even knew what it was. M would sometimes mince her own beef (Child's fingers beware!) and the un- cooked spaghetti came all the way from Italy (I assumed) in long brittle strips wrapped in blue paper. Once, when I was a badly behaved early-teenager she lost her temper with me (Very rare), chase me into the hall and hit me on the shoulder with the packet causing the spaghetti to burst all over the carpet, but I couldn't help but laugh when she stomped off with a crunching sound underfoot. We made it up very quickly and laughed about it always.

Italian restaurants were a half-hour drive away in East London (Barking and Ilford) but I can only remember *Coq au vin* as the solitary exotic foreign dish in most other restaurants in our area. I was brought up to understand that French food was special and rather superior, but no-one ever explained why.

M had two signature dishes, neither of which would appear in a fine-dining cookery book, but they were delicious and there was never any left for the birds. One was an onion crumble baked in the oven until crisp on top, and the other was 'afters' (Pudding) made from a packet of chocolate chip cookies, soaked (*Marinated* if you are posh) in sherry and covered in home-made

Instant Whip, a non-cream, cream-like substance.

M didn't generally eat *fast food*, she asked me if fish and chips were fast food because you often had to wait a long time in a queue, particularly on a Friday night. I said that fish and chips was '*slow, fast-food*' but she said that was ridiculous.

M thought there were too many cooking programmes on telly and she was irritated by all the fanciful recipes, tiny portions and sauce-swirls on a big plate 'to make it look like there's more food on the plate than there really is,' and she frowned at 'chef-speak' like the instruction to *drizzle* something on your food. M said: "Drizzle is rain, what they mean is sprinkle or pour." You obviously don't question your Mum on a subject like that as they know best.

High Tea: '*Afternoon Tea.Co.Uk*' claim that the likely reason why this meal was called *High Tea* is because it was eaten at a table, unlike *Afternoon Tea* which was taken while sitting in a low, comfortable chair or sofa. At some point the 'upper-class' *High Tea* amalgamated with *Afternoon Tea* with the addition of pigeon, veal, salmon and fruit.

M and I didn't believe there was such a thing as '*Low Tea*,' and so we unofficially claimed it for the '*lower-class*.' After consultation with M it was deemed to be '*A mug of tea with three spoons of sugar, a portion of jellied eels and a generous helping of spotted dick and custard* (Custard to be hot and thick). Enjoy it standing, sitting, in a shed or van, down a hole or up a ladder.

'*The Barnsley Chop*': This magnificent chop deserves its own sub-heading on account of its consistently high quality over many years. It's a double loin lamb chop which is also referred to as a *saddle chop* because it's cut across the saddle, creating the double loin chop with a small under-fillet.

The Barnsley Chronicle claims that the Barnsley chop is thought to have originated at the *King's Head Hotel* on Market Hill in 1849, however, it is more commonly agreed to have originated at *Brooklands Hotel* in Barnsley where it is still beautifully served to this day, I know this because I took lunch at the *Brooklands* (I feel the reader is impressed) and my chosen word to describe it is sumptuous *(*Splendid)*.

A famous man-of-Barnsley is the retired cricketer and umpire *Harold Dennis "Dickie" Bird, OBE, who* is known for his like of the Barnsley chop, along with I believe, the very famous Yorkshire and England batsman *Sir Geoffrey Boycott.* Dickie was born in Barnsley and given the *Freedom of the City* and a 6 feet high statue of him was erected in 2009. He is 5'10" but appeared shorter on account of a stooping standing position when umpiring. The statue was subsequently placed on a 5 feet plinth to prevent rowdy passers-by placing inappropriate objects on his erect finger which was used during a game of cricket for signalling his decision that a batsman was 'Out' and must leave the pitch.

In a test match between England and Australia, a very-fast, very good Aussie bowler called *Dennis Lilley* who was known for his fiery temperament and 'never-say-die' attitude, appealed to Dickie for an LBW decision (*Leg before wicket*) which was turned down. Dickie later confirmed that Dennis, while standing a close distance from his face said: '*Dickie Bird, you are a legend.*' High praise indeed.

School Days: In the final year of *Primary School* before moving on to the big *Secondary School* we would have to do (hard) mental arithmetic tests every morning, scores were totalled at the end of the month and the results determined where you sat in the classroom the following month. Classes had 48-50 pupils sitting in 4 rows of double desks (With a lift up lid and an inkwell for your fountain pen) with the top of the class pair sitting at the front of the first row nearest the door, and in my class if you were last you sat at the back of the 4th row in the far corner of the classroom near the stick insect glass tank.

I enjoyed Primary school but not these tests. If you don't want to know where I sat look away now (I started at the back of row three with Bobby Thomson and grappled my way to the back of row one before we left). I never found the tests easy and had no idea why I slowly got relatively better, but they did help us all when the time eventually came to take the national '11-Plus' exam which determined the type of school you could apply to go to. It's good to know that the school curriculum is a little broader and less driven by punishing mental arithmetic tests. I never really got to know the stick insects well.

Dogs: A dog's sense of smell is 40 times better than humans which is obviously very powerful, and we should be grateful that they never complain about the smells that humans naturally generate. Joni and I have had between 1-3 dogs since we were married in 1981 and can't imagine life without one, most of our dogs have been 'rescued' and then become a part of our family. Last year I filled two large photo albums with pictures of our lives with dogs as a Christmas gift for Joni who is an unofficial *Dog Whisperer* and it's obvious how our dogs feature quietly and prominently in most of everything the family have done together, even when sometimes it's only a furry bum and tail sticking out from under a table or a beady pair of kind round eyes nestling under the bed (Against my strict instructions).

M was a little afraid of dogs but grew in confidence over the years as her sons had them and they became part of her own family, one of her favourites was '*Buddy*' our *Cairn Terrier* who was relatively small (A runt) in a small breed of funny, multi- personality dogs. She always made M laugh with her terrier antics like charging round the room or garden in an ever-decreasing circle, Buddy well understood that she was not to jump on M's lap or lick her and so she would jump on her lap and lick her face at every opportunity. Those two together are a memory to cherish.

Joni and I have been blessed with our dogs including two magnificent black *Labradors*, M loved them both because they were intelligent and gentle and were too big to jump on her lap. *Cassie was* a 'worse-for-wear' old lady from a dog rescue centre that we had for too few years towards the end of her life, one summer's evening we took her on a charity walk in the woods, she disappeared but was spotted at the half-way refreshment point queueing for a burger with onions (No ketchup). It was swallowed intact then she went to the back of the queue and waited for another one.

When Cassie died, the rescue centre asked if we would like to take a young Labrador that had been rejected by the London *Metropolitan Police*. *Stormy* (By name not nature) was not an *Alpha* male and was a clown all his life, we don't know why he was rejected but the Constabulary's loss was our gain and he lived a very contented 14 years. He was very smart but never really understood that his tail was something attached to him and not an occasional visitor, and he was always curious of the origin of the sound of his own frequent farts.

M came on several holidays with us in England and Wales and a dog or three were always present. M was capable of snoring a little (Or a lot) but it was always to be understood that the culprit was a dog with a snoring issue.
God rest you gentle furry souls.

Sport: M and I talked often about sport and watched it on the telly when I was interested. She would generally do her knitting. She thought it was ridiculous when some years ago the Government instructed schools to reduce competition in sport as she believed competition in sport can be a very positive thing if managed effectively.

We talked about how the British have progressed from war-faring to using sport as a (Mostly) peaceful way to satisfy their instinctive warrior traits. There is passionate rivalry when *Celtic* play *Rangers* at football and England play Wales, Scotland or Ireland at rugby (Or anything else), yet when Scotland play an international match the Scots come together to form the magnificent *Tartan Army* and when *The British Lions* Rugby squad go overseas there is always an 'army' of English, Welsh, Irish and Scots standing shoulder to shoulder supporting the Lions.

So, if sport can channel and control passion without warfare, M and I agreed that the sporting battlefield should become the only legal way to go to 'war.' I declared that I would write to the *United Nations*. I haven't got around to it yet.

Triathlon: Arguably (Dad, my brother and I loved a good argument) this is the sport that Mother Nature intended us to do. It reflects the story of mankind developing over a very long time from small, jellified blobs (Amoeba) that floated in water, to creatures that crawled on to land, stood up, walked, ran, invented the wheel and created the bicycle.

Cricket: A personal favourite discussion topic with M, although the discussion was always a bit one-sided Cricket is the second most popular spectator sport in the world after football (Soccer), it was probably created in Saxon or Norman times in the late 16th Century by children from the Weald, a woodland area across Kent and Sussex.

The Dutch word *Krickstoel* means 'a long low stool' used for kneeling in church, which was similar to the long, low wicket with two stumps used in early cricket. The first famous clubs were *London* and *Dartford* in the early 18th century but there were also notable early clubs at *Maidenhead, Hornchurch, Maidstone, Sevenoaks, Bromley, Addington, Hadlow, Chertsey* and the most famous early club *Hambledon* in Hampshire.

I played cricket against *Hornchurch* many times over the years and remember losing there in *'The Romford Recorder Cup'* in May 1985 on the day *Liverpool* played *Juventus* in the *European Cup Final* at the *Heysel Stadium* in Brussels. During some crowd disturbance before the game a wall collapsed killing 39 people and injuring hundreds more. We all sat in the pavilion after our match watching the tragedy in near silence.

~

Here are two favourite historical cricket stories from the two World Wars: (*Source: Peter Fitzsimons. 'Sydney Morning Herald' April 2019):*

"In the first world War, a cricket match was played by the *New South World 4th Battalion* at *Shell Green* in the final days of the infamous *Gallipoli* campaign (Turkey). In an effort to confuse the Turks and disguise the evacuation of allied soldiers which took place every night, our blokes **(Aussies)** thought cricket might be just the thing. And it was, until enemy shells started whistling down on the pitch at third man and long-off, meaning they had to pull up stumps early for fear of everyone having to retire hurt!

My favourite moment in the Australian year is the moment's pause after the *Last Post* is played at the *Essendon/Collingwood* match at the Melbourne Cricket Ground when 90,000 people are so silent you can hear the flag flapping in the middle.

~

In World War II, after *Singapore* had fallen and our blokes were marched off to *Changi,* among others they found themselves in the same compound as the *Royal Norfolk Regiment* of Britain.

Back in the early 90s I interviewed in his Canberra home, a former POW, *Richard Conway*, who set the scene. Both the Brits and the Australians had to provide forced labour for the Japanese war effort, but "every three weeks or so, the Japanese would announce ashita yasumi desu or 'holiday tomorrow', and on these occasions a few of us Australians would often play a rough game of cricket in the middle of the clay compound."

And one day in August 1942, a couple of officers of the Norfolk regiment made Lieutenant Conway, who'd played first grade cricket for *Sydney's Waverley Cricket Club,* an offer – "How about a "Test match," next yasumi, between the English and the Australians in the compound?" "Done"! was the reply.

Conway was appointed captain and all the prisoners of war waited for the occasion with great impatience. Three weeks later Conway was amazed to be handed by the English officers a carefully typed list, setting out the team members, the umpire and the scorer, and informing the Australians that the wicket would be "pitched at 10.30 am."

The next day, the Australians turned out, rough and ready, in "ragged shorts and thongs to find the English, extremely well turned out in their Bombay bloomers." The Poms being the Poms, they even had a full canvas cricket kit with stumps, pads, bats and a new ball while they had prepared a clay pitch that gave an even bounce.

For men living on only eight grams of rice a day, worked endlessly and ravaged by dysentery, various skin diseases, Singapore foot and the dreadful *beri-beri*, it was not easy to play a full-blown cricket match, but the way Conway told it, this was different.

"All of us, Australians and Brits, had always dreamed since we were little boys of playing cricket for our countries, and this was it," he said. "Our POW status didn't exist and we were prisoners no longer. It was a Test match between England and Australia and that was it. All of us forgot everything else."

Sadly, the English won that first 'Test' which was designated as being in "Sydney," but they were clobbered in another two Tests in "Brisbane" and "Melbourne" over the next six weeks on successive *yasumis* before the Tests had to break up, as many of the POWs were sent to other camps. Lieutenant Conway was sent to the infamous *Thai- Burma Railway*, and was very lucky to survive. But even in the toughest of those times the memory of the Changi cricket "Tests," was able to raise a wry smile, and still nourished his soul, fifty years on!"

This unique cricketing rivalry and respect remains strong today.

~

After the War Dad started a cricket club with his brother Jack and they named it after Dad and Uncle Bill's business, *Rontays*. M spent many hours over many years watching cricket from the boundary and on the telly while knitting. When Tom and I were kids M would sit on the boundary with the other ladies and we would disappear up trees and in fields and ditches with the other children. The first home ground the club occupied every other Saturday afternoon was in the countryside at *Noak Hill* in *Harold Wood* where the changing rooms were a farm hut with a cold-water sink in each changing room and a single toilet. Today there is a well-resourced pavilion at *Noak Hill*.

The women would talk together in their mostly deck chairs for the five hours the game was played, pausing to make tea in the community hall next door, serving sandwiches and cake for the cricketers between innings which was always triggered by an *Umpire* who called out *'Tea'!* What else would he shout?

These were great days for small children left to find their own fun, no harm came of us, the worse that happened was cousin Wayne getting stuck, fairly often in the big old Oak tree that sat within the boundary of the cricket outfield. Four runs were scored if the batsman struck the ball and it hit the tree.

Many years later at *Noak Hill*, which was no longer our home pitch, one of my own children fell out of a different tree, landing on her head. The same child also opened the driver's door of my parked car while I was fielding*, wound down the window and with her friend sat with their legs through the open window. The hinges groaned a bit in the following winter months. Stories of 'the problem middle child' abound.

*Note: Fielding is done on the playing area or pitch. These days 'the field' is still used regularly in the cricketing vocabulary but top-level cricket is played on a grass carpet rather than a farmer's field.

M rarely actually watched the game from the boundary or on the tv, but she was happy to sit and do her own things while it was on like knitting, talking, crochet or reading, she had an endless supply of the *Reader's Digest* short stories and Women's Magazines that were passed around her friends and neighbours. M&D were always heavy users of their local library and insisted Tom and I did so when we were young. If you were a grubby youth in the 1960s it was definitely not cool* to be seen walking anywhere near a library (*Cool* was not a word used in those days other than to describe temperature).

Originally, cricketers were referred to as either 'Gentlemen' (*'Amateurs usually of sound breeding and/or ancestry'*) or 'professionals' (Players who were paid to play and tended to be from the 'working-classes'). Miners were renowned for their fast-bowling ability, not least in Yorkshire. It was common for the 'Players' and 'Gentlemen' to have separate changing rooms despite playing in the same team. I would say that was prejudice and not fair play old chap.

I have always been interested in cricket because Dad played, and I was lucky to have coaching at the Essex indoor nets in *Ilford* when I was a teenager. The coach was a young Essex County cricketer *John Lever** who had a successful career with Essex and England. I often watched him play and it was possible to chat with the players at most County grounds in those days.

*Note: *John Kenneth Lever* (Nicknames, JK, Jake, and Stanley) was born in *Stepney* in 1949 and played 21 Test matches for England taking 73 wickets. He was banned from playing for England for three years along with all England players who had taken part in the 'Rebel' tour to South Africa in 1982 during the *Apartheid* era. In the warm-up match against *Western Province*, John broke down after bowling just two balls and X-rays showed he had a curvature in his spine. He had bowled for ten years with a sore back but didn't know about his spinal problem. He recovered quickly and carried on with the tour and his career.

Between 1967 and 1989, John played 529 first Class matches for Essex and took 1,722 wickets. Well played sir!

John and his Essex team-mates loved a joke and there is an old expression when a bowler delivers a particularly good ball to a batsman which is described as a '*Jaffa*' (Like the orange). A well-known Lancashire and England batsman, *David Lloyd*, a popular commentator on *Sky Sport* known as *Bumble,* made his debut as a First Class umpire in April 1985 in a pre-season match between Cambridge University and Essex and John Lever was the first bowler to deliver a ball with Bumble standing as the umpire. John in fact bowled an orange not a cricket ball and the batsman wacked it and it burst into a cloud of fruit mush. Fortunately, the bowler and umpire were well matched in terms of a sense of humour.

I played cricket with enthusiasm until I was 55 when I ran out of it. I played at school for Harold Wood Colts and the 3rd eleven; Havering District; and at University, but for 44 years whoever else I was playing for I hardly missed a game for *Rontays Cricket Club*, the team Dad and Uncle Jack had formed in the 1950's. I made my debut on a rainy day in a Council park in Elm Park, Hornchurch, I borrowed a pair of boots from Mick Ridley which had spikes in them (Which were hammered in the leather soles), so naturally I used them for tap dancing on the concrete path. Mick was not amused.

Cricket was fun, why else play it, not least on an end of summer term tour with *Loughborough University* to Devon and Cornwall where we played cricket and après-cricketed with equal vim and vigour. We lodged in a pub that had been visited by the *Somerset County Cricket* team the week before and the chalk marks were still on the floor in the bar where fuelled by beer they had played games to test their strength.

One challenge was to reach forward as far as possible from a press-up position with an empty beer bottle in each hand (No 'risk assessments' undertaken). We were young and fit but generally not as strong as two of the Somerset team's better known players, *Brian Close*, a big, rotund man-of-steel (Captain of Yorkshire and England) and a young up-and-coming all-rounder called *Ian Botham* (Known as *"Iron Bottom"* across the cricket-playing *Subcontinent** (*Bangladesh, Bhutan, India, Maldives, Nepal, Pakistan and Sri Lanka).

Another of my favourite cricketing experiences involved one of England's best ever batsman, *Graham Gooch,* Essex and England Captain; 118 Test matches for England/MCC; he scored the most first-class runs in a season (2,559, in 1984); made more first-class centuries (94) for Essex than any other player; scored 44,846 runs in all first-class cricket at an average of 49.01 including 128 centuries; and with 44,846 first-class runs and 22,211 First Class runs Graham Gooch is the highest scoring professional batsman of all time to date. Well played old boy.

Despite his world class status and achievements, I bowled him out (I feel the reader is impressed) and my lasting memory is of his stumps displayed in all directions of the compass, and the sound of ball on wooden stumps was loud and magnificent. I was bowling at him with some other local club cricketers at the Essex County indoor cricket nets in *Ilford*, East London before he went off to play for England in India in 1981-2. We were using old leather balls that had been used many times before, I tried to bowl as fast as possible and so lost control of the ball which shot along the floor and under his bat while he was trying to smash it to the boundary for at least 6 runs.

Graham was not pleased at being bowled out by me (Did I mention that I bowled him out?) and he bounced the ball on the floor to show that it was not fit for its purpose (If you were the batsman), I changed the ball to stop the highest scoring professional batsman of all-time whinging, and nearly took his wicket again approximately 15 times (It may have been 2 times?) with a plastic indoor ball.

Some years later I found myself standing next to Graham in the boy's toilets at *Lords Cricket Ground* (The Home of cricket), we were attending a charitable event and he was a speaker. It was my opportunity to remind him that I had bowled him out in 1981 (Noisily knocking all his stumps over etc), I had dreamed of this very opportunity since that infamous day and I said: "Nothing" - I couldn't say what I wanted to say and anyway he looked a bit miserable and was concentrating on the job in hand.

Coincidentally, we left the event at the same time ahead of most others and were striding out through *The Grace Gate* by *The Lord's Tavern* pub* almost side by side. I had a second chance! So this time I said: "Nothing" - once again I couldn't do it, and in a trice he'd crossed the road, climbed into a waiting car and was whisked away while I walked to the Underground station and ruefully made my long journey home.

Sometime later I read an autobiography that Graham had written and realised that as a boy he had played in his local team with his Dad (In the Ilford/East Ham area I think?) against me and my Dad, we were both in our early teens and I remembered him from a photo in his book. The memory was of his distinct stripy cap and how confident he was for his age as a wicket keeper and batsman. I can't remember the game but suspect I probably nearly bowled him out a number of times (15 maybe?)

Notes For Folk From Overseas On 'Cricket':

If you want to watch a professional game of cricket, which can be made a very sociable occasion for spectators with lots of food and drink available whatever the weather, I recommend the shortest form of the game which is when each side has 20 overs to bat and bowl and the winners are the team with the most runs. There's lots of whacking the white ball all over the place, stumps being hit, catches taken, fielders running, jumping, diving and rolling around on the grass, batsmen being run out, players shouting Owzat! (*A question shouted at the umpire asking if the batsman is out) and much more.

If you don't understand the rules of the game, it doesn't matter just go along and enjoy the refreshments on sale and maybe join in the shouting and singing with the other spectators. You will be welcome. The game takes about 2.5 hours from start to finish.

If you decide to go to an international 'Test' match it can last 5 days and finish in a draw (No result) between the two teams so only go for one day or half a day otherwise you will probably be bored.

Some spectators like to wear fancy dress at Test matches, usually on the Saturday of the game e.g. Napoleon Bonaparte, Superman/Woman, the Sugar Plumb Fairy or a duck etc. Avoid costumes that threaten your personal safety like the Eiffel Tower (Cumbersome), a red post box (Poor visibility) or a pantomime horse (A costume for two people that is difficult to walk or climb in). I recommend you think carefully about your costume as you will have to wear it all day and at the end of the day's play you may have to journey home on public transport e.g. a busy bus or train, and so may feel a little embarrassed. You don't want your costume attracting the wrong kind of attention so choose with care, perhaps avoid going as a vegetable e.g. a turnip, or dressing as a Nun if you are a man, particularly if you have a beard (British Nuns usually don't have beards). Personally, I would avoid Superheroes e.g. Thor, as there may be fellow travellers who will want to challenge your super-powers or ask to see your chopper (Axe).

Fancy dress parties are common in the UK (Reason not known) and some will have a dressing-up theme like 'Vicars and Tarts' or 'The Only Way Is Essex' (TOWIE) and if you are hosting your own party then why not be creative and think of a new, fresh idea like *'Peasants and Politicians'; 'Confused Bishops';* or *'Angry Librarians'.* Your part will make a strong statement about you and the kind of people you invite to your parties.

~

Football: I have a younger cousin, Ron, who was a professional footballer, I don't think he ever scored a goal but then he was a goalkeeper. His career lasted from 1980 to 2000 and his clubs were: Reading; Sutton United; Ipswich Town; Brighton & Hove Albion *(Loan);* Wichita Wings *(USA);* Walsall; Southend United; Ashford Town; Leyton Orient; Columbus Crew *(USA);* Chelmsford City; Dover Athletic; Barnet; *and* Hendon. *His one adult cricket club was* Rontays - *playing for anyone else would have been a family scandal.*

In the early 1990's I was sleeping on the couch through *Match Of The Day* on BBC1 on a Saturday night when I was woken by the legendary tv commentator *Barry Davies* who shouted my name loudly declaring that I had made a great save for *Sutton United* in the FA Cup. The slow-motion replay clearly showed that cousin Ron, with whom I share a surname name had made the save. Thanks Ron, it was a nice, brief moment of illusion for me.

Ron was friends from school days with footballer *Clive Allen* whose Dad Les played for *Spurs* in the League and FA Cup winning team of 1960–61; his younger brother Bradley and his cousins Martin and Paul Allen all played professional football very well.

Clive was a top-class footballer and prolific goal scorer, he played 407 professional club games and scored 194 goals; played 8 times for England (It should have been many more); played for 10 clubs and had his most successful spell at *Spurs (Like Father like son)* where he played 105 games and scored 60 goals including 49 goals in the 1986/7 season - WOW!

In 1997 Clive played 'American Football' as a 'kicker' for *London Monarchs* in the *NFL Europe* league making 7 'conversions' (Kicking the ball through the posts after a 'try' has been scored) and 6 out of 6 'field goals' (Like a 'free kick' in soccer). Clive played a few games of cricket with *Rontays CC,* and his younger brother Andy was a reliable regular for a good few years. An exceptional sporting family!

Clive's Dad Les would visit the Rontays warehouse in *Chadwell Heath* as did a number of players from *West Ham United* and *Spurs* including *Terry Venable's* Dad who secured a good number of autographs for me . Terry had a long-playing career including *Chelsea, QPR, Spurs, Crystal Palace* and was manager of *Barcelona, QPR, Spurs, Crystal Palace, Leeds United, Middlesboro* and England.

My earliest football memories are watching Dad play for Collier Row British Legion, when he was too old to get a game in the 1st or 2nd team he started a 3rd team and went in goal and recruited a good bunch of young players who then moved up the club ladder. The footballs were big, heavy leather lumps with a lace tied up to keep the bladder inside. If you headed the lace on the ball the indentation took a couple of days to disappear from your forehead. If the ball was wet it took on the weight of a 'medicine ball', the boots had leather studs that were nailed into the bottom of the boot and they had a hard, round toe cap for kicking the ball and the players in the other team.

In 1966 aged 11 years I watched all of England's games at Wembley in the *World Cup* apart from the final. Being the oldest, brother Tom had a ticket, but Dad couldn't find a spare ticket for me from anywhere (I never let Tom forget the injustice), so I watched it on telly in black and white while mostly standing on my head for good luck. I remember collapsing in a heap when Germany equalised in the final minutes of the game.

A disappointing football memory amongst many was going for a trial for *Havering District* Under 12's and being put in the '*Possibles*' group which sounds ok, but you really needed to be in the '*Probables.*' My group (Of failures) was sent to play a game amongst ourselves refereed by a young West Ham United player called *Trevor Brooking* (647 games for West Ham and 47 for England). I volunteered to go in goal because there wasn't a proper goalie in the group, I didn't have anything to do but made one single save whereupon Trevor came over and told me that if I wanted to play in goal I should use my hands and not my feet to make a save. Thank you Sir Trevor.

In 1977/78 while I was a student at *Loughborough University*, I completed the Football Association Preliminary Coaching Award on a Sunday morning in a public park in Nottingham. It was extra fun because some of the players from *Nottingham Forest* and *Notts County* were on the course. Forest were promoted from the old 2nd Division the previous season and weren't expected to achieve much that year but with their manager Brian Clough they won the *First Division* (The Premier League today) and the *League Cup*. I've often wondered if the FA coaching course helped them in any way and I suspect playing against footballers like me on a Sunday morning over the park instilled a deep and enduring sense of self-confidence.

My first proper job was teaching in *Thurrock* in Essex and in 1979 I attended a foggy Friday morning training session at *Chelmsford City FC's* ground where *Bobby Robson* (Later *Sir Bobby*) manager of *Ipswich Town* took a session with his players. For a couple of hours around a hundred schoolteachers and club coaches sat in the main stand while Bobby gave us a running commentary on the session, what he was trying to achieve and some amusing insights into to some of his players. The squad had many successful international players like *Terry Butcher, Mick Mills, Kevin Beattie* and *Paul Mariner* (All England internationals), *Alan Brazil, John Wark (*Scotland) and *Arnold Mühren* (Holland) and they won the *FA Cup* in 1977/78, were *Premier League* runners up in 1980/81 and '81/'82 and *UEFA Europa League* winners in 1980/81.

Bobby Robson voluntarily brought his squad to Chelmsford for an early morning session for the benefit of a bunch of mostly schoolteachers, he was obviously a top-quality coach and outstanding communicator and consequently he became a long-standing favourite of M's from about 1979. Thankyou Sir Bobby.

In 1982, an ex-professional footballer, *Mark Lazarus*, who ran a house removal business (He moved the contents not the house), *Lazarus Brothers*, moved my family to *Cranham* in Essex. On the day we moved his partner was unwell and he only had a boy of around 11 years old to help him, despite this, Mark who was an exceptionally strong man, completed the move into our new house pretty much on his own. I am sure at one point I saw him with a wardrobe under one arm and a large plant pot in the other hand ? Thank you, Mark.

Note: Mark Lazarus chose football over boxing and played as a right-winger, moving into midfield later in his career making more than 400 Football League appearances and scoring over 100 goals. Most of his games were played with *Leyton Orient* and *Queen's Park Rangers* for whom he scored the winning goal in the *1967 League Cup Final* against *West Bromwich Albion*.

I attended the *League Cup* final at Wembley as a neutral supporter and was impressed with the friendly attitude of the West Brom supporters after the game. They were in the First Division and favourites to win but were beaten by a QPR, a 2nd Division team. I wrote to the Editor of *Football Monthly*, a popular magazine at the time, expressing how impressed I was with the West Brom fans, the letter was published and as a result I received a £5 cheque in the post and a letter from a supporter of *Hajduk Split* in the then Yugoslavia, asking if I would like to be his 'pen pal.' We wrote to each other for some time swapping football club lapel badges and match programmes.

Today, *Hajduk Split* are one of the most successful teams in Croatia, I don't know what became of my pen pal in the unrest that occurred for a number of years during and after the break-up of Yugoslavia? If foreign folk wish to support a Croatia team, I recommend *Hajduk Split*.

As a younger man I had a favourite Welsh, Scottish and Irish football club, my Irish favourite remains *Glentoran* from where the football legend *Danny Blanchflower* came, he was a favourite of M's and captain of Spurs between 1954–1964 making 337 appearances.

My *Scottish* choice was *Motherwell* who played Spurs in the *Texaco Cup*, Second Round, First Leg, on Wednesday 21 October 1970. Spurs won 3-2 but in the second leg Motherwell beat Spurs 3-1 and won the tie. In the first game at *White Hart Lane, Tottenham*, a very tall, elderly *Motherwell* supporter with a loud

Scottish voice and a small hip flask for liquid refreshment shouted out throughout the game: *"Come on the wee Well! You can beat this million-pound team"!!* Ultimately, he was right.

Motherwell Manager *Bobby Howitt* said after the match: *"This was Motherwell Football Club's* finest hour. I am over the moon. This was a wonderful, wonderful result for us and Scottish football. Surely this proves once and for all that the English game is not superior to ours."

I struggled a bit to find a Welsh team but settled on *Swansea City* because they have a wonderful beach right next to the City Centre, and Wales has always been a favourite holiday venue for my family.

Note For Folk From Overseas On 'Football':

England has two national games, cricket and football, it will be an advantage when talking to an English person to have some conversational topics on football, as together with the weather it should provide sufficient vocabulary to enjoy a good conversation.

First, choose a football team that you can claim to support, you don't have to attend any of their matches but do a little research and maybe watch them occasionally to keep up to date. M suggested that *Leyton Orient* would be a good choice, they are known as *'The O's'* and they are not controversial because they haven't had much success over the years and so no-one apart from their proper fans knows much about them. A good choice by M, I think.

The *'O's* stadium is in the shadow of the *London Stadium* at *Stratford* which was built for athletics in the *2012 Olympic Games,* currently *West Ham United* (*The Hammers*) play there. They used to be famous in the 1960s because three of their players were in the 1966 winning England *World Cup* Final team (Have I already mentioned that I didn't have a ticket for the final but my older brother Tom did?) The England and West Ham Captain was *Robert Frederick Chelsea Moore, OBE.* For some years Sir Bobby drank beer in *The Optimist* pub in *Upminster* with his footballing colleagues including another 'Great' English footballer *Jimmy Greaves,* and my Uncle Harry who lived near the pub.

~

More Miscellany...

Christmas: In the 1960's and 70's we enjoyed large family gatherings at Christmas on Boxing Day, often at Uncle Gordon and Aunty Kit's big house in *Emerson Park, Hornchurch.* Uncle Jack was a very good amateur MC (*Master of Ceremonies*) and it was custom for everyone to 'do a little turn' which meant singing or maybe just telling a joke. There were one or two talented performers but mostly not, yet despite the lack of star quality, Uncle Jack made the whole thing seem like we were in our own private little theatre. The best of times.

These are joyous memories with two generations enjoying each other's company, not least in the terrible winter of 1962/63 known as *The Big Freeze of '63*. The kids and the more energetic adults made a very long slide in the road and we skated and slid along it on most of our body parts until long after dark.

Years later, after Dad died, Tom and I took it in turns to invite M to our houses for the Xmas festivities, she was always a happy, sociable guest and is remembered for her Christmas earrings (Bells), singing, hand-jive (Of course) and enjoyment of red wine - *Merlot, Shiraz* and *'Cab Sav'* were her favourites to name but three.

The Telephone: M didn't like using the phone unless she was talking to friends and family. She spoke with her lifetime friend Myrt and her sister Jess every week and they were sit-down conversations that often went on for an hour or more. She would say: "*Myrt is a good listener and Jess is a good talker.*" Sibling rivalry can last a lifetime.

Religion: M lost any religious faith that she may have had when her younger sister Ivy died of cancer in her thirties, she would say, "*How can there be a God when two young children and a husband can be left alone with no Mother or wife*"?

M had a Christian education at school and always enjoyed singing in church at Christmas, weddings and baptisms. She had no prejudice of religion, race, ethnicity or anything else and we sort of agreed that the prayers we offered up were probably more akin to a wish for good fortune, maybe a prayer to 'Lady Luck'? We agreed that *Mother Nature* gave some fuel to our faith. Did we have faith? Definitely!

'The Swinging Sixties - 'Fact or Fiction'?: M enjoyed a lot about the 1960's but said it swung according to your age and frame of mind. With two young children, the musical 'revolution' in the 60's passed her by to some extent, she liked the *Beatles* but said that *Cilla Black, "Sings like she's being strangled."* Brother Tom was the one who swung the most in the '60s, he dug the groove and favoured the '*Mod*' style - haircut; music; clothes; the *Ilford Palais*; but no *Vespa* scooter (So no tiger's tail on the back).

Technology: Technology in its common household forms highlighted a significant difference between my and M's generation, I generally embrace it without having good knowledge or understanding of much of it, but M avoided it whenever possible. I bought her a mobile phone designed for older folk in case she got into trouble indoors or out, but she didn't use it once. In the early 1980's her music centre (Radio, record and CD player) replaced her post-war '*Radiogram*' (*Radio and record player in a hardwood cabinet*) and she had it playing all day every day unless the tv was on.

M didn't want a dishwasher, she couldn't/wouldn't see the benefits and would gently scoff my pre-dishwasher rinse in the sink when she was round our house. An electric oven, small microwave, kettle and toaster made up her full armoury of techno items.

Alcohol: On Sundays M would cook a roast dinner, listen to her (LP) records and enjoy a *Schooner (*Small pear-shaped glass)* or two of warmish, medium dry sherry before lunch and Dad would meet male family and friends down the local pub, usually *The Drill* in *Gidea Park* for a couple of pints and be home in time for lunch.

I remember 'tipsy' occasions but never drunkenness and have a black and white photo of M in a bar in the *Lloret de Mar* on the *Costa Brava* with a guitar she couldn't play and a *Matador* black Sombrero (Think *Clint Eastwood's film 'Man With No Name')* looking a little mellow *(Sozzled).* It's a family treasure.

The local pub had an *Off-License (*A small box room with a little serving hatch attached to the pub where you could buy a limited range of beer, wine, spirits, soft drinks and salted crisps with the salt in a small piece of blue paper inside the bag – then came 'Cheese and Onion').* It had a very loud doorbell so the people serving in the pub could here you come in and it always struck me as a downbeat experience, perhaps for people who weren't allowed in the pub by the management or their husband or wife?

We could smell the *Ind Coope Brewery* for most of the years we lived in and around *Romford,* it was founded at the *Star Inn, Romford* in 1708, in 1799 the Inn and brewery were purchased by *Edward Ind* and *J Grosvenor,* and *C.Coope* joined the firm in 1845. In 1856 the Company opened their brewery at *Burton-upon-Trent* and registered as *Ind Coope & Co. Ltd* in November 1886. The *Romford* brewery closed in 1992.

I worked at the brewery one summer holiday in the section where the old barrels were brought back from the pubs and clubs and the dregs were poured into a drain or re- processed in a very large open tank the size of a small swimming pool. The foul smell was constant and reminded me of liquid vomit and it had the effect of encouraging that very thing. I couldn't drink beer for about 3 months as the smell in the glass transported me to the dark cellar of the brewery with its distinctive stench, cock roaches and Ferrell cats who seemed to thrive on the dark, dank conditions. I didn't go back the next summer.

Films and Theatre: M watched 'films' not 'movies,' and M&D went to the 'pictures' (not the movies) quite often, and when I was a kid, they would sometimes take me to see the latest *Epic* in Leicester Square. Films like *How the West Was Won, The Longest Day, Zulu* and of course *El Cid* and Ben Hur are my lifelong favourites. I've seen *Zulu* approximately 15 times, mostly on the telly and I watched it in a cinema in Belgium with sub-titles, an excellent way for a young person to learn some words from a foreign language (*Flemish* not *Zulu*).

M didn't like scary films, she preferred to be entertained while watching a film and didn't see the point of being made to feel miserable or frightened, she would say: 'Real life gives you plenty of misery and so I like a nice film with a happy ending.' She would definitely not have enjoyed my scariest film ever, *The Exorcist.*

M&D preferred the theatre, particularly musicals and they would go to the *West End* regularly, M often talked about *Sammy Davis Junior's* performance at *The Talk of The Town* in *Piccadilly* and of course the time she played the hooter for *Val Doonican.*

As an elderly person living alone M watched telly during the day and old films would often be on in the background when I visited. On more than one occasion it was *South Pacific,* quote: "*There's a woman behind every tree in Guam*"! (Why?) and the big hit number, '*There's Nothin' Like A Dame*' in which "*Sailors, Seabees and Marines*" sing: "We got sunlight on the sand, We got moonlight on the sea, We got mangoes and bananas, You can pick right off the tree, We got volleyball and ping-pong, And a lot of dandy games! What ain't we got? We ain't got dames!"
They don't make 'em like that anymore.

For information, *Guam* is defined as '*an unincorporated and organized territory of the United States.'* I wonder what a '*disorganised*' territory of the US looks like? It's in the north western Pacific Ocean with a population of around 165,000 and I very much doubt there is a woman behind every tree anymore.

Interesting Footnote: M didn't like **tattoos,** she said, 'They are for sailors.' Like *Popeye the sailor man* I suppose?

The London Marathon: My son Dave ran his first Marathon in London in 2015, I had never been to watch it before and was blown away (Not *amazed*) by the scale of the event. The London I know was transformed into a running track flanked by hundreds of thousands of stewards and spectators from all over the world. The noise of the crowd shouting support for the runners was constant for 6 hours plus. Dave was not a runner of any distinction but had done the necessary training then characteristically injured his knee while "making some shapes" on the dance floor in a club about a month beforehand. M had died just two months earlier and I think it gave him a determination to complete the marathon for his Nan come what may I was surprised by the emotion I felt for the amateur runners and many of them looked as though they would struggle to finish even if they walked the whole way around the course. We saw Dave run past a few times by changing our viewing spot and on one occasion he characteristically nearly knocked over the entire water station trying to reach his Mum in the crowd to give her a hug. I think there should be a team of Daves, *'Team Dave,'* running the London Marathon every year with their own first aid team and additional 'catastrophe response' stewards along the course.

I was unsurprisingly very proud of our Dave, he ran for the *Alzheimer Society* in memory of his Grandad Tom, we were invited to a pub off *Trafalgar Square* by the charity and all agreed that his *'Nanny Peck'* (M) was there in spirit to give him support. After a pleasant hour we had to assist him out of the pub because he had stiffened to the texture of a 6'5" length of plasterboard.

About 40,000 runners and circa 750,000 people reside in harmony at the London Marathon each yea, it is an inspirational day and if you haven't experienced it you should go sometime soon as a spectator, volunteer or runner.

Camping: When my brother Tom and I were small we enjoyed holidays in caravans by the seaside. Uncle Bill and Auntie Jess had a caravan at *Jaywick* at *Clacton on Sea* which in the 1950's and 60's was a 'go to' holiday destination, it was close to *Clacton-on-Sea* which hosted *Butlins Holiday Camp*, and all other typically English seaside resort entertainment. We had fun with our cousins and did the things kids typically did and still do when they are *'beside the seaside beside the sea,'* like donkey rides, *Punch & Judy,* amusement parks, candy floss, sand-castles and associated bucket and spade, splashing in the sea, crab fishing, shell collecting, riding on the train with wheels that goes on the road, fish and chips, roller-skating, trampolining, cricket, volleyball and football on the beach and sleeping well at night.

You can only do those very British things properly in Great Britain and what more could anyone want for a kid's holiday? Apart from a brolly and waterproof clothing and sturdy footwear.

M didn't favour all the work that went with a holiday in a tent or a caravan and so our family holidays switched in the '60s mainly to the new flight and hotel 'package' which were relatively cheap. Unlike M, I have enjoyed all forms of camping through life and feel equipped to offer a few camping-craft tips to anyone thinking of holidaying on a campsite in a tent, caravan, pod (*A small flimsy capsule sold under the illusion of 'glamour'), lodge (*a caravan in disguise) or camping-van/motor home.

Camping Tips:
If possible, *wear shorts if sitting in the toilet block*, suspend them above the floor by creating outward tension with your knees. If you have weak knees, camping may not be for you?

Etiquette - 'Hello' is the only word you need on a camp site anywhere in the world. Everyone understands what it means, and most people say it back in English or their own language. Campers who don't return a cheery 'hello' are probably camping to lie low and hide from someone eg. the police, tax inspector, a jilted lover etc.

- *Assume you will need to have a pee in the middle of the night* and keep an empty vessel to hand - avoid narrow neck bottles. This particular in-tent activity can be both messy and potentially embarrassing so seek prior approval from tent mates.
- *Avoid 'one-upmanship'* with fellow campers - this is more typical of caravan and motor-home owners as tent-dwellers are generally have smaller egos. Do not compete to be seen to own the best sun loungers or camping chair*; avoid plastic flower displays in your front window or external table, this is an unnecessary 'territorial' manoeuvre; refrain from using a large satellite dish as some men see the size as a symbol of their fertility; avoid presenting a chrome-edged bar-b-que that is larger than the smaller caravans on the site - campers will talk about you behind your back, and you may be labelled a show-off.

*Note: Re the sun lounger/chair - avoid eye contact with the camper with an exceptionally high-back chair as in their mind it's a throne and depicts power and authority (Ref the 'Iron Throne' in *The Game of Thrones*). Self-important campers consider the high-back camping chair as the modern form of the Edwardian 'high hat'* which depicts high status and elegance.

*Another Note: The *'top hat'* is the most common form of *'high hat'* and is a tall, crowned hat usually of silk these days. The top hat is a descendent of the *'sugar loaf hat'* worn in *Medieval* times. Further historical information is available from *'Oliver Brown' of Chelsea*, England.

Prioritise warmth over glamorous appearance at night. Take excessive sleeping-wear for all eventualities and if residing in a tent plan ahead of arrival to minimise drafts and the ingress of water. The Labrador dog is an excellent multi-purpose barrier and internal heater - prepare for farting, and if possible, keep them dry to reduce their indigenous odour. Tent dwellers must obviously secure the tent with good quality ground pegs to ensure it doesn't blow away - if it does, go and sleep in the car - if you don't have a car and weather permits spend one night only sleeping rough like a vagrant (*A homeless person). If the weather doesn't permit, go to a nearby Bed & Breakfast. If all else fails, go home.

- Please *consider your noise volumes* after 9pm e.g. music or drunken shouting; and similarly, before 7.30 a.m. e.g. whistling.

~

SILLY THINGS

If you have clung on heroically and are still reading as we approach the end of this little book you will know that the sections marked *'Chat's With M'* are mostly light-hearted and on the silly side, but this final Chapter, while again based on chats with M, contains topics of conversation that didn't qualify for the previous *'Miscellaneous'* chapter, clearly indicating their unclassifiable, *higgledy-piggledy** content (**Chaos and disorder*). They were sifted along with the other mountain of notes on scraps of paper recording chats with M, but they were left effectively homeless and labelled 'silly' for want of a better description.

Consequently, please answer the following questions to determine if you are likely to cope with the content of this Chapter:

* *Do you have a middle name?* Yes/No.
* *Are the Highlands and Islands of Scotland in* A. England or B. Scotland?
* *Which is the darker chocolate in colour* A. Milk or B. Dark?
* *Name one of your favourite smells?* (There is no correct/incorrect answer
* to this question.)

Please mark your own answers.

If you answered all four of the questions correctly you may wish to skip the Chapter and move on to the *Conclusions* at the end of the book where you will find some important information regarding 'children in need.'

If your score was low, congratulations, you have passed the test. Please proceed with caution.

~

The last time I ever pulled M's leg was while she was putting her daily medication into her weekly container to make sure she took the right pills at the right time and I told her that I was feeling very anxious that I might be a hypochondriac.

M and I laughed a lot but rarely shared a 'proper' joke, neither of us was very good at remembering or telling them and most of my favourites were rude and inappropriate to share with my Mother. I did tell her a joke by *Andy Hamilton* (**Comedian, novelist and screenwriter): 'Claustrophobia is the fear of Father Christmas.'* M didn't understand it and after I had explained it I wished I hadn't bothered in the first place. The failed joke reminded me of one of my favourite *Homer Simpson* declarations: *"These days people forget the true meaning of Christmas. The birth of Santa Clause."* M laughed at this.

New Year Resolutions: One year, M and I discussed New Year resolutions and decided we were bored with the usual self-promises to go on a diet and do more exercise to lose weight after Christmas, so we committed to two ground-breaking resolutions. M said she would do more 'hand jives' while listening to music indoors, her reasoning was that it was mild exercise and she enjoyed it, so it was good for stress. I resolved to give more cuddles as M, Joni and our kids and dogs all liked a regular cuddle. I have since worked at my resolution and have progressed to approximately the mid-point of the *'Cuddle spectrum.'*

A German Football Manager: M seemed unusually interested while we watched the football *World Cup Final* between Germany and Argentina in 2014 and in the second half she announced: *"It's the Swinging Blue Jeans!"** She explained that she had been trying to remember the name of the group in the 1960s who had a member who looked like the German manager *Joachim Löw*.

Note: 'The Swinging Blue Jeans' were a four-piece British 'Merseybeat' band whose hit singles were "*Hippy Hippy Shake,*" "*Good Golly Miss Molly*" and "*You're No Good.*" I don't know which *Swinging Blue Jean* looked like *Joachim Löw* but vocalist/guitarist *Ray Ennis* had a mop of black hair in the 60's so maybe it was him?

Daring a Friend: When I was 12 years old, I had a short story published in the school magazine, it was called *'Scream'* and described the sound my friend David made when I should have shouted "STOP!" before he fell in the river with his eyes closed. It was a game of trust that we played together, and I failed David who was a particularly nice and trusting chap. I remain disappointed with myself.

Katherine Tate's Nan: M had a badly kept secret which was that she watched the comedy series in which the comedian *Katherine Tate* impersonates her Nan, an old lady from South London. Unlike her many other favourite tv programmes, M didn't mention this one because of the very bad language and felt guilty that she enjoyed it. I saw her just once, clutching her rib cage in pain while laughing at Nan's foul language and outrageous behaviour.

Gravy and Custard: Question: What place would the world be without thick, hot gravy and custard!? Answer: It would be a lesser place.

Note: *They should not be consumed together. This excludes pregnant women who may feel the need to do so, for example, with a lump of coal and a boiled egg?

Showering: I told M that the *Romans* invented 'the shower' as a way of washing the body clean, she believed me which allowed me to confirm that the name of the inventor of the very first shower ever built in the *Holy Roman Empire* was S*tarcus Bolocus.* She instinctively believed me but the penny soon dropped and she picked up a large ball of wool which was destined to be a multi-coloured jumper with stripes worn by an unknown child in *Rumania,* and threw it at me.

Clothing for Golf: I bought a bright red V-neck jumper and M said it looked very nice, I said it was from a golf shop, so she changed her view and pulled a face with her nostrils flared. I asked what was wrong and she declared she didn't like golf clothes on men because there were too many strutting peacocks on the golf course wearing garish (*Obtrusively showy, bright and lurid*) colours when green, grey, black and brown were more appropriate for a game which involved walking about on grass and in woodlands etc.

Face-lifts: M never wanted to have a face-lift, she said there is no escape from Nature's face wrinkles or a 'turkey neck' and there is always a slightly evil smile etched on the stretched face of the recipient like *The Joker* in *Batman.* Harsh.

Painting: Dad was always supportive and would praise my painting skills (*Artisan* not *artistic),* as soon as I could hold a paint brush the right way up Dad gave me little painting projects like a garden fence or a shed door, as a child I did on one occasion apply a little paint to our rabbit, *Snudge,* but that was my own initiative. I was almost out of short trousers when Dad sent me up my first ladder to paint a window-sill and frame, he stood with his foot on the bottom rung which made me more nervous because it hadn't really occurred to me that there was anything but fun in what I was doing.

In my teens I was given pocket money for painting during school holidays and at 17 years I was managing a long ladder with an extension ie. pull a rope and the ladder extends further - not common these days I suspect? While painting the wooden soffits (*The base of the roof underneath the gutter*) I saw that some of the concrete rendering was peeling away from the wall and I helped it on its way with my paint stripping metal blade. I had excavated a patch of brickwork about 12 inches in diameter when our next-door neighbour, a nice man called Bill who was the *Mayor* of *Romford* at the time, called over to me and said: "*I wouldn't strip off any more of that from the wall if I were you, once you start, you'll have to take the whole lot off.*" Momentarily I thought he should mind his own business, then I thought I should do what the Mayor of Romford said. Subsequently, a bunch of men repaired the entire wall with scaffolding and ladders and all sorts of paraphernalia. The *Mayor* was indeed wise.

Oil Paintings: If you are told "*you are no oil painting*" it generally means that you are not considered good looking by your accuser, but M and I agreed that very few portraits of people in oil paintings through history appear to be particularly attractive. A high proportion have bulging eyeballs, looking like they are sitting on something uncomfortable, with pale pudding-shaped faces and rosy cheeks. M said her mother Ada insisted that portrait paintings were mostly of the upper class and they all looked the same due to the in-breeding of the Aristocracy (*An aristocrat is someone whose family has a high social rank Aristocracy). A little far-fetched I feel and ironic in so far as Ada quietly claimed a Royal bastard ancestral line (She was round faced and often had rosy cheeks?)

Crisps: We shared some hand cooked crisps and M said, 'How can so many bags of crisps be cooked by hand!?' I said, 'they're not, the crisps are made from hands not by them.' She gave me a look that I can't easily describe.

The Colour Ginger: It's not uncommon for males with gingery coloured hair to have to put up with rude jibes as though having ginger hair is a misfortune. M and I agreed that it was a load of tosh.* (*Pretentious, silly, baloney, bilgewater, drool, humbug, tommyrot, twaddle, taradiddle, hokum, meaninglessness, nonsensicality, bunk - thanks go to The Free Dictionary) I suggested that if you gather a group of people together with 'ginger' in their hair colour and if they stand closely together in a huddle and the sun shines on them there would be a lovely golden glowing aura around the group in the form of a 'golden orb.' We agreed that ginger is golden!

Sharing A Pair of Reading Spectacles: Friends of mine, Sue and Dave, shared a pair of old, broken glasses, the arm was missing on one side which allowed them to have one lens each by putting their faces together and holding on to each other. They are long and happily married and I feel that sharing a pair of reading glasses helps keep them close. Try it with your partner. Why not?

Night Clubbing: M asked me what 'clubbing' was? I explained what goes on in a club and how people generally behave. She said "Why"?

Baldness: All the various parts of our body are obviously inherited from our parents' genes but who decides which bit comes from which parent? Allegedly men take hair genes from their Mum. Says who!? I would have liked my hair genes from my Dad because unlike M's family of frequently bald or balding men, Dad's male relatives are mostly well thatched through until old age. I'm fortunate that while my hair has slowly and quietly disappeared for years, I am told that the shape of my head is not particularly grotesque (A rare complement from my wife).

Joni recently took a photo of me and proudly announced: "I am adjusting you in the picture to hopefully give you more hair."

Fortunately, baldness can now offer itself as a fashion accessory and many handsome men carry the flag of the Baldy, like Bruce Willis, Jason Statham, Yul Brynner, Pep Guardiola (Pep and I share a liking for home-knitted cardigans), John Travolta, Prince William and in the near future David Beckham, unless Posh Spice requires him to have a hair transplant.

Nimbleness: M was short and nimble whereas I am tall and slightly gawky (*Awkward and ungainly*). I don't feel that is a fair allocation from the gene pool, surely it would be fairer if Mother Nature balanced the negatives with the positives. With just a couple of different genes from M and not Dad I could have been an English version of a fabulous West Indian cricketer, *Brian Lara* i.e. a diminutive batsman who scored the highest number of runs in first-class cricket including 501 not out for Warwickshire; he also holds the record for the highest score in a Test Match innings *(See 'Cricket' for a definition of Test Match)* scoring 400 not out against England in *Antigua* in 2004.

Swapping Birthday Cards: Mum-in-law Jean and I sent the same birthday card back and forward to each other for a few years until one of us refreshed the exchange. Cards with reference to farting* (*Passing wind from the bum*) are our favourites, Jean has a hard-earned reputation for passing wind and to her credit she feels no need to explain or apologise for an audible burst of gas (One of her younger great grandsons calls them '*love puff's*) but if I am present she will look at me and say: "*A real Gentleman would claim responsibility for a lady's wind,*" to which I reply: "Yes, but I'm no Gentleman," to which she agrees.

By sheer coincidence, my brother Tom and I often exchange cards with a farting theme, the challenge is to avoid repeating a card that has previously been sent. Life is complex and challenging.

Druids: M and I were watching the telly and saw a short video clip of Druids celebrating the *Summer Solstice* at *Stonehenge,* I asked her if she knew much about Druids, she didn't so I looked them up on a search engine of my choice and found this visionary statement from the *British Druid Order* on their website: "*Rekindling the sacred fires of Druidry as a living, breathing, animistic, shamanistic, life-affirming, Earth-honouring spirituality for the 21st century, drawing inspiration from the threefold stream of Awen's flow from its source, the Cauldron of the goddess Ceridwen. Hail and Welcome!*" (Their marketing 'strap line' has surely moved on since the Roman's left?)

M and I were unsure of some elements of the statement, so we changed the subject to the *Eurovision Song Contest* that was on the telly the following Saturday.

A Guarantee of Nothing: M didn't buy a lot of household cleaning sprays she preferred old fashioned soap and hot water and a clean cloth and swore by vinegar. Lots of household cleaners for the kitchen and bathroom promote the fact that they kill 99% of germs or bacteria etc. Well I'm afraid that doesn't inspire my confidence, with average bad luck any one of us could catch one of the alleged 1% of bad bacteria who are alive and well and looking for a host body to infect.

The same principle would apply to a security company advertising a home security system that was 'guaranteed to prevent 99% of mad axe murderers from entering your home'. No thanks. Not good enough I'm afraid, very afraid.

The One Arm Bandit: Also known as the *'slot machine'*, Joni recalled when she was a child in the 1960's watching news on the tv about dangerous gangsters in the U.S. and linked it to robberies from *'one arm bandits'* who she assumed were gangsters with one arm. She pictured them with an arm that was stiff like a cricket bat (Baseball would have been more appropriate) and they would swing them up and then down on people's heads from behind: *"They wore long dark overcoats and trilby hats but they obviously couldn't drive a car with only one arm."* She remains a creative thinker.

Holes In The Ground: M had a grandson who worked for gas installers which often involved working in dark, deep holes in the ground. She worried about his health and wellbeing (He's grown up to be a fine, fit fellow) and we talked about how tough it must be to get out of bed day in and out and find the motivation to go back to the hole in the ground you were working in yesterday or will need to dig today. Where would we be in the world if there wasn't enough people of substance who are willing and able to do it?

Eating Spaghetti: The actress *Sophia Loren* is a proclaimed beauty and international treasure and consequently her advice warrants attention when she says: "Spaghetti can be eaten most successfully if you inhale it like a vacuum cleaner." M said: "I doubt she's ever used one."

Eaves Droppings: *The eaves are the edges of a roof which overhang the face of a wall.* Joni also pointed out to M and I that when she was that same child in the 60's she asked her Dad what he was doing up a long ladder outside the house. He said he was: "Cleaning the eaves because of the pigeon shit," and consequently Joni understood that pigeon droppings were called 'eaves' but was unsure what other types of birds' mess was called?

England v France: Wensleydale cheese was first created by French *Cistercian monks* from the *Roquefort* region who had settled in *Wensleydale, Yorkshire*. It was the English that first introduced the wine making method that allowed the French to make *Champagne*. A 1-1 draw.

The Appearance of Women and Men: It is not uncommon (*Avoid a double negative when possible*) across the animal kingdom for the male to be the physically more attractive or colourful of the species, M explained that this is nature's way of the male trying to appear attractive to the female with the hope of mating in order to make babies. In contrast, it's common in the human race (*Homo Sapien*) for the female to be the more attractive of the species, so why are human men different from the rest of the animal kingdom?

'And Now the News': M was a *'newsaholic,'* (* Habitual consumer of BBC news etc).

Soup: M called me a *'soupaholic'* because I eat (Or drink?) it often, she said it was the type of food which 'warms the cockles* of your heart' (**The cockles** *of the heart are its ventricles which is from the Latin 'cochlea' (snail) referring to their shape).* Peas feature strongly in my favourite soups and are the oldest known vegetable, they were very popular with the ancient Greeks, Egyptians and Romans.

M was not impressed with chefs on the tv who used large amounts of cream, butter and sugar and she thought the ingredients (Nosh) of the dish being cooked were often expensive as she was of the school of thought that it's better to *'buy cheap and chew harder.'* Despite having a number of dentures (*False teeth*) M actively supported this doctrine and enjoyed a sirloin or filet steak throughout her adult life.

Cup-Cakes: A few years ago, cup-cakes (**Small sponge cakes made in a circular* *paper container with crinkly edges*) became popular after years in the shadows and M wanted to know why: *"Who decides that we should all start eating them again?"* Fair question?

The Meaning of Life: M and I agreed that *'What is the meaning of life?'* is a less interesting question than, *'What is the purpose of life.'* But we didn't have an informed answer for either.

*Sunday Morning i*s ideally a time for relaxation and reflection, for example, one Sunday morning I relaxed by washing the car, visiting M, walking our dog and on returning home received a reflection from Joni that *"In the 40 years I've known you your eyebrows have shifted closer to your eyes."*

~

Notes For Folk From Overseas On 'Silly Things':

Rice Pudding: This is a desert dish (*Follows the main course, not from the *Sahara* or other desert) which has been enjoyed in the UK for many years and is readily available cheaply in cans and other environmentally unfriendly packaging. If you hear the comment: *"He could not knock the skin off a rice pudding"* this will be an opinion about someone's alleged lack of physical strength which is not directly linked to activity involving a rice pudding, or the removal of its skin which has formed after cooling off.

An alternative condemnation is: *"He/she could not punch his/her way out of a paper bag,"* again this is not a literal expression but rather an *analogy** intended to emphasise someone's view of another person's lack of physical prowess.

It's a silly expression because people in the UK do not wear paper bags due to the wet weather (*Analogy - a similarity between like features of two things, on which a comparison may be based).

'The National Trust - Don't confuse the word 'Trust' with 'Truss*.'The National Trust state that they: "Look after the places you love, from houses, buildings and gardens to coast and countryside." Please note that they select the places we love ie. we pay to go into the places that they own and have decided we love.

(*Note: Truss: (Noun) this word has a range of definitions including: a framework consisting of posts and struts supporting a roof, bridge, or other structure; a surgical appliance worn to support a hernia; bundle of old hay (56 lb), new hay (60 lb), or straw (36 lb).

"At the end of the day," you will hear this popular expression often and it means 'when something is finished,' it's a generalised expression and is not specific about one particular day, for example: "At the end of the day it doesn't matter how hard I try I can't iron a shirt nicely or resist eating a whole bar of chocolate in one go."

~

THE FINAL CHAPTER

In this little book of life and death I have candidly shared some of my memories of my Mum, her experiences, and our discussions in order to give you the lovely reader, a glimmer of insight into the people of her generation from *Stepney* to *Romford* and surrounding areas where she lived all of her life.

An enduring memory of M is how grateful she always was for the smallest kindness or contact with a fellow human being, from a cup of tea given or taken, a passing nod from a neighbour, a new family photo for the album or a wet and windy weekend in a British Bed & Breakfast.

Another abiding memory is her instinctive love of children, her own and the children of the world at large, she had a strong maternal instinct that shone brightly, which brings me to the main purpose of my concluding Chapter.

M and I had a discussion one dark, cold November day while listening to the *BBC Children In Need* fund-raising Friday on Radio 2, she was knitting multi-coloured jumpers with stripes for children in Romania and we talked about the many awful situations of children in the UK and around the world, some long standing and others current.

M suggested there could be a compulsory *Children's Tax* on big businesses, and I thought it could replace a proportion of their *Corporation Tax* with a 'gift tax' rebate as an incentive to businesses. "*Everyone's a winner!*" I exclaimed enthusiastically and M replied, "*That's a nice idea dear*" then returned her attention to her knitting. I don't think I had managed to make the sale?

At the beginning of this ambitious little book, I suggested that *NASA* should leave a copy of it on every planet that astronauts from Planet Earth land upon in order to allow friendly aliens to read it and donate their version of money (Cheese; kryptonite; ancient Egyptian skulls etc.) to a children's charity of their choice.

Now at the end of the book I further extend ambition and invite one of the world's leading nations (Perhaps the ancient civilisation of China?) to lead the way on the introduction of a new *Children's Tax*, and hopefully once the benefits are seen there will be a world-wide snowball effect and other countries will follow suit. Certainly, the UK, who historically are tied up in an antiquated political sticky morass of policies, procedures, pantomime shouting, countless resolutions, bills and laws and colourful fancy dress pageants in the Houses of Parliament, could cast aside their caterpillar ermine cloaks and *Marks & Spencer* suits, spread their butterfly wings and fly with a new *Children's Tax*. *"Here! Here!"*

~

Very finally, because all the author's royalties will go directly to the *BBC Children In Need* charity, I ask again that if while reading you noticed yourself making an audible noise as explained in *The Introduction*, please make a donation to a children's charity of your choice.

Please donate at least one unit of your home country's currency as I am hopeful of a donation from each of the 95 currencies in the world. At the time of writing, I believe (From memory) they are:

Afghani; Antillean Guilder; Ariary; Aruban Florin; Australian Dollar; Bahamian Dollar; Baht; Balboa; Barbadian Dollar; Belize Dollar; Bermudian Dollar; Birr; Venezuela Bolívar Soberano (Replacing the *Bolívar Fuerte* in 2018 – what a shame *; Bolivian Boliviano* (How do they think of these great names!)*; Brunei Dollar; Canadian Dollar; CFA-franc; Colon; Congolese Franc; Convertible Mark; Nicaraguan Cordoba; Dalasi; Denar; Dinar; Dirham; Dobra; Dong; Dram; Euro; Fijian Dollar; Forint; Franc; Ghanaian Cedi; Gourde; Guarani; Hong Kong Dollar; Hryvnia; Iraqi Dinar; Kina; Kip; Koruna; Krona; Krone; Kuna; Kwacha; Kwanza; Kyat; Lari; Lats; Lebanese Pound; Lek; Lempira; Leone; Leu; Lev; Liberian Dollar; Lilangeni; Lira; Litas; Loti; Maldivian Rufiyaa; Manat; Metical; Naira; Nakfa; Ngultrum; Nuevo Sol; Pa'anga; Peso; Pound; Pound Sterling; Pula; Quetzal; Rand; Real; Rial; Riel; Ringgit; Riyal; Ruble; Rupee; Rupiah; Shekel; Shilling; Som; Sudanese Pound; Swiss Franc; Taka; Tala; Tögrög; US Dollar; Vatu; Won; Yen; Yuan; Złoty.*

Thank you very much for staying the course, for hopefully making an audible noise and consequently a little donation to charity.

~

Making a Compliant About This Little Book

If you wish to complain about this little book, please read the following instructions:

1. Keep your complaint to yourself and get over it.
2. Alternatively, contact our *Customer Services Department* whose contact details may be hidden somewhere in the small print if you can find any.
3. If you send an email you will receive the reply: '*Do not respond to this email address as it is not monitored by human beings.*'
4. Any complaint will almost certainly be against Company policy. There is no Company and, therefore, no policy.

Please note: Our main priority is the satisfaction and enjoyment of our readers. If you have suffered discomfort during the reading of this little book, please accept the following statement with our compliments together with two fingers forming a 'V' shape:

We are very sorry for any inconvenience you may have experienced.

THE END

Top: Newlywed lovers.

Below: Post-war, pre-Mum dancing.

Top: Butlins Holiday Camp 1958. Dreaming of a white Christmas.

Below: A day to remember. Mum's parents, Fred and Ada are seen early 'photo-bombing'.

Top: Grandad Fred in First World War uniform with his young wife Ada.

Below: My crazy in-laws John and Jean. Looks can be deceptive.

Top: A full page poster of a Michael Caine lookalike.

Below: Joni (Right) with sister Marion holding up their Mum.

Top: Two of my favourite cuddly people- Mum and small Small.

Below: Mum in her last decade during our random chats. I miss them.

Blood, Sweat & Joy

Printed in Great Britain
by Amazon

54177440R00129